**Cowtown Wichita and
the Wild, Wicked West**

COWTOWN WICHITA

AND THE

Wild, Wicked West

Stan Hoig

University of New Mexico Press
Albuquerque

12 11 10 09 08 07   1 2 3 4 5 6

Library of Congress Cataloging-in-Publication Data

Hoig, Stan.
   Cowtown Wichita and the wild, wicked West / Stan Hoig.
      p. cm.
   Includes bibliographical references and index.
   ISBN 978-0-8263-4155-6 (pbk. : alk. paper)
   1. Wichita (Kan.)—History—19th century. 2. Frontier and pioneer
life—Kansas—Wichita. 3. Wichita (Kan.)—Social life and customs—
19th century. 4. Wichita (Kan.)—Biography. 5. Frontier and pioneer
life—West (U.S.) 6. West (U.S.)—History—1860–1890. I. Title.
   F689.W6H65 2007
   978.1'8602—dc22

                              2006035807

Book design and composition by Damien Shay
Body type is Utopia 9.5/13
Display is Phidian and Belwe

Contents

LIST OF ILLUSTRATIONS   vii

PREFACE   ix

INTRODUCTION   xiii

Chapter One
    LEGENDS OF GOLD   1

Chapter Two
    BEFORE THE PIONEERS   15

Chapter Three
    THE TALKING GROUND   25

Chapter Four
    A FINAL FAREWELL   33

Chapter Five
    OLD JESSE'S TRAIL   45

Chapter Six
    DUTCH BILL, KNIGHT ERRANT   57

Chapter Seven
    OUTPOST ON THE ARKANSAS   69

Chapter Eight
    FOR A SPAN OF MULES   85

Chapter Nine
     GATEWAY TO ADVENTURE   97

Chapter Ten
     NEAR BRIMSTONE   109

Chapter Eleven
     "SOMEDAY THEY'LL GET ME!"   119

Chapter Twelve
     GUESTS IN TOWN   129

Chapter Thirteen
     BOOMER BASTION   139

Chapter Fourteen
     THE FADING FRONTIER   153

Chapter Fifteen
     SHOW BIZ WEST   161

     NOTES   169

     BIBLIOGRAPHY   185

     INDEX   193

List of Illustrations

1. The Little Arkansas country served as a favorite buffalo   9
    hunting ground for Osage warriors.

2. The Wichita Indians resided in conical grass-hut   21
    communities on the Arkansas.

3. Indian agent Jesse Leavenworth helped initiate the   27
    Treaty of the Little Arkansas held at the site of
    Wichita in 1865.

4. Buffalo Bill Mathewson was a buffalo hunter, Indian   37
    trader, banker, and pioneer of Wichita.

5. The Chisholm Cattle Trail was named for half-Cherokee   46
    Jesse Chisholm who once resided on the Little Arkansas.

6. Former Indian trader James Mead was a founding father   49
    and promoter of Wichita.

7. Cowboys wave good-bye after delivering a herd of   52
    Texas longhorns to Wichita.

8. His contemporaries hailed "Dutch Bill" Greiffenstein   58
    as the "Father of Wichita."

9. This "ranch stop" at the Ninnescah River on the Chisholm   71
    Trail was located just south of present Wichita.

10. Governor Samuel Crawford promoted the founding of   74
    Camp Beecher and joined in establishing Wichita.

11. The Munger House became the first rooming and   87
    boarding house on the site of Wichita.

12. Herds of Texas cattle once forded the Arkansas River   98
    at the head of Wichita's Douglas Avenue.

13. Marsh Murdock, editor and publisher of the *Wichita Eagle*,   104
    played a significant role in the town's early history.

14. Saloonkeeper Rowdy Joe Lowe contributed much to   114
    Wichita's Wild West reputation.

15. Mike Meagher (left), the man who tamed Wichita, died   120
    in a blaze of gunfire at Caldwell.

16. Wichita had become a model western town in 1874.   130

17. David L. Payne, an early settler at Wichita, led the   140
    Oklahoma Boomer movement to settle Indian Territory.

18. The Wichita Corn Train of 1884 repaid Ohio farmers who   158
    had once sent aid to Kansas.

19. Oklahoma Harry Hill operated a livery stable in Wichita   159
    and formed a Wild West Show.

20. Showman "Pawnee Bill" Lillie was called on by the   162
    Wichita Board of Trade to take over after the death
    of David Payne.

Preface

For a brief span of time, during the two decades between 1870 and 1890, Wichita was a model community of what has come to be known as the American Wild West. Even before that it had been at the center of early exploration and frontier activity. Wichita had it all: native tribal life; early visitations by Spanish conquistadors; a concourse of fur traders to and from the mountains; the passage of American and Mexican traders between Missouri and New Mexico; military expeditions; buffalo hunters; trail herds and rowdy Texas cowboys; contiguous Indian battles; colorful Indian treaty councils; gun-toting outlaws and stalwart lawmen; Indian-fighting military men; a bevy of notable Indian traders and frontiersmen; and supporting characters that were in themselves reflections of the flamboyant western America that once existed. It was a day that once burned brightly, and will never be again.

Wichita's history is by no means limited to events within its city limits. In truth, the influence of Wichita and those who resided there extended well beyond the town, and the town was conversely affected by events in the surrounding countryside. Its commerce, its civic progress, the welfare and safety of its citizens, and its evolution as a community were often directly related to and influenced by happenings that occurred on the trail and the itinerant clientele that arrived thereby.

An essential part of Wichita's early history was its relationship to affairs in nearby Indian Territory where key roles were played by a number of Wichita's early citizens, such as Greiffenstein, Mead, Mathewson, Chisholm, Payne, Meagher, and many others. The *Wichita Eagle* regularly reported on events in Indian Territory and continued to do so well after white settlement.

Further, Wichita was economically and culturally connected to the Indian Territory, now Oklahoma, where many eastern tribes had been relocated alongside the Plains tribes. The Territory, policed by only a handful of deputy U.S. marshals, was also a bastion for white renegades who often sought refuge across the Kansas border. During the early years, Territorial army units were largely dependent on Wichita as a supply point and port of entry.

During Wichita's first twenty years of existence, its Wild West mystique underwent an interesting metamorphosis. As the town began to develop more and more as a commercial center and take on the airs of eastern civilization, the old Wild Westness began to change. The advent of nearby communities, increase of the white population, demise of the Indian threat, extension of rail lines, tillage of the land, arrival of the merchant class with its stores and homes, establishment of law and order, and drift of the frontier element to the west and south all contributed to a gradual demise of Wichita's Wild West days.

By the end of the 1880s—as white demands for free land were threatening Indian autonomy and frontier rule in the neighboring Indian Territory—Wichita began to lose much of its original Wild West identity. Trail herds were no longer being driven along Douglas Avenue. The men who now walked the streets did not wear spurs or six-guns strapped about their waists. Disputes were no longer settled "in the street" but in the court of law. The sight of a blanketed form on Wichita's streets became a novelty.

This change was dramatically reflected in 1889 by the organization of Oklahoma Harry Hill's Wild West show. Though by no means original, this Wichita-based show was a postmortem of Wichita's Wild West period. It was a fantasized embellishment of the days of stagecoach holdups, Indian battles, and six-gun duels, all aimed at lionizing the dead shot, the expert rider, the western outlaw, and the heroic lawman.

This book leaves it to others to fit Wichita into a particular sociological concept. Both Robert Dystra in *Cattle Towns* and Craig Miner in *Wichita: the Early Years* address this complex matter. Rather this work simply traces the rise and fall of the frontier West in a community that was both typical and distinctively American. Much of Wichita's history could serve as a model for a frontier town of the American West as it evolved from an unruly frontier settlement into a prosperous community of farmers, merchants, and professional folk.

Wichita, Dystra argues statistically, was no wilder nor more lawless than its sister cowtowns of Caldwell, Wellington, Newton, Abilene, Ellsworth, or Dodge City. Yet, to have so many of the representative elements of the Old West present in one place was unique in itself. This, plus Wichita's location for a time as a principal point of entry to the Indian Territory, gave the city a sharp singularity. Wichita's historical involvement in the affairs of the Territory sociologically, commercially, and militarily, as well as its demise as a haven for America's Indian tribes, imprinted the character of the town.

This book seeks to provide readers with some of the colorful events of Wichita's history and characters, letting them vicariously share, as does the city's Cowboy Museum, in the experience of her Wild West days. It is my hope that these chapters will lend tribute to those sometimes valiant, sometimes wicked, sometimes hilarious, and often audacious characters who played their part in Wichita's drama of the western frontier.

I extend thanks to the good folks at the Wichita City Library; Wichita-Sedgwick County Historical Museum; Barker Texas History Center, University of Texas; Western History Collection, University of Oklahoma; University of Central Oklahoma Library; Division of Archives/Manuscripts of the Oklahoma Historical Society; Kansas Historical Society; and, as ever, to my wife, Pat Corbell Hoig, for her gracious help in preparing this manuscript.

Introduction

Once she had been only a nameless collection of grass huts, her existence unknown to recorded history until those who rode upon animals and wore iron upon their chests first came to bare her presence to the world. Humble though she was, men were lustful of her from the start, thinking she possessed great treasures of gold and silver.

Alas, she had no gold or silver, but she *did* have great herds of buffalo whose hides brought men with long guns a'visiting. Behind them came others who exchanged her buckskins and beads for calico and gingham, combed the raffish tangles from her hair, adorned her neatly with streets and stores and houses of freshly sawed pine, and gave her a name.

Gradually, day by day, she became more and more the lady, and the men more and more prideful. They saw in her the image of their dreams. She was a princess, they said, this Wichita. A Peerless Princess of the Plains!

Now she stood in shining splendor at the edge of the great ocean of undulating prairie, giving port to the lusty drovers who sailed their armadas of Texas longhorns up the Chisholm Trail, offering respite to the flotsam and jetsam that floated westward with the tide of post–Civil War immigration—men such as Billy the Kid, Wyatt Earp, and Bat Masterson.

From her harbor on the Arkansas River, she sent forth hardy souls to ply the wilderness as explorers, soldiers, Indian traders, buffalo hunters, and others who hearkened to the call of western adventure. Through them she remained bound to the frontier whose receding shadow still swathed the land of the Indian to the south.

At the same time she flirted with grim-eyed border ruffians and occasionally played hostess to stately warrior-chiefs, who in recess of battle came blanketed and with feathers perked above their heads to stroll her boardwalked streets and gape into windowpanes with skeptical curiosity. And all the while she was mistress to the ambitions of farsighted captains of enterprise who planted in her womb their dreams of tomorrow.

A princess, perhaps, but a tough-minded gal; and no prude she. There was mud on her boots and something of a wicked smile on her lips as she tripped the lively fandangos of history. Bright of eye, quick to laugh, she was none the less compassionate and caring when there was need. But when she was in her Sunday dress and sweetly bonneted, who would guess her at other times to be a brawling, hair-pulling hussy?

Indeed, she was of royal lineage, Lady Wichita; not of European or East Coast aristocracy, but the stuff of Chisholm, Mead, and Greiffenstein. Molded of Kansas clay and cradled in the lap of the Indian country, she was pure American West and damn proud of it!

Chapter One

Legends of Gold

> He [the Turk] said also that the lord of that country
> took his afternoon nap under a great tree on which hung
> a great number of little gold bells.... He said also that
> everyone had their ordinary dishes made of wrought plate,
> and the jugs and bowls were of gold.
> — George Parker Winship, *The Coronado Expedition*, 1964

In the year 1826, long after Coronado's visit of 1541, a group of twenty well-armed men on horseback, with seven pack horses in tow, came up the Arkansas River from the south. At their lead was Nathaniel Pryor, once a member of the Lewis and Clark expedition and leader of an expedition that fought the Arikaras on the upper Missouri in 1807. Pryor had since established himself as an Indian trader near recently founded Cantonment Gibson in Indian Territory. His party consisted of several Arkansas men along with officers and enlisted men from Gibson. Scouting for them was a young Scot-Cherokee half blood in his early twenties named Jesse Chisholm.[1]

The men were searching for gold. They had been lured there by stories they had heard of an El Dorado waiting to be found in this region. Only the year before, Pryor had made a trip to New Orleans. While there he met a wealthy merchant who said he had been a member of the Zebulon Pike expedition to New Mexico in 1806. The merchant told an intriguing story.[2]

He claimed that he had been with that portion of Pike's party that had been taken captive by the Spaniards of New Mexico and

1

imprisoned at Santa Fe. He had escaped with another man, the two of them retreating northward to the Arkansas River and following its course eastward. When they reached Walnut Creek in present Kansas, the two men encountered signs of a smelting operation having taken place there.

Their curiosity impelled them to investigate further and eventually they discovered gold. They melted a large quantity over a makeshift furnace and ran it into bars. Then, splitting and hollowing out a log, they constructed a canoe and carried their bonanza on downriver to Natchez. It was this gold, the merchant claimed, that had enabled him to embark into commerce and make his large fortune.

While wading a small creek below the Little Arkansas, two of the Pryor party found large quantities of shining particles in the riverbed sand. The particles glistened in the sunlight. The men eagerly filled their handkerchiefs with the sand and took it in to camp. An excited debate regarding the particles ensued among the men.

Only one of them, a soldier named Mixen from North Carolina, had any mineral knowledge whatever. He said he had never seen gold in that form. Others, who held visions of finding gold in lumps as big as hen eggs, did not feel it would be worth the trouble to wash the particles and pack them home. It was decided that if this were gold, it had been washed down from a mother lode upstream.

Hopefully, the party continued its search on north up the stream. Reaching its headwaters, they moved west over to the Arkansas River, which they explored extensively to the vicinity of the Little Arkansas. Their search was fruitless. Finally, after seven long weeks in the field, the men were weary, discouraged, and ready to return home. Killing sixteen elk and curing the meat, the Pryor party turned their horses back down the Arkansas toward Gibson with only some worthless quartz to show for their efforts. Still, some of the men remained convinced that a lost gold mine existed somewhere above on the river. They were determined to return someday to find it.

The legend of gold on the Arkansas had been spawned three centuries earlier when stories of a golden city called Quivira had caused the Spanish conquistadors under Francisco Vasquez de Coronado to explore this region—the first known visit from the outside world. Visions of great wealth described to them by an Indian-slave guide whom they called the Turk had lured them deeper and deeper into a strange land.[3]

Coronado's misled army wandered about the Texas Panhandle and stumbled into the maze of Palo Duro Canyon. Finally, with only a party of thirty chosen horsemen and six foot soldiers, four grooms, pack animals, and a remuda of extra horses, Coronado turned northward across the Oklahoma Panhandle to the Arkansas River of western Kansas. Traveling with Coronado was Father Juan de Padilla, whose proclaimed mission was to Christianize the heathen Indians. The Turk, now under bitter suspicion of purposefully misleading them, was placed in chains, and the Spaniards turned to another Indian guide named Sopete.[4]

On the morning of July 2, 1541, the Spanish entourage came onto a buffalo hunt being conducted by a band of Indians just southwest of present Larned, Kansas. The Indians were greatly alarmed to see men dressed in metal helmets and armored coats that glistened blindingly in the sun. Nor had the Indians ever before seen a horse. With altogether natural fright at such an alien sight, they fled for their lives. But Sopete called to them in their own tongue, and the Indians were persuaded to return and meet the Spaniards in friendship.

This, the first European contact with the native inhabitants of Kansas, was a historic moment. With it the clock of recorded history had begun to tick after eons of silence, marking the start of the modern era for the region of Wichita, Kansas. It was also a step in creating a myth that would not die. For three centuries, men would continue to come to the Arkansas River of southern Kansas in search of the treasure chest of the Quiviras, the supposed El Dorado of North America. Even as late as 1849, men were scouring the sands of the Arkansas for signs of precious metals.[5]

The Indians met by Coronado led the Spaniards to their villages. For more than a month the visitors remained to explore the region. In New Mexico, the conquistadors had found Indians, the Pueblos, who lived in flat-topped, multistoried houses. Then in their march across the buffalo-covered prairies, they had encountered other Indians, the Apaches, who lived in "small huts" made from long poles that were tied together at the top and were covered with skins. But the natives that they met along the "River of Quivira" were different still.

The Quivira Indians, now presumed by most historians to have been the Wichitas, resided in round-topped grass huts constructed with a covered entry door and a place at the roof's center through which the smoke from lodge fires could escape. These Indians were remarkably tall to the Spaniards, who measured them at ten palms or well over six feet in height. Seen as they were in July and August, the dark skinned, tattooed Indian men went about virtually naked except for skimpy breechclouts about their waists. Custom permitted their women to go bare breasted, and the Spaniards found them well proportioned with facial features much like Moorish women.

These Indians lived by the hunt and, like other prairie Indians, procured meat (which they ate uncooked), moccasins, and other needs from the buffalo. They also planted and raised corn and melons and baked bread under the ashes of their lodge fires. To this diet the Quivirians added beans, plums, mulberries, and nuts.

Their villages, in which the grass huts had no particular arrangement, were scattered along the river bottoms of the streams feeding into the Arkansas basin. Archeological evidence shows these tributaries to be Cow Creek in the vicinity of Lyons, Kansas, and, to the east, the Little Arkansas, the mouth of which is engulfed today by the most populous city in Kansas.[6]

To his great disappointment, Coronado and his men found no signs of gold or mineral wealth in the Quivira villages. There was no lord with gold-draped canoes or glistening plates and bowls and jugs. They found only primitive grass hut villages and swarms of dark-skinned, tattooed people. The only merits to report, the Spaniards soon discovered, was a land with rich, black soil and great herds of buffalo that grazed the virgin prairie.

When Coronado summoned the native chief, the headman arrived with some two hundred warriors. All were well armed with bows and arrows and wore headdresses along with their breechclouts. The elderly chief was a huge man, and about his neck dangled the only metal discovered by the Spaniards at Quivira—a copper ornament of unknown origin.

It is believed that Coronado, well aware that his small force stood surrounded by a vast army of native warriors, made no attempt to explore beyond the Quivira villages. Still suspicious of the Turk and fearing he would use his influence against them, the Spaniards strangled him to death and buried his body secretly. Fear of reprisal, along with the lateness of the season and the torrid weather, caused them to turn back for New Mexico in early August. They planted a cross, at the foot of which was a message proclaiming the fact of their visit, and departed.[7] Though they carried not one grain of gold with them, the Spaniards had helped perpetuate a myth that would live on and on.

Padilla was so zealous and determined in his wish to Christianize the Indians that he returned to Kansas the following spring. With him were a Portuguese, two Indian lay assistants from the Pueblos, a few servants, and six Quivira Indians who had guided Coronado back to New Mexico. The priest brought with him a horse, some mules, and a flock of sheep along with a few church ornaments.

After spending some time among the Quiviras, Padilla set out to the northeast to visit another tribe known as the "Guas," thought by some to have been the Kansa (or Kaw) Indians. However, his party encountered hostile Indians who attacked them with bows and arrows. Father Padilla was slain, but the rest of his party escaped. The Pueblo lay assistants returned later and buried the priest. Historians believe Padilla's grave to be near Herington, Kansas, where a park monument stands in his memory.[8]

There is no record of the Spanish having visited Kansas again for half a century. In 1593 Francisco de Leyva y Bonilla and Antonio Gutierrez de Humaña led an unauthorized expedition to the north in another quest to reap of the fabled wealth that still haunted the men of Spain.[9] This party is thought to have reached the Quivira villages on the Arkansas, then continued northward until they were attacked by Indians who set the prairie on fire around them in all directions. Only one person with the expedition, a Pueblo Indian, escaped. On his return to New Mexico, the man was captured by an Apache band and held in captivity for a year before finally reaching home to tell his story.[10]

In June 1601, the Spanish governor of New Mexico, Don Juan de Oñate, led a force of seventy well-armed men, attendants, two Franciscan friars, Humaña's Indian guide, more than seven hundred horses and mules, plus carts and artillery into southern Kansas. In part, Oñate hoped to learn more about the fate of the Leyva-Humaña party. In the main, though, he and the New Mexico Spaniards he recruited for the expedition were driven by resurgent tales that wealths of gold were waiting to be found.

Near the end of its march, most likely in southern Kansas, the Oñate expedition encountered a large body of Indians whom they called Escanjaques.[11] These Indians resided in leather tents and lived by the hunt. They told the Spaniards of other villages, enemies to them, to the north and followed the conquistadors to a heavily wooded river believed to be the Arkansas. There Oñate found a large settlement consisting of more than twelve hundred grass huts populated by natives whose bodies were painted with stripes and who planted crops in much the same manner as those Indians met by Coronado. These the Spaniards called Rayados, though they undoubtedly were the Quiviras. Oñate's official report described the first known human community of the region:

> We came to a settlement containing more than twelve hundred houses...made of forked wooden poles joined together by sticks and on the outside covered with straw....We stayed a day at this pleasant place, surrounded everywhere by Indian cornfields and gardens....There were many beans and some calabashes, and plum trees between the planted fields....It was thought that it doubtless bordered on the tropics, as the people we saw went about naked, although some used skins.[12]

When Oñate took some of the Rayados captive in an attempt to learn the fate of the Bonilla party, the rest of the village inhabitants fled. When the Escanjaques began looting and burning the Rayado houses, Oñate ordered his men to stop them. This so angered the Escanjaques that as the Spaniards began their return march they were attacked by an estimated fifteen hundred Escanjaque warriors—"the arrows came down thick."[13] The outnumbered but better armed Spaniards successfully drove the Escanjaques off and made their way safely back to New Mexico. Still, like Coronado, they had failed to find the storied gold they sought.

In 1606 a party of six hundred Quivira Indians made the long journey to Santa Fe to offer their friendship and, even, some of their land to the Spanish in return for help against their enemies.[14] What may have resulted from this offer is not known, for the records become silent again concerning the Spanish connection with the Quivira region of Kansas.

There is record, however, of a Spanish visit to far western Kansas some time between 1664 and 1680. Juan de Archuleta was sent with a military force to capture and bring back some Taos Indians who had fled Spanish rule and established a fortified settlement called El Curatelejo.[15] This site, near present Scott City, Kansas, was well west of Quivira. Archuleta was told that the land of the Quiviras was on a route from El Curatelejo to the country of the Pawnees to the east.

During a period of nearly a century and a half (1606–1748), no further visits to the Quivira area by the Spanish are recorded. During this time, it is believed, the Wichitas were defeated by the Apaches, who had the enormous advantages of horses and metal weapons that they had procured from the Spaniards. The Wichita villages were attacked and destroyed repeatedly, their women and children being carried off into the rampant slave trade of Spanish New Mexico.[16]

As a result, the Wichitas deserted the region of southern Kansas and moved down the Arkansas River into present eastern Oklahoma. There they were met by French explorer Bernard de la Harpe in 1719. After the Comanches migrated from the northern Rocky Mountains and drove the Apaches south into Texas and New Mexico, the Wichitas returned to their Quivira homeland.

We are left to wonder what unchronicled visits may have been made by the Spanish from New Mexico, the French from Louisiana, the British from Canada, or the Americans from the east during this century and a half. An intriguing hint of one possible visit is to be found on a 1757 map by Antoine S. Le Page du Pratz, though its accuracy is subject to question. Du Pratz himself added to the legend of gold on the Arkansas by stating: "I found, upon the river of the Arkansas, a rivulet that rolled down with its water, gold dust."[17]

Another story told by early Kansas Indian trader James R. Mead (he may well have gotten it from his friend, Jesse Chisholm) indicates that a Spanish party from New Mexico once descended the Arkansas River in boats loaded with gold and silver. The party was supposedly surrounded by Indians one night as it camped at the mouth of the Little Arkansas. After a siege of several days, they were all but one killed. This one survivor buried the gold and silver before he made his escape.[18]

Other unpredictable visits could easily have occurred during the ensuing time, as an event in 1748 illustrates. In the fall of that year, three French soldiers deserted their post in Arkansas and joined a party of twelve men headed for New Mexico. They followed the winding Arkansas into Kansas, where they came onto two Indian villages. The Indians conducted them to a Comanche encampment, and from there the men eventually made it to Taos and on to Santa Fe.[19]

During the year following, Felipe de Sandoval, a Spaniard from the same French post on the Arkansas, and two others canoed up the Arkansas on their way to Santa Fe. After fifty days' travel, they reached what is thought to have been the Wichita settlements at the

Little Arkansas. The Indians there, who were much the same as Coronado had described them two centuries earlier, were conducting a brisk trade with the French. A party of Frenchmen had only recently visited them and left gifts, including a French flag that now flew over their village.[20]

Sandoval reported that these people, who were warring with the Apaches, indulged in cannibalism. He claimed that he had seen them eat two captives. It was a year later, 1750, when a command of Spanish soldiers under Lt. Gen. Bernardo de Bustamente y Tagle pursued a band of Comanches and followed the Arkansas River eastward to a large Indian village.[21]

Another piece adding to the historical puzzle of Quivira is the story told by James Mead of his once discovering a cave on the Smoky Hill River, forty miles west of Salina, Kansas. On the wall of the cave were numerous hieroglyphics and drawings of animals and figures of men in battle scenes. And in one place Mead found an inscription that read "TVREDO, 1786," indicating the probability of a Spanish visit to that area then.[22]

Throughout the eighteenth century, Kansas and much of the Indian-inhabited Central Plains saw a continued struggle between the French and the Spanish over trading dominance with the fur-and-horse-rich tribes. But with the proprietorship of Louisiana Territory transferring from Spain to France and then to the United States in 1804, the Americans entered into the contest.

United States exploration of the vast new territory saw Lewis and Clark traversing the Missouri River to the far Pacific coast during 1804–5. Even as Lewis and Clark were returning in 1806, another exploring expedition under Lt. Zebulon M. Pike departed Missouri and marched across central Kansas to the Great Bend of the Arkansas River. There Pike divided his command, sending Lt. James B. Wilkinson down the Arkansas River southeastward to Little Rock, Arkansas, while he explored present-day Colorado.

Accompanied by five soldiers and two Osage guides, Wilkinson attempted to float down the ice-crusted river in a skin canoe and another hewn from a tree trunk. Unsuccessful in this, he and his small party proceeded on foot across the prairie land of southern Kansas, encountering herds of elk, antelope, deer, and buffalo: "If I saw one, I saw more than nine thousand buffalos during the day's march," Wilkinson noted in his log for November 10, 1806.[23]

The Little Arkansas country served as a favorite buffalo hunting ground for Osage warriors. George Catlin drawing.

Wilkinson found no Indian villages as his small party passed the mouth of the Little Arkansas. Gone now were the Wichitas, having been driven south by the pressure of the Apaches and the Osages of Missouri who now came there regularly to hunt. While at the Little Arkansas, Wilkinson and his men paused to fell a tree, split it, and hew out two new canoes. As they started on down the river, one of the craft overturned. The party's meat supply and valuable ammunition were dumped into the stream.

By good fortune, they were met soon after by a party of Osages. The tribesmen insisted on sending out hunters to replenish the lost meat. After a short delay, the explorers moved on; but the water in the Arkansas was so low that they were forced to portage the boats for a distance. As they passed the mouth of the Ninnescah on November 26, a raging blizzard struck, causing the scantly clothed and often wet group great hardship and suffering.

There would be others to follow the Wilkinson exploration of the region. In March 1815 the fur-trading party of A. P. Chouteau, Jules de Mun, and Joseph Philibert passed by the Little Arkansas on their way west to trap and hunt in the Colorado Rockies.[24] The next year, soon after his famous battle with the Pawnees at Chouteau's Island near present Lakin, Kansas, Chouteau returned to the Little Arkansas to erect what was the first log house to exist temporarily at the site of present Wichita.[25]

By the time the Stephen H. Long detachment traversed the Arkansas in August 1820, the Little Arkansas had been named, so the expedition chronicler noted, by "a few hunters, who have had an opportunity to visit it."[26] Arriving at the mouth of the river on August 14, 1820, the Long expedition found a "fine limpid stream of cool flowing water, meandering through a dense growth of trees and bushes" with "honey locust and buttonwood, though the principal growth was cottonwood, elm and ash."[27]

Captain John R. Bell of the expedition reported of the Little Arkansas site: "We discovered an old (Osage) Indian village, or [it] may more likely be an Indian hunting camp for the winter season, as many of the cabins were enclosed and covered with bark."[28] While such was typical of an Osage camp, Bell also noted that watermelons, pumpkins, and corn were seen growing at random in the fields around the cabin. These summertime crops could well have indicated a remaining Wichita presence.

A year later, in October 1821, the Hugh Glenn party of trappers and traders marched up the Arkansas River from Fort Smith, Arkansas— twenty men in all with thirty horses and mules, traps, and supplies. Jacob Fowler, who kept a journal of the trek, noted on October 13 that while they were camped on the bank of the Little Arkansas they were visited by Indians they supposed to be Pawnees from the region of present Nebraska.[29]

The Arkansas River was now on its way to becoming a standard route for the first westward movement of trappers and Indian traders who worked the beaver-rich streams of the West as well as for buffalo hunters and travelers headed for the Rocky Mountains or California. The Glenn-Fowler party, accompanied by the McKnight-James group who had traveled to New Mexico via the Canadian River earlier, came down the Arkansas in 1822. After separating at the Big Bend, the

McKnight-James men continued on to the Little Arkansas and from there followed the Osage hunting trail to the Neosho River.[30]

The notion of a lost gold mine at the Little Arkansas was by no means forgotten following the Pryor expedition of 1826. In 1847, Arkansas native William Black told of other gold-seeking efforts up the Arkansas River:

> So fully impressed with the evidences in that region, Mixen soon after our return made up a small party, and tried it again, though without success. Richard Bean, of Cane Hill [Arkansas], went with him on that occasion, who is not satisfied with his failure, is willing to go again, also, to go with us this summer. Mixen, then, with a party of Cherokees, made another exploration in vain, and I have no doubt, if he is living and learns that we are about to try it again, will join us.
>
> In the summer of 1847, James McNab, Nicholas McNair of the Cherokee Nation, who live about 6 miles from the Grand Saline, [name unclear] Childers, and James Callan, of the Creek Nation, who live on the Verdigris, were out in the prairies, up the Big Bend, and found some gold sands on *Walnut Creek*, 15 miles above its mouth, and brought some of the dust back in quills, which proved to be pure gold. They went down the creek, and there saw the beaver dam, which identifies the creek. They also went up Walnut Creek to be about 35 miles below the Little Arkansas. I have no doubt but it is the same creek, and down it were washed the sands we saw.[31]

The hope of discovering gold was most likely in the back of the minds of the forty-eight trappers and hunters led by Robert Bean from Fort Smith to the Rocky Mountains in 1830. This group followed up the Canadian River. After a fight with some Comanches, they turned north to strike the Arkansas below the Big Bend.[32]

Still further stimulus to the Arkansas River gold fever was supplied by another Arkansas man. He claimed that in 1835 a man who lived near Fort Towson on the Red River had returned with a lump of "pure stuff" from the southern Kansas region.[33] James Mead's statement that Jesse Chisholm led a gold-seeking expedition to the mouth of the Little Arkansas in 1836 may be correct. More likely, however, Mead simply misremembered the date of the 1826 venture.[34]

Further encouragement was given to the gold myth by a story that an Arkansas man told of hearing from a Spanish gentleman in Havana in 1843. The Cuban said that in 1783 he had been a surgeon with a Spanish party that explored the upper Arkansas and Yellowstone. Somewhere (the story is not clear as to just where) they discovered a large body of silver ore. While boating it downstream, the Spaniards were attacked by Indians. All of the group but the Havanan and eight others were killed.[35]

Those who escaped later returned to the scene, reclaimed their ore, and carried it on downstream in buffalo-hide canoes. At a point along the Arkansas, the Havana man said, they landed, constructed furnaces, and ran their silver into bars. This story, the Arkansas man believed, gave credence to the account told by the New Orleans merchant in 1806.

In 1843 Captain Enoch Steen and fifty-four dragoons marched from Fort Gibson to an escort assignment on the Santa Fe Trail, establishing a route that would be followed by California gold rush parties in 1849. During that year a member, William Black of Crawford County, Arkansas, who had been with the Pryor-Chisholm excursion of 1826, led still another gold-seeking group to the Little Arkansas area.[36]

In May a party of gold seekers on their way to California from the Cherokee country blazed a new trail past the Little Arkansas. They were followed in 1850 by another California-bound group of Cherokees that searched for gold as they went. The Cherokees found nothing until they reached the South Platte, where traces of gold dust were discovered.[37]

For many years the Santa Fe Trail was a principal concourse of American travel westward, one camping stop being at the Little Arkansas a few miles above its entry into the main Arkansas. Past here plodded the oxen bull teams, their wagons loaded with trade goods for Santa Fe. They returned later with cargoes of Mexican silver or buffalo hides and sometimes escorting herds of cattle, horses, and mules. Here, too, came the early emigrants moving west to Colorado, New Mexico, Arizona, and California. Sometimes they were escorted by foot soldiers or mounted dragoons, which provided some small protection against attacks by the warring tribes of the Plains.

Beyond the limits of the trail, southern Kansas remained the active arena of the Indian well beyond the time of the American Civil War—a hunting and warring ground for the Cheyennes, Arapahos,

Comanches, Kiowas, Osages, Kansa, Pawnees, and other tribes of the Central Plains. For the white man, the Little Arkansas area was still a land of mystery and danger. And there were still those who believed that somewhere along the sandy bed of the Arkansas a great lode of gold or silver lay waiting to be discovered.

Chapter Two

Before the Pioneers

The Little Arkansas was a gem; a ribbon of stately trees
winding down to the parent river through a broad, level
valley of green, as I first saw it, dotted over with the black
bodies of fat, sleek buffalo and an occasional group of
antelope or straggling elk, and not a living human soul
in all the country now known as Sedgwick county.
Such was the Little Arkansas as the writer first saw it
from the highlands to the east, overlooking the valley,
on a sunny afternoon in June, 1863.
— James R. Mead, "The Little Arkansas," *Collections of the
Kansas State Historical Society*, 1908

When the Wichitas departed during the eighteenth century, the country around the Little Arkansas became the hunting grounds for other tribes such as the Iowa and Kansa of northeastern Kansas, the Osages of southwestern Missouri and southeastern Kansas, and the Pawnees of Nebraska. The Little Arkansas marked an approximate eastern limit of the buffalo range, and for the Osages it was a line of demarcation for their hunting excursions westward. They chased the herds of the prairie adjacent to the river, but beyond that they went no farther for fear of the Paducas (Comanches) and other hostile tribes of the Plains.

To the Osages, the Arkansas River was "Ne Shutsa," or Red Water, while the Little Arkansas was "Ne Shutsa Shinka," or the Little or Younger Red Water. They associated the two as parent and child.[1]

The Osage Trail from the east—in long use, James Mead judged from its deep ruts in places—struck the Little Arkansas six miles above its mouth. There the gravel ford, which became known as the Osage Crossing, witnessed the passage of Indian villages and hunting parties as well as military expeditions and westward wandering frontiersmen.[2] The Osages were particularly fond of the area and often came with their families to construct temporary lodges along the river.

The structures, unlike the Plains Indian buffalo-skin tepees, were made by setting rows of green-cut poles in the ground some eight feet apart, then bending them over and lashing them together to form an arch some six feet high. Other poles were then tied to the sides with willow withes, and the whole was covered with buffalo skins and reed mats to make a comfortable abode some ten to twenty feet in length.

The Osage hunters usually came twice a year, in June and September, to chase the countless American bison that grazed in the Arkansas valley and on the rolling sweeps of prairie beyond the river. Following behind the hunters came the Osage women, they to butcher the fallen game and load the meat and hides aboard their twin-pole travois or onto horses to carry their kill back to camp.[3]

At times independent war parties of Osages came west, not necessarily to hunt the buffalo but to ride forth simply for whatever adventure they might turn up. A. F. Greenway, then a trader with the Osages and a brother to their agent, accompanied one such party in the spring of 1852. Greenway wrote an interesting account of this trip to the Little Arkansas, giving us an intriguing glimpse of Osage activity on the Little Arkansas long before the site was reached by white civilization.

Ever since he had first arrived at the Osage reservation in southeastern Kansas, Greenway had been anxious to take part in a buffalo hunt. His opportunity came when a party of eighty-five young Osages prepared to make a reconnoitering tour westward to the Little Arkansas. Greenway felt he would be safe with the group, which was armed with shiny new Leman flintlock rifles. As Greenway made his preparations to "see the buffalo," some of the Osage elders held a medicine ceremony to bring him good luck.[4]

He outfitted himself with three blankets, a wagon sheet to serve as a tent, ten pounds of cheese, twenty pounds of crackers, one small box of dried herring, a two-gallon coffee boiler, one sack of ground coffee, and other smaller articles. He loaded these supplies and other accouterments onto a pack pony and recruited a young Osage boy as his own personal aide. From an old white hunter, Greenway borrowed a heavy, long-barreled buffalo gun. The gun weighed more than fifteen pounds and used a ball that weighed an ounce.

The Osage party made an imposing sight as it headed westward, moving along nicely without incident all that first day. It was nearly sundown when the group reached a blackjack ridge overlooking a large valley and flushed a deer from a thicket. Immediately a wild chase ensued with Greenway joining in. The deer disappeared into a deep marsh area where the grass was almost as high as the riders' heads and escaped. The Osage party regrouped and crossed the marsh to go into camp on its west bank for the night.

It was then that Greenway discovered that he had not only lost his hat during the chase but the coffee boiler from his pack animal as well. He also learned a hard lesson about Osage hunting parties. It was against their medicine to bring along much of anything to eat, relying on their hunting prowess for food. A few of them had brought a little dried meat but nothing more. Thus when Greenway set out his supper of crackers, cheese, and herring, he was soon joined by the entire party of famished warriors. In a very short time, all of his food supply had disappeared with the exception of the herring, which the Indians did not like.

The loss of his hat was more serious to Greenway than his coffee pot. As they rode, the warming sun began to burn his neck and face badly. The bandanna he had tied around his head did little good. His youthful Osage helper proffered his medicine bag and suggested that Greenway should paint his face for protection. Thinking that the more he used the better, Greenway applied the paint freely. Soon, however, he noticed blood-looking drops on his hands, shirt and saddle. He asked the boy about this and was told that he should have first used tallow to prevent the paint from melting off.

"I asked where the tallow was, and they said it was in the buffalo [none of which had yet been killed], so that point was settled."

The party continued at a lively gait, while the hungry Greenway had only his herring to munch on. The salty fish satisfied his hunger, but he had no water to overcome the great thirst it created. That night he made coffee in a tin cup and drank several cupfuls. The Indians joined him, and by morning the coffee sack lay discarded inside out, the coffee all gone.

Finally, on the following morning the first buffalo were sighted. The Osages killed several animals, but Greenway, his eyes full of sweat and paint, failed to get in a shot. Choice buffalo cuts were roasted that evening, and the party glutted itself on "straight buffalo." The diet was too much for Greenway, who became ill as the party moved on toward the Little Arkansas.

In anticipation of meeting enemy warriors, the Osages put out scouts on either side of their march. With Greenway and his helper in the rear, the party advanced cautiously over each rise until the Arkansas River was reached. There they found the wide river valley black with thousands of buffalo. Indeed, the herd was so vast and so thick that it took the party some time to work its way through it.

The Osages went into camp at sundown in an area between the Arkansas and Little Arkansas rivers near their juncture. Though the site was a beautiful camping ground, Greenway was feeling so ill that he could little appreciate it. Rejecting the idea of having more buffalo for supper, he retired into his blankets early. He had slept for nearly two hours when he was suddenly awakened by a commotion among the horses. Something had frightened them, and their alarm quickly spread among the Osages as well. Some suspected that enemy warriors might be lurking in the dark. One of the Osages told Greenway to catch his horses, calling his attention to a strange noise that sounded "like a wind before a storm."

There was a good deal of thunder, and flashes of lightning revealed an ominous black cloud moving in. Pronouncing the whole thing as a bad omen, the Osages jumped aboard their horses and headed back through the buffalo herd, which stampeded in all directions. In the wild decampment, Greenway's pack horse broke loose from the Osage boy and disappeared into the night, the youth in pursuit.

Now all alone, Greenway waited for a time before realizing that the boy would not be able to rejoin him in the dark. During a flash of lightning, he spotted a dark object moving toward him. Quickly deciding that he would be better off with the rest of his party, Greenway gave free rein to his horse and headed out. He caught up with the Osages in about an hour, his aide arriving later without his packhorse or pack.

The next morning a council was held, and it was agreed among the Osages that they would go back and see what frightened them. But Greenway had had enough. He held his own council with five of the group, offering them the equivalent of twenty dollars in trade goods to take him on to the reservation. Three days later they arrived at the post. When Greenway had recovered he went to the old medicine counselors and told them their medicine was all foolishness, that it hadn't done him a great deal of good. Their answer was simple. Sometimes their medicine didn't work for palefaces.

Five days after Greenway had returned, the Osage party came in with seventy-two ponies and Mexican mules and three scalps. Greenway thought that the trophies had likely been taken from Mexicans traveling the Santa Fe Trail.

During the sojourn, Greenway had thrown away the heavy buffalo rifle loaned him by the old hunter. The frontiersman valued the gun highly. Though Greenway gave him two ponies in repayment, the old man never forgave him.

"His friendship and mine ceased and was never resumed," Greenway commented.

Greenway returned to the mouth of the Little Arkansas in April 1854 with another Osage group. In two days there they killed 132 buffalo. They took the best part of the kill and were preparing to leave when Pawnee horse thieves slipped in and stole seventeen of their ponies. Two young Indians were sent back for more horses, while Greenway "passed the time in profanity." Some of the Osages went on their own way, later coming in with several ponies and two scalps that were either Cheyenne or Arapaho.[5]

In 1857 a small party of white hunters and trappers arrived at the Little Arkansas to indulge themselves in the rich coffers of buffalo, beaver, and other game. This group consisted of C. C. Arnold, Ed Moseley, Thompson Crawford, Robert Dunlap, Robert Durackin, Jacob Carey, and a man named Maxley. Arnold, who remained in the region for an extended period, is considered by some to have been the first bona fide white settler in the vicinity of Wichita.[6]

A year later Moseley and Maxley located a trading post at the Osage Crossing. There they trapped for beaver and conducted a whiskey trade with the visiting Osages. Both men eventually became victims of the frontier. Moseley was killed in a fight with a party of Indians near Kiowa, Kansas; Maxley drowned while trying to cross a flooded stream.[7]

Bob Durackin and Jake Carey built a cabin on the banks of the Arkansas River west of the Osage Crossing at the location of what later became Park City and resided there for a time. They cultivated a small patch of land and went into the business of capturing buffalo calves and cows to sell to eastern animal parks and traveling menagerie shows.[8]

The first farmer by trade settled three miles north of the Osage Crossing on a high bank of the Little Arkansas in 1860.[9] His name was John Ross, and he brought with him his wife and two children. Ross built a cabin and began breaking the land. But his enterprise came to a tragic end one day in October. Ross and a hired hand hitched up a wagon and headed southwest toward Cowskin Grove, located due west of present Wichita on Cowskin Creek, to kill a buffalo or two for meat.

Ross's wife and children were left at home alone. When night came, the two men had not returned; nor did they do so on the following day. Finally the frantic wife enlisted the aid of a passing hunter and sent word to the closest settlement on Walnut Creek that her husband was missing. A search party of about twenty horsemen was collected from among the Walnut Creek settlers, and the men hurried to the Cowskin Grove area. They found no sign of the missing men that day and went into camp at dusk.

When the search was resumed on the following morning, one of the party made a gruesome find—a human leg with a boot still on it. A short distance away, Ross's dismembered head was discovered. Further search failed to locate anything more of the missing men, their wagon, or horses. The remains were taken back to his home and buried on the bank of the river near Ross's house, with stones piled atop to stymie predators. It was believed that the two men were murdered by a band of Osages (it was their warring style to decapitate their victims) who resented Ross's intrusion onto their hunting grounds. Mrs. Ross and the children quit Kansas and returned to the East.[10]

The advent of the Civil War in 1861 brought the return of the site's former settlers, the Wichita Indians. After departing the Little Arkansas region, the Wichitas had relocated first on the lower Arkansas in present northern Oklahoma at a site known as Ferdinandina near present Ponca City, Oklahoma; then on the Red River at what is today known as the Spanish Forts just north of Nocona, Texas. From there they migrated to the North Fork of the Red where Col. Henry Dodge found them in 1834. Later they moved to Cache Creek in the Wichita Mountains of present Oklahoma and eventually on to Rush Creek east of the mountains.

During this time, they maintained their traditional mode of livelihood, cultivating small fields of corn, beans, and pumpkins. They lived in peace with the more dominant Comanches and Kiowas,

The Wichita Indians resided in conical grass-hut communities on the Arkansas. Courtesy Manuscript Division, Oklahoma Historical Society.

whose warrior bands fiercely opposed white encroachment onto their lands. Because of the Wichitas' friendship with both the Plains tribes and the whites, they were prevailed on in 1858 to act as an intermediary in persuading the Comanches to come in to Fort Arbuckle for peace talks.[11]

While the Comanche chiefs and their families—some six hundred tribespeople—were on their way to Arbuckle, they stopped for a visit at the Wichita village on Rush Creek. There they were victimized by a surprise attack of U.S. troops under the command of Maj. Earl Van Dorn, who was unaware of the government's peace initiative. More than seventy Comanches as well as a number of Wichitas were killed, 120 lodges were torched, and all of the camp equipage was destroyed.

The angry Comanches blamed the Wichitas for the disaster, and the tribe was forced to move to near Fort Arbuckle for protection. They remained there until 1859 when the government leased an area between the Washita and Red rivers from the Choctaws and Chickasaws as a reserve for them and other Indians of the region. An agency for the Wichitas was created, and Fort Cobb was established nearby to provide protection for the tribes.[12]

The protection was short-lived. The Civil War erupted in the spring of 1861, and the Union abandoned its Indian Territory forts along with its Indian charges. Colonel William H. Emory led the Union retreat northward to Kansas. His entourage consisted of more than a thousand soldiers and civilians with a caravan of army ambulances, ox teams, eighty wagons, and six hundred horses and mules. Emory crossed the Arkansas near the Little Arkansas and made camp there before reaching the frontier settlement of newly founded El Dorado, Kansas.[13] El Dorado had been established in July 1857 by William and H. Bemis, who were later joined there by the trading establishment of Stein and Dunlap.[14]

The Wichitas and others now became wards of the Texas Confederates, with whom they had long been at odds. It was an uneasy relationship at best, the Reserve Indians being very displeased with their situation and with their agent, Matthew Leeper. Matters came to such a state by August 1862 that a large number of Reserve Indians deserted the agency. Rumors were heard that some of the Indians who had moved to Kansas earlier now planned to send down a war party to attack the agency.[15]

The rumors were true enough, and in early September a well-armed group of Delawares and Shawnees arrived on the Washita River to join the Leased District tribes in an attack on the agency. The Tonkawas, whom the others disliked intensely because of their cannibalistic habits and their support of the Texans, were excluded from participation. Just after dark on the evening of October 23, the allied force of Indians entered the agency, murdered four white men who worked there, and burned their bodies along with the agency structures.

The Tonkawas, who lived nearby, decamped and disappeared into the night. On the following morning, however they were found hiding in a grove of trees, surrounded, and brutally massacred. Out of some 390 Tonkawas, only about 150 managed to make it to safety at Fort Arbuckle.

Word now reached the Leased District that a large unit of Texans and Indians was on the march for Fort Cobb. The Wichitas had no choice but to flee with the other tribes to Union-controlled Kansas, traveling some three hundred miles in a month and a day to reach Walnut Creek.[16]

The pitiful retreat of the Wichitas back to Kansas in 1862 has been little noted by historians. James Mead, who knew the Wichitas well, told how they, along with Shawnees, Delawares, Kickapoos, and other loyal Indians, fled the Leased District with few of their belongings. Mostly they were afoot, only a few having wagons, most of which soon broke down on the roadless prairie. Some of the loyalists were caught by the Confederates on the Salt Fork of the Arkansas and killed. Those that reached Kansas went into camp on Walnut Creek near a place called Belmont. The Wichitas and other refugee tribes huddled there that winter, utterly destitute, living virtually without shelter, food, or clothing. Their situation was corrupted even further when virtually all of their horses died from starvation.[17]

Despite Union promises to help them, by 1863 some fifteen to twenty thousand Indian refugees were residing, diseased and starved, in southern Kansas in extremely dire conditions. Though some small amounts of food were supplied by the government and a physician was sent to vaccinate some against smallpox, the tribes received little help. The Wichitas and Caddos, being planters by tradition, had brought along their seed corn, but the season had been too far advanced to plant when they arrived.[18]

The refugee tribes were still on the Walnut when James Mead first visited the Little Arkansas in the spring of 1863. Mead found the area to be a hunter's paradise. He and his two companions camped in Ross's old cabin near the Osage Crossing, killing sixteen buffalo and a big-horned elk in the vicinity of the cabin.[19]

That fall Mead established a trading post at a large spring on the Walnut where the refugee tribes were then congregated, the site eventually becoming the town of Towanda.[20] He returned to the Little Arkansas that fall to conduct trade with Indian bands that came there to hunt.

Mead, a descendant of Maj. Gen. Ebenezer Mead of the Revolutionary War and the son of a Yale-educated Presbyterian minister, had come to Kansas in 1859 at the age of twenty-three from Davenport, Ohio. After attending Iowa College, he had embarked on a lumber career on the Mississippi River, but the financial crisis of 1857 caused him to go broke. Having been introduced to the Indian trade in north-central Kansas while attending a buffalo hunt on the Smoky Hill River, he established a trading post on the Saline River in the fall of 1859. Being impressed with the fur trading potential of southern Kansas, he moved his operations to Towanda in 1863.[21]

During the spring of 1864 the Wichitas, destitute and mostly afoot, moved back to their old home site on the Little Arkansas, erected new grass huts, and planted gardens in the rich soil of the river bends. They were joined there by the Wacos, Kichais (Keechies), and Tonkawas while the Caddos, Delawares, and Absentee Shawnees located ten miles to the east on Dry Creek. Warriors from these tribes regularly went south to gather up horses and cattle—theirs and any others—roaming freely there.

Through the fall, Mead conducted trading operations on the Little Arkansas with the refugee tribes as well as with the Osages who still came there to hunt.[22] On August 6, 1864, the *Emporia News* reported: "J. R. Mead of Towanda passed through this place on Tuesday with several large loads of hides and furs, mostly buffalo robes, for Leavenworth. He traded for them west of the Arkansas."

Joining Mead in the fall of 1864 was Jesse Chisholm, who arrived to build "some comfortable cabins for his family in a fine grove of hackberry timber, just below the forks of the creek which flows through our city bearing his name."[23] Chisholm also initiated a trading post there, capitalizing on his Indian connections and the high regard in which he was held by both the refugee tribes and the bands who lived on the prairie beyond the Arkansas.

Thus, as the Civil War was still being fought in the fall of 1864, the site of present Wichita once again featured a settlement of Wichita Indian grass huts nestled in the forested juncture of the two rivers. The Wichitas were now accompanied by the log cabins and corrals of Mead, Chisholm, and others such as I. J. L. Don Carlos and his Indian wife, who resided there. Other white men had arrived, but mostly they were those who lived beyond the advance of towns and cities. These men hearkened to places that were still a part of the Indian country, where the land was abundant with game and unfettered by the conventions of formal society. Soon there would be more arriving to form the nucleus of a permanent village. Before then, however, the Little Arkansas would host a treaty council, sponsored by the U.S. government and featuring some of the most prominent names of the American frontier.

Chapter Three

The Talking Ground

To-haw-son, or Little Mountain, a Kiowa chief, spoke as
follows: The Kiowas own from Fort Laramie and the north
fork of the Platte to Texas, and have always owned it.
That all the branches, creeks, rivers and ponds that you see;
all the deer and buffalo, wolves and turtles, all belong to
him—were given to him by the Great Spirit.
White man did not give it to him.
— John B. Sanborn, *Report of the Commissioner*
of Indian Affairs, 1866

Even as it conducted the conflict with the rebellious states of the
South, the federal government found itself faced with serious
problems on the Central Plains where the Sioux, Cheyennes,
Arapahos, Kiowas, and Comanches were beginning to offer increased
resistance to white encroachment across and onto their lands. At
stake were not only the frontier settlements in Kansas, Nebraska, and
Colorado but also the commerce, supply, and immigration routes
westward. Indian depredations against transportation on the Santa
Fe Trail, the Platte Trail, and the new Smoky Hill road to Colorado
were increasing; and the military was ill prepared to provide the protection that citizens were demanding.

During the summer of 1864, an Indian war burst into flames all
across the region. It had been exacerbated when U.S. troops shot
Cheyenne chief Lean Bear down without provocation on the Smoky
Hill River. Lean Bear had only recently met with President Lincoln in

the White House and carried a voucher as a friendly Indian. In an effort at making peace, Maj. E. W. Wynkoop at Fort Lyon, Colorado Territory, led a daring military expedition into western Kansas. He was successful in persuading Cheyenne principal chief Black Kettle and six other Cheyenne and Arapaho leaders to attend a peace council at Denver's Camp Weld. The chiefs left Denver thinking that Col. John M. Chivington had promised them safety if they took their camps in to Fort Lyon. But the Indian situation took a fateful turn when Chivington launched a surprise attack on Black Kettle's village at Sand Creek, Colorado Territory, on November 29, 1864, killing many Cheyennes.

Both Sand Creek and the aftermath of the Civil War had left the Kansas frontier in chaos, not only from its severely disturbed Indian residents but from an often-corrupt and inept military leadership, rampant thievery of Indian annuity goods and livestock, a frontier population that passionately believed in simply annihilating the Indians, dishonest politicians, and army generals who held vested financial interest in the westward-extending railroads.[1]

The cause of making peace with the tribes was taken up in the spring of 1865 by Comanche-Kiowa agent Jesse Leavenworth, a graduate of West Point and son of Gen. Henry Leavenworth, namesake of Fort Leavenworth. There was also the problem of returning the destitute refugee tribes to their assigned home area in the Indian Territory. These bands quickly agreed to a grand council of all the tribes, requesting that it be held near their Little Arkansas villages.

They preferred to meet at this location, they said, for several reasons. It was farther away from the whites, who in the past had broken their fences, stolen their horses, and caused other friction during their stay in southern Kansas. Further, their horses were in wretched condition and too poor to travel.[2]

It was another matter to persuade the more hostile, less dependent tribes to come in. Leavenworth sent Jesse Chisholm and William "Buffalo Bill" Mathewson into the Indian Territory to talk in the scattered bands of Comanches, Kiowas, and Plains Apaches. Eventually chiefs of these tribes arrived at the Little Arkansas, and on August 15, 1865, signed a temporary truce.

There was still no word from those Cheyennes and Arapahos ranging below the Arkansas under the domination of the angry and belligerent Cheyenne Dog Soldiers. Black Kettle, accompanied by George Bent, the half-blood son of William Bent, risked the dire

Indian agent Jesse Leavenworth helped initiate the Treaty of the Little Arkansas held at the site of Wichita in 1865. Manuscript Division, Oklahoma Historical Society.

threats of the Dog Soldiers and came up to Dutch Bill Greiffenstein's trading post on Cow Creek. From there they rode to the Little Arkansas where they met with Leavenworth and Maj. Gen. John B. Sanborn, agreeing to return in October to effect a treaty.[3]

When the full treaty talks got under way on October 11 at the council grounds, which extended from five to eight miles above the Little Arkansas-Arkansas River juncture, the government was represented by a wide range of important figures. Leavenworth and Sanborn were now joined by Maj. Gen. William Harney, an athletically slim, snow-haired army veteran who stood six-feet-four in his moccasins and was famous as a storyteller; Thomas Murphy, Indian superintendent of much western experience; Judge James Steele of St. Louis; and two men of great frontier notoriety—William Bent of Bent's Fort and the most famous man of the West at the time, Kit Carson.

Other western notables were present to interpret and lend their long experience among the Indians to the occasion: John Simpson

Smith, who had lived among the Blackfoot and the Cheyennes for thirty-five years; Jesse Chisholm, known and respected by whites and Indians alike for his sagacity and humaneness; German immigrant William Greiffenstein, an experienced and well-liked Indian trader who was married to a Cheyenne woman; William Mathewson, a veteran of twelve years on the plains as a fur trapper and trader; and James Mead, another successful hunter and Indian trader of the Kansas frontier.

By the time the complete commission arrived, there were some three thousand Indians camped along the Little Arkansas, these being members of the Wichita, Caddo, Waco, Ioni, Tawakoni, and Kichai tribes, as well as splinter groups of tribes removed from the East.[4]

The peace commission arrived at the council site from various directions. Kit Carson, now a U.S. Army colonel, came up from Fort Bascom in New Mexico accompanied by six soldiers in an army ambulance and two wagons. William Bent traveled down the Arkansas River from his fort in eastern Colorado Territory. General Harney came in from Fort Riley, escorted by two companies of First Colorado Cavalry and two of the Second U.S. Mounted Infantry, while Sanborn arrived with an escort of one hundred mounted infantrymen.

Leavenworth, Judge Steele, and Superintendent Murphy left Atchison on September 28 with three ambulances and a wagon train, accompanied by lawyer Samuel A. Kingman, who would serve as one of the three secretaries for the treaty council.[5] Kingman's diary of the journey and ensuing events provides a far more personal view of the affair than is revealed by the council transcripts.

Kingman's group, which had been joined by Sanborn's escort near Junction City, arrived at the Little Arkansas site on October 4 to find the council at a standstill. The Cheyennes, fearing another Sand Creek affair, were reluctant to come in. Sanborn and Harney refused to cross the Arkansas to meet them for fear of being detained there by high waters.[6]

So the commission waited for more than a week, during which time the monotony of camp life grew more and more intolerable. Kingman reported in his diary that "the same faces, the same ideas and the same routine of daily sensation and occupations soon became tiresome. Eating, smoking, talking and sleeping make the whole day."[7] Some of the commission party fished and some hunted without much luck, and others visited the refugee Indian camps.

By October 12, however, the Cheyennes had arrived, and the treaty site overflowed with people. Never before had this spot of western geography seen such a collection of grass huts, tepees, Sibley tents, horses, mules, wagons, commissioners, agents, soldiers, teamsters, clerks, traders, frontiersmen, and Indians of many tribes, all engulfing the land between the two rivers.

Representing the Indian tribes were some of the most notable chiefs of the Plains: Black Kettle and Little Robe of the Cheyennes; Little Raven, Storm, and Big Mouth of the Arapahos; Poor Bear and Iron Shirt of the Plains Apaches; Satank and Little Mountain of the Kiowas; Eagle Drinking, Horse Back, and Buffalo Hump of the Comanches.

James Mead, who shared a tent with Kit Carson, described the famous frontiersman as a short-legged, short-armed, stout man with a ruddy face and flaxen hair that fell to his shoulders. By nature a kind and unassuming man, Carson was, nonetheless, a man of strong determination and a fierce countenance.[8]

On one occasion, Mead recalled, a rumor swept the council grounds that a party of Indians on their way to the treaty had been attacked by troops on the Santa Fe Trail and thirteen of them killed. On hearing the story Carson declared that he didn't believe a word of it. However, he said, if the account was true then "the treaty is gone to hell. I had six soldiers coming down, but I'll need a hundred going back!"[9]

The rumor was false, and the treaty talks were conducted with the various tribes, the first council being held on October 12 with the Cheyennes and Arapahos. Commission president Sanborn addressed the two tribes with John Smith interpreting for the Cheyennes and Mrs. Margaret Wilmarth, Indian widow of mountain man Thomas Fitzpatrick who had been the first agent for the two tribes, translating for the Arapahos.

On behalf of the government, Sanborn apologized to the Cheyennes for Chivington's attack on the village at Sand Creek and offered governmental restitution for Indian losses there. He also stated the government's desire to locate all of the Indian tribes either north of the Platte or south of the Arkansas. He had already rejected William Bent's proposal for a Cheyenne-Arapaho reservation on their hunting grounds in western Kansas between the Smoky Hill and the Republican rivers. Sanborn well knew that the Kansas-Pacific Railroad was building westward along the Smoky Hill.[10]

Secretary Kingman was impressed with the speeches made by the Indian chiefs, even though he found the bare legs and nearly naked bodies of the Indians around the council circle a bit undignified for such a solemn occasion. He felt the speech of Black Kettle was especially eloquent: "When he spoke of the desolated wigwams, murdered braves, squaws and children on that occasion, [he] sent a thrill throughout the whole of the Indians present and even in translation touched every heart there."[11]

"My shame [mortification] is as big as the earth," Black Kettle told the commissioners. "I once thought that I was the only man that persevered to be the friend of the white man, but since they have come and cleaned out our lodges, horses, and everything else, it is hard for me to believe the white men any more."[12]

He then brought forth his wife and had her display the nine bullet wounds she had received as she lay on the ground at Sand Creek and was potshot repeatedly by Chivington's men. He complained, too, that some of the Indian children taken captive in the attack had not been returned as promised.[13]

The Cheyenne principal chief noted the presence of General Harney, whom as a small boy he had seen on the Missouri River with Gen. Henry Atkinson's party of explorers. "I don't know how small I was," he observed. "The general must have a great and strong heart."[14] Harney later made Black Kettle the gift of a handsome bay horse.

Black Kettle and other Cheyenne chiefs signed the treaty proffered by the commissioners. In doing so, they agreed to live on a new reservation area to be laid off for them in northern Indian Territory. This done, the commission undertook talks with the Kiowas, Comanches, and Plains Apaches. The principal issue for the whites was the attacks being made on wagon trains along the Santa Fe Trail. In return for promises of annuity goods and other assistance, the three tribes were asked to cede all lands north of the Canadian River to the government, with permission granted for them to visit the Salt Plains just south of the Kansas line to obtain salt.

Also of issue to the whites was the matter of white captives held by the Indians, in particular those of the Kiowas and Comanches who had long raided into Texas and Mexico. Eagle Drinking, a Comanche, admitted to holding some white captives, but he noted that some of his people, captured by Maj. Earl Van Dorn seven years before, were still being held prisoner in Texas.

Regarding the ceding of land, Eagle Drinking declared: "I am fond of the land I was born on. The white man has land enough. I don't want to divide again."[15] Kiowa chief Little Mountain insisted that the Kiowas, like the whites, had long wanted peace; but "the Great Father is always promising to do something for him, but never does anything."[16]

On October 18 the Cheyennes, Arapahos, and Plains Apaches, their treaties signed, departed for the Salt Plains. Talks with the Kiowas and Comanches were stalemated while the Kiowas dispatched a party with an army ambulance to go south and bring back the white captives held there by others of their tribes who were not ready to make peace.

The odds did not appear favorable for success, especially when a black man from Texas rode into camp. The man reported that though he had recently been able to redeem his wife and two children from the Comanches at the price of seven ponies, the Indians had reneged on the release of two others who were supposed to have been a part of the trade. They were a woman of about forty years of age and her four-year-old granddaughter. The woman was said to be the widow of a Union man who had been hanged in Texas because he refused to join the Confederacy during the war.[17]

The envoys to the Kiowas returned with five white prisoners. They were Mrs. Caroline McDonald, age twenty-six, whose residence had been near Fredericksburg, Texas; her daughter, one-year-old Rebecca; a nephew, seven-year-old James Taylor; a niece, three-year-old Dorcas Taylor; and James Burrow, age seven, of Georgetown, Texas.[18]

The talks with the Kiowas and Comanches were resumed, the tribes now being represented by other chiefs: Lone Wolf, Black Eagle, Kicking Eagle (Kicking Bird), Stinking Saddle Cloth, and others for the Kiowas; Iron Mountain, Iron Shirt, and Silver Broach for the Comanches. William and John Shirley, Indian Territory traders, interpreted for the Comanches, while Jesse Chisholm assisted with the Kiowas.

Silver Broach issued a final reminder that the Texans were still holding some of his children; also that "the Great Father at Washington promised me presents some time ago, such as houses, utensils, grain, etc., and I have got none yet. I think before I get any of them I will die an old man, as I am pretty old now."[19]

During the time the Kiowas were sending for the captives, a council had been held with a group of Osages who were passing by on a hunting expedition. The commission talked with them concerning the purchase of the Osage lands in Kansas south of the Arkansas River. The Osages said that they had relinquished much of their territory without seeing any reward. "Heap talk, no money," they observed and said that they would wait to see what happened regarding past promises by the coming spring.[20]

Now the attention of the commissioners was finally turned to the Wichitas, Caddos, Anadarkos, Wacos, Kichais, Tawakonis, and Ionis who most desperately needed help. These bands were so destitute and living in such sordid conditions that four of their people had died from starvation only recently. Kingman judged that the coming winter would likely finish them off.[21] They expressed their great desire to return to their homeland in the Indian Territory.

In response the treaty commission recommended that their agency at old Fort Cobb, which they had been forced to abandon during the war, be reestablished. The refugee tribes would find, however, that the white man's promises were empty. They would continue to suffer and die at the mouth of the Little Arkansas for two long years before being permitted to return south.

By now the weather had turned cold and windy, and the trouser-clad and bare-legged orators alike were compelled to cut short their speech making. Some of the commission party had already packed up and headed homeward, yearning for the comforts of hearth and featherbed where, as Kingman put it, there would be "no broken slumbers, no aching bones, weary of their contact with solid earth."[22]

Soon they were gone—the Cheyennes, Arapahos, Plains Apaches, Kiowas, Comanches, commissioners, soldiers, and the other temporary guests—from the mouth of the Little Arkansas. All that was left were the starving, nonwarring tribes who had gained nothing for the coming winter except promises. But already the potential of this place sitting ideally on the edge of the Indian and buffalo frontier had caught the eye of the white man. Soon he would come in force.

Kansas politician Sam Wood, who on November 15 following the treaty camped on the Little Arkansas while en route to New Mexico with a herd of cattle, made a prediction in a letter he wrote home:

"At some point on the Little Arkansas," he prophesied, "will yet be the greatest town in the West."[23]

Chapter Four

A Final Farewell

I travelled with them one day's march and really it was
a pitiful sight to see the women and children, old men
and old women trudging along on foot, most of them
barefooted and nearly naked and yet these people are the
best disposed to the whites of any Indians in the south.
— Philip McCusker, Letter to Wichita Agency,
Office of Indian Affairs, November 15, 1867

Somewhat as it had been when Coronado first arrived, the site of
present downtown Wichita in the fall of 1865 was dotted with villages of cone-shaped grass huts. The houses stood well over fifteen
feet tall and were ten to twenty-five feet in diameter.[1] Though
Kingman had expressed disdain for the Wichitas, whom he considered indolent and lewd, he sympathized with their sorry plight on the
Little Arkansas. Even so he did not know them as intimately as did
James Mead, who found them to be a kind, gentle, and honest people.

The Wichita women, their faces and bodies tattooed with pink
and blue zigzag lines, did most of the camp work and took a hand in
construction of their thatched huts. Forked poles standing about five
feet tall were planted in the ground. To these, other poles were tied
horizontally. Smooth top poles twenty feet or longer were then set
upright in the ground outside the vertical posts, bent, and lashed
together at the top. The women would then weave the long, reddish
bunch grass in and out of the poles, overlapping the bunches so that
the finished structure effectively resisted both wind and water.[2]

Sometimes the insides were plastered with gypsum mud. Low doors made of grass or skins were placed on the east and west. Inside the lodges were raised bunks for sleeping, each with storage space beneath, while the fire was at the center of the house. The smoke from the fire filtered through an opening at the top of the hut where the poles were joined. The ground was kept smooth, hard, and clean for about fifty feet in a circle outside of the house. The Wichitas' gardens—called "squaw patches" by the frontier whites— were not far away. These plots were protected by small poles set upright in the ground. At harvest time, scaffolds were erected to store their produce.[3]

The Wichitas still existed in much the same fashion as they had when Coronado was there three centuries earlier, subsisting on buffalo meat along with the corn, beans, squash, and melons they cultivated. Only now there was much less of all to feed the people. The harvest this season had been very poor. A severe lack of food, combined with a great deal of illness, had left the Wichitas and others in woeful condition.

They complained that their agent, Maj. Milo Gookins, had often failed to issue them their annuities and cheated them when he did. They said that the agent did not "talk straight" with them. This proved to be true. Gookins had been ordered to issue the refugee tribes fifty rifles, two hundred fifty pounds of powder, fifty thousand caps, and five hundred pounds of lead for them to use in hunting buffalo and procuring meat for their people. The Indians had never received the arms.[4]

The peace commissioners sympathized with the Wichitas, observing that "they are poorly supplied is evident from their appearance."[5] Moreover, the twenty-five miles they had to travel to obtain their goods at Gookins's residence was much too far for them to go on foot. To improve the situation, the agent purchased a log house nearer the Wichita village from a settler named Don Carlos to serve as an agency storehouse.[6]

The Wichitas and other refugee Indians in the area struggled through the winter of 1865–66 in continued destitution. A number of their people perished during the cold winter months from disease and starvation, leaving many orphans and widows.[7] Large plots of corn and other vegetables were planted during the spring of 1866, and good rains gave promise of a bountiful year. But the rains would not stop, continuing incessantly through the month of June. As a result, the Little Arkansas and other streams of the area overflowed and washed out the direly needed crops.[8]

Equally as detrimental to the food supply of the refugee bands were the Cheyenne warriors who drove the Wichita hunters from the buffalo range. The Cheyenne Dog Soldiers also threatened to kill any of the refugee Indians who attempted to move south to their old homes.[9]

In July 1866, the government relieved Gookins of his assignment and replaced him with Maj. Henry M. Shanklin. On arriving at the Little Arkansas, the new agent inspected the Wichitas in their lodges. He found his new charges in deplorable condition. They were, he reported, poorly fed, naked, sick with diarrhea from eating green plums, and in utter despondency as to their future. Shanklin distributed some of his own supplies to the aged and ill and made arrangements to provide them with flour, beef, salt, and medicines.[10]

A count of the Indians in the agency tallied 392 Wichitas, 155 Wacos, 151 Tawakonis, 362 Caddos, 520 Absentee Shawnees, 114 Delawares, 144 Kichais, and 70 Creeks and Cherokees. Late in September of 1866 the commissioner of Indian affairs, Dennis N. Colley, approved a contract with Charles B. Johnson of Sherman, Texas, to subsist and remove the Wichitas and associated tribes from Kansas. They were to be taken back to their old agency in the Leased District of Indian Territory.

Johnson was to supply each tribal member with one pound of fresh beef, three to four pounds of flour or corn, and salt. In return he would receive eleven and one half cents for each ration furnished and eight dollars for each Indian removed, excluding children under one year of age. Johnson made plans to conduct the removal in late November or early December at the latest.[11]

Shanklin, however, had received no official notice of this removal plan. When Johnson contacted him regarding it, the agent refused to permit his charges to leave until he had been given official instruction on the matter.[12]

Eventually Shanklin was notified by Indian Superintendent William Byers that Congress had appropriated some sixty thousand dollars for the removal. This would, Byers said, enable Shanklin to move the Indians early the following spring and have them in the Leased District in time for them to make a crop the coming season. Contractor Johnson was instructed to begin delivery of his subsistence goods to either Chisholm's ranch at the site of present Wichita or to Paul's ranch in the Chickasaw Nation of the Indian Territory.[13]

In January 1867, the commissioner of Indian affairs directed Shanklin to accompany a delegation of Shawnees to Washington, D.C., for the purpose of reestablishing their claim to lands in Kansas.[14] He was in St. Louis on his way back when orders reached him from Secretary of Interior P. H. Browning to begin removal of his charges immediately. Funds were placed at his disposal with which he was to purchase farming equipment, milk cows, wagons, teams, and other items that would permit the Indians to begin active farming operations as soon as they arrived in the Leased District.[15]

While still in St. Louis, Shanklin learned that the refugee Indians had not received their supplies from Johnson and were in dire straits. Accordingly, he used some of his allowance to purchase flour and meal and have it shipped to the agency. While at Lawrence, Kansas, he learned further that the Indians were reluctant to move that spring because of troubles with the Cheyennes. They feared that the government would not protect them if they went south. This concern had been intensified by Shanklin's absence from the agency.[16]

Other complications were developing, also. The Kansas lands occupied by the Shawnees were being surveyed for settlement. The whites, who lost no time moving in, complained that the Indians were stealing their horses and cattle. The Osages, too, caused problems by insisting that the refugee tribes pay for the use of their lands during the past four years.[17]

Shanklin duly made arrangements for the 260-mile, twenty-day trip, securing eighty teams and wagons for transporting the Indian camp equipage, lodge materials, and subsistence stores from the Little Arkansas to the Leased District. But once again an unprecedented rainy season caused the streams and rivers of southern Kansas and the Indian Territory to remain in virtual flood stage until the last of June. William Mathewson said later that during this occasion he had to swim his horses several miles to escape the floodwaters of the Little Arkansas.[18]

In an effort to overcome the flooding problem, Shanklin had a small boat hauled nearly a hundred miles to the Arkansas River. But in trying to transport some of the Indians across the rampaging stream, one of them drowned. Shanklin, whose son had also drowned in the Whitewater while seining fish the previous August, gave up the venture.[19]

In early June, he received new orders to remove the tribes at once. But now the agent learned that Johnson, his contract having expired,

Buffalo Bill Mathewson was a buffalo hunter, Indian trader, banker, and pioneer of Wichita. Wichita-Sedgwick County Historical Museum.

refused to furnish supplies to the Indians. This forced Shanklin to delay the removal until July while he purchased sixty-two hundred dollars worth of flour, beef, and salt.[20]

Meanwhile, on June 20, Superintendent Byers was replaced by James Wortham, who assumed control of removing the tribes. Wortham first advertised in the Lawrence newspapers for a contractor who would effect the removal of the Little Arkansas tribes. When it was learned that Frank A. Rector, an ex-Confederate army general and Indian commissioner, was about to be awarded the contract, people in Lawrence rose up in indignation and sent letters of protest to the secretary of the interior. Wortham then named J. J. Chollar as a special agent to oversee the removal.[21]

Chollar immediately headed for the Wichita agency, where Shanklin had been ordered to render all assistance to him. On arriving there, however, Chollar found that still another calamity had befallen the Wichitas, causing further delay in their departure.[22] The dreaded disease cholera had been raging all across Kansas, striking immigrants along the Platte Trail, construction workers on the Kansas Pacific Railroad, which was then inching its way along the Smoky Hill, and military posts such as Fort Harker. It had also struck inside the Indian Territory.

One of the military units that had been infected was the Eighteenth Kansas Volunteer Regiment. It had hastily departed Fort Harker on a summer's campaign against the Cheyennes, leaving ahead of schedule to escape the scourge. The Eighteenth was at Walnut Creek ten miles above Fort Zarah on July 21 when cholera struck the unit, making many of the soldiers violently ill and killing seven.[23]

Undoubtedly it was the Eighteenth Regiment that brought the disease to the Wichita Indians. The propensity of soldiers to seek sexual relations with Indian women cannot be overlooked as a possible contact. By late July, the Wichitas had became dangerously infected with cholera. Within five days, Wichita people began dying.

A physician, Dr. Kellogg of Emporia, was sent for. Though he correctly identified the disease as *cholera morbus*, he mistakenly placed the blame for the illnesses on green plums and melons the Indians had been eating. The disease quickly spread. A few days later several of the Tawakonis became afflicted and now a general panic set in among the Indians.[24]

The doctor recommended that the Indians be removed at once as the best way for them to escape the plague, but the Wichitas refused to leave. The Great Spirit had given them the strength to plant their corn that spring, they said, and if they did not protect their seed corn by harvesting it, they might not be given that strength again. Further, they were bound strongly by tribal custom to attending their dead and mourning over the graves of loved ones and friends.[25] The Wichitas were fastidious about the burial of their dead, which they did with great seriousness and purpose. The family always accompanied the body to the grave, but it was not uncommon for them to employ others, usually women, to conduct the burial.

A hole was dug, and the deceased was laid on buffalo robes and blankets within. The head of the corpse was placed to the west and the feet to the east. Wichita men were buried with their bows and arrows or guns; women with their cooking utensils. When the personal possessions had been arranged beside the body, sticks were placed over it all, followed by a blanket of grass.

Once the hole had been filled in with soil, the grave was protected with poles that crisscrossed over the mound. Grass was scraped away from around the grave for several feet. Horses were often killed at the graveside to accompany the warriors into their other world. When the grave was thus prepared, relatives went into mourning about it, wailing for long periods and fasting. The women survivors often cut off their hair.[26]

Among those who fell victim to cholera during the summer of 1867 was the Wichitas' second chief A-wa-he (or O-was-he) who had been a signatory to a treaty with the Confederacy in 1861. Possibly it was his bones that were uncovered by men digging for brick clay at Wichita in 1872. The discovered grave contained a skeleton wrapped in a buffalo robe, two decayed moccasins, two silver earrings, a bow, quiver, six arrows, a brass army plate, and two silver peace medallions. One medallion bore the likeness of Andrew Jackson and the other of Franklin Pierce.[27]

Even as plans were being laid for the removal of the refugee tribes, preparations were under way also for another treaty with the prairie tribes that the Treaty of the Little Arkansas had failed to extricate from Kansas. The hoped-for peace had not come about, and Congress had authorized another treaty effort. A new peace commission was established on July 20, 1867—the same day on which Indian agent Jesse Leavenworth and Cheyenne chief Black Kettle once again met at the Wichita village relative to conducting still another treaty council.[28]

At first the Cheyenne leader was reluctant to enter the Wichita village. His reason related to a raid into Texas by a Wichita war party. The warriors had gone south across the Indian Territory on a horse-stealing raid, supposedly to make up for their own loss of horses to the Osages. No one in the tribe would talk with Shanklin about it. However, it was eventually learned that while they were on their way back with a fine herd of horses and some scalps, the Wichitas had been attacked by a band of Cheyennes. Several of them had been killed, and Black Kettle feared that the Wichitas might seek revenge.[29]

When Buffalo Goad, the Wichita principal chief, sent his word guaranteeing safety, the Cheyenne leader, accompanied by a small party including George Bent, swam their ponies across the still-flooded Arkansas. On the north bank Black Kettle was met by Leavenworth, Jesse Chisholm, Dutch Bill Greiffenstein, and James Mead and escorted into the Wichita village. There they found the Wichita headmen seated in a circle smoking. Outside of the ring, an old Wichita man and his wife sat wailing at the loss of their son who had been killed on the Texas raid.[30]

Jesse Chisholm and a Comanche party under Chief Ten Bears were also there when a council was held on the following day. Leavenworth read a long letter from the commissioner of Indian affairs, it being interpreted for Black Kettle by Bent. A number of big men were coming to make a new peace, the letter said. Leavenworth wanted Black Kettle to take the news back to his people. The Cheyenne leader agreed to do so, then rode back across the river and disappeared to the south.

George Bent remained with Greiffenstein for a time before going to talk to the various bands of Cheyennes and Arapahos, who were still under pressure from the recalcitrant Dog Soldiers. The ultimate result of these efforts would be the Treaty of Medicine Lodge in October 1867.[31]

Leavenworth had other matters to attend to while at the Little Arkansas. A herd of Texas longhorn cattle, to be used as stock cattle by the tribes, had been purchased from Robert H. Taylor of Texas. It was necessary to meet the herd in the Territory and hold it there for the refugee tribes when they arrived. Also there was a load of annuity goods to be delivered to the Comanches and Kiowas, and still one other matter. Two young Texas boys, ransomed from the Kiowas, had to be delivered to Fort Arbuckle where they would be met by friends from Texas.

To accomplish all of these things, Leavenworth contracted traders Greiffenstein and Mathewson to freight the annuity goods from the Little Arkansas into the Territory. Mathewson would go on to Arbuckle, deliver the boys, and take charge of the herd. The two frontiersmen departed in early August.[32]

Even as Leavenworth was involved in these matters, Chollar and Maj. C. F. Garrett departed the Little Arkansas with a contingent of 313 Absentee Shawnees, 98 Caddos, 58 Delawares, and 8 Ionis for Fort Cobb in the Leased District. They were to be guided by the Delaware scout Black Beaver. The Indians were in good health when they departed on August 3, apparently having escaped the cholera menace. But they were not so fortunate as it seemed.

Things were going fine for a time, but while encamped at Buffalo Springs just north of the Cimarron River, the caravan of Indians was struck by the disease with devastating results. According to Garrett, the Shawnees lost fifty of their number before they reached the Washita River and the Caddos forty-seven, including several of their headmen.[33]

On returning from the Territory, Mathewson reported that the dead Indians had been left along the road like "rotten sheep."[34] Garrett, who was stricken himself, remained with the sick at the Canadian River along with Black Beaver, whom he gave great credit for keeping the Indians together. Chollar later claimed that he had taken the others on to Fort Cobb, but Rector charged that Chollar had fled in panic and deserted his charges. The Indians were left at Fort Cobb under the supervision of Black Beaver.[35]

Leavenworth was back at the Little Arkansas in October to distribute annuity goods to the Comanches and others. The chiefs were to bring in their own wagons and haul the goods back to their camps at the Salt Plains. However, a virtual state of war existed between the army and Plains tribes in Kansas. Because military authorities considered Leavenworth to be a traitor because of his Indian sympathies, they seized the wagons of annuity goods and hauled them off to Fort Larned. The agent was left to explain to his charges why his promises were not to be fulfilled.

On October 21, even as the great peace council at Medicine Lodge was taking place, the Wichitas were finally placed on their way back to their homes in the Leased District. On that date Shanklin issued his last report from the Little Arkansas agency, saying that he had moved all of his goods, supplies, and office equipment across the Arkansas and would take up the march on the following day. His charges were complaining, he said, that the government had not issued them warm clothing as had been done for the warring Comanches and Kiowas.[36]

After moving only twenty miles in the direction of Fort Cobb, the Wichitas refused to go any farther in fear that the Cheyennes and Osages would come south in the spring and make war on them. Shanklin, assisted by Garrett, finally persuaded them to continue. Having learned that the grass had been burned off the trail as far south as the Cimarron River, he divided his caravan into two sections. The supplies were sent on the direct route and the Indians on a more westerly course.

The exodus of the Wichitas, Wacos, Tawakonis, and Kichais was even more tragic than that of the group that had preceded them. Philip McCusker, a frontiersman then serving as official U.S. interpreter, gave an account of the march:

> About the last of October and while the council was in session the agent arrived there again telling them he had

orders to move them at once, that they must pack up immediately and be ready to start when the wagons come. This the Indians proceeded to do at once, some of them crossing the Arkansas River and awaiting the agent on the other side. A great many of them were sick, two Wacos dying after they crossed the Arkansas, and were waiting for the wagons; and when the wagons did come up never were a people so disappointed as they. There was 10 wagons in all, wagons that had been hired from farmers in the country, some of them with two poor broken down horses or mules and some with oxen that gave out before they got back. The wagons were in a measure already loaded with materials for building an agency when they got there, with stores and with annuity goods that had lain at Towanda a long time and now that cold weather has set in the Indians need those goods very much. They have already suffered a great deal after getting over to Cow Skin Creek some 10 miles south of the Arkansas. The Agent with his ten wagons left them to shift for themselves without a word of warning. Up to that time he had been hurrying the Indians to pack up and get away as fast as they could. They used every exertion to comply with his request, in fact leaving one sick woman on the south bank of the Arkansas who was too sick to be removed. And as they had no wagon to put her in they left her to her fate to linger out her miserable existence. How long the poor creature lived I don't know, but when I passed there some days after, the wolves and ravens were disputing over her unburied remains. When the Indians got over to Cow Skin Creek, a great many of them were very sick and two of them about to die there; the Indians would not abandon. And as the agent would not wait for them they remained in camp on Cow Skin about 5 days. When these two Indians died they buried them right at the crossing and then moved over to the Ninnescah. The night they encamped on this stream the prairie fires were burning in all directions but the Indians did not consider them dangerous. But toward morning the wind changed 'round to the north, and then a terrific gale bringing a fire down on the Indian camp with the speed of a race horse. They made every effort to save their stock but [in] spite of all exertions they lost one hundred and thirty-one head of saddle horses besides mares and colts. A great many of those they saved were so badly burned that I think they cannot live through the winter. This is the worse thing that could have befallen these people as they depended entirely upon their horses for supplies of meat and buffalo robes.[37]

In succeeding years, white men would view the bleaching bones of the cholera victims on a stream north of the Cimarron and dub it Skeleton Creek. The remains were still there in 1870 when Josiah Butler, traveling with a Mathewson train headed for Fort Sill, witnessed the "many human bones scattered around."[38]

The Wichitas thus departed from the Little Arkansas for the final time, though in early December 1867 a war party returned to the region to recoup the loss of their horses. When settlers on Spring Creek near Eureka discovered several of their horses missing and moccasin tracks about, a posse was dispatched to the Little Arkansas. There they encountered a party of Kansa Indians who told them that seven Wichitas who were camped nearby had taken the horses. The Kansa warrior led the posse to the Wichita camp.

When they spied the posse, the Wichitas drew their bows and warned the white men not to come any closer. The settlers insisted that they wanted only to talk, and the Wichitas were persuaded to come forward to shake hands. But when one of the posse members cut the string of a Wichita's bow, a fight commenced. The Wichitas fought as they retreated, wounding one settler seriously and two others slightly. The Kansa warriors came in after the fight and scavenged the Wichita's bows, arrows, and blankets.[39]

For a time after the tribe had been returned to the Leased District, the Wichitas suffered badly. By 1869, however, they had settled back into their familiar rounded straw houses, surrounded by neatly fenced fields of corn and watermelon patches much the same as they had once had on the Little Arkansas when they were first met by the conquistadors.

Chapter Five

Old Jesse's Trail

> The next spring he returned, camped by my place
> with his train. I took supper with him and he said,
> "I am owing you. I have no money, but have buffalo robes,
> wolf skins, beaver, buckskins, and you can take your pay
> from any of them." I chose coyote skins, which were legal
> tender for a dollar, and he counted out three thousand.
> — James Mead, from O. H. Bentley, ed.,
> *History of Wichita*, 1910

Jesse Chisholm had first visited the site of Wichita at the mouth of the Little Arkansas in 1826 searching for gold. According to James Mead, Jesse abandoned his Indian Territory trading post in 1864 during the Civil War and returned to the Little Arkansas. Confederate military correspondence, however, shows that both he and Black Beaver had accompanied the refugee tribes in their flight north from their rebel-controlled agency by September 1863.[1]

Jesse built a house, trading post, and corrals on a small creek feeding into the Arkansas. It would soon bear his name—Chisholm Creek.[2] During the following four years, he operated from there in several capacities—Indian trader, cattle dealer, and scout for the U.S. government. More significantly, however, Jesse established a wagon road northward from his Indian Territory location that became the famous Chisholm Trail. In the years to follow, Texas cattlemen drove thousands upon thousands of longhorns up the trail to Kansas railheads.

The Chisholm Cattle
Trail was named for
half-Cherokee Jesse
Chisholm who once
resided on the Little
Arkansas. Wichita-
Sedgwick County
Historical Museum.

For more than thirty years the half-Scot, half-Cherokee frontiersman had roamed the distant sweeps of Indian country below
the Canadian River and south of the Red River into the wilds of
Texas, taking his goods out among the Comanches, Kiowas,
Wichitas, and other prairie tribes to trade for horses, Mexican
mules, buffalo robes, furs, and at times even captive children. From
his home on the Canadian River, his wagons traveled as far south as
Torrey's Trading Post and the Guadalupe River of Texas in the conduct of his trade.[3]

During these years, Chisholm became the friend and confidant
of many tribal leaders. Because of this and his ability to speak many
different tongues, Chisholm's services became invaluable to the
Cherokee Nation, the Republic of Texas, and the United States in
dealing with the prairie tribes. On numerous occasions Chisholm
rode far afield to contact Indian leaders and persuade them to

attend peace councils. He served as interpreter and as an adviser to both whites and Indians in settling their problems.

In 1839 Jesse and a small group of friends trekked from the Cherokee country to California by way of El Paso, and in 1845 he traveled to Mexico to verify the death there of the famed Sequoyah, inventor of the Cherokee alphabet. In 1846, following the Treaty of Comanche Peak on the Brazos River, Jesse helped escort a delegation of Comanches and other Indians via New Orleans to Washington, D.C. While there he acted as a translator between the Indians and President Polk.

During these years, Jesse sired children, first by Eliza Edwards and then, on her death, by Sah-kah-kee, both half-blood Creek women. In addition to his natural children, Jesse took into his family entourage a number of Mexican children whom he rescued from Indian captivity on the Plains. When the Civil War broke out Jesse was engaged in trade with Indians of the Leased District and the other tribes of western Indian Territory, working from Council Grove (now west Oklahoma City) on the North Canadian. He also operated a salt works north of his post, hauling the salt to Texas and other points to market.

Chisholm had longstanding ties to the South both through his Cherokee heritage and by virtue of his many white friends who became associated with the Confederacy. Because of this, Confederate general Albert Pike persuaded him to assist in concluding treaties with the Indians of western Indian Territory in 1861. But his first loyalties were to the Indian people he knew and associated with. Even though he had been appointed as a confederate Indian agent in 1862, when the Leased District Indians were forced to flee the Indian Territory following a bloody uprising at their agency, Chisholm came north with them.[4]

Jesse became involved in the buying and reselling of cattle that warriors of the refugee tribes retrieved from the Indian Territory. The Caddos were particularly active in securing cattle from the unattended herds the tribes had left behind. It is possible that some of the cows came from Texas herds as well.

This trade in what was generally considered to be contraband cattle had become epidemic all along the Kansas-Indian Territory border. The "fast cattle" brought good prices in Kansas. Agent Gookins complained about this "illicit and immoral traffic" and said that loyalist Indians were threatening to get their cattle back after the war was over by raiding in Kansas.[5] Charges were made in Kansas newspapers that a conspiracy existed among prominent Kansas businessmen and traders, high-ranking military officers, and white cattle thieves concerning contraband cattle.[6]

It was counterargued that the cattle were fair game, they being left unclaimed in the upheaval of war and many belonging to the disloyal Indians still in the Territory. In the west, it was argued, the refugee tribes were simply recovering their own stock that they had been forced to abandon. Rightly or wrongly, Chisholm played a role in this.

In the spring of 1865, Fort Leavenworth merchant John Stevens backed Chisholm with several wagonloads of trade goods. Using these goods, Chisholm hired Indian drovers to gather up some three thousand head of cattle in the Territory and drive them to the Little Arkansas. He grazed the cattle on the west side of the river for a time before having some driven to New Mexico and some to the Sac and Fox reserve in eastern Kansas.[7] The trade ended in September 1865, however, when Stevens drowned while driving a buggy across a swollen stream near the Sac and Fox Agency in eastern Indian Territory.[8]

Mead came to know Chisholm well and had numerous business dealings with him.[9] One such occasion occurred during the summer of 1865 when Mead purchased a herd that Chisholm had brought up from the Territory. He held the cows at Chisholm's place "using the corral and buildings he had turned over to me."[10] Mead stated that in January 1866:

> Jesse Chisholm loaded some wagons with the usual
> hunter's and trader's outfit—coffee, tobacco, sugar, blan-
> kets, etc.—and with his usual retinue of followers and
> employees, started south to mark out a trail to his old
> ranch at Council Grove on the North Canadian. . . . I accom-
> panied him on this trip with some of my own teams.
> Chisholm and his Indians knew the country well, were
> expert plainsmen and selected the best possible
> route. . . . As we progressed southward, we soon mapped out
> a plain road and we named the streams from some inci-
> dent or occurrence that would happen in the locality.[11]

Mead thought this was the first Chisholm wagon train to travel the route that became the Chisholm Cattle Trail.[12] Even if so, it was by no means Chisholm's first trip back into the Territory from Kansas.

Former Indian
trader James Mead
was a founding
father and pro-
moter of Wichita.
Wichita-Sedgwick
County Historical
Museum.

During the period from the fall of 1864 through the fall of 1867, Chisholm was employed intermittently as a guide, scout, and inter- preter by Jesse Leavenworth. Chisholm's pay vouchers show him to have been engaged from December 1, 1864, to February 15, 1865; from April 15 to May 25, 1865; and from June 22 to August 31, 1865, at seven dollars a day.[13]

During the winter of 1864–65, Leavenworth sent Chisholm into the Territory to persuade the Comanches, Kiowas, and others to come north for peace talks. In preparation for the Treaty of Little Arkansas council, Chisholm carried Leavenworth's message from vil- lage to village. In June 1865 the agent reported from the mouth of the Little Arkansas that Chisholm would leave there again on the next day to locate the Comanches and others who had gone south to the Wichita Mountains.[14]

Several days later, on July 14, Chisholm wrote a letter to agent Leavenworth from Fort Arbuckle, reporting: "I have the honor to inform you that I have seen Ten Bears Comanche chief, and he has agreed to see and bring all the chiefs to council in the coming 20 or 25 days at which time you may expect to meet me with them at Bluff Creek near the mound of rock on the hill."[15]

He penned another note from the Cowskin on August 1 saying: "I am here with 125 Indians and nothing for them to eat. What shall I do with them? Fetch them over in the morning or not? Please let me know."[16]

Though he moved back to the Territory in 1866, Chisholm did not sever his relationship with Kansas, taking up a trading relationship with E. H. Durfee of Leavenworth. Most likely it was Chisholm whom Capt. Henry Brandley met near Emporia in December 1866. Brandley told of meeting a small train of heavily loaded wagons belonging to a trader on the Canadian River in the Indian Territory. These wagons had delivered a load of furs to Fort Leavenworth where, their owner said, goods could be purchased cheaply enough to justify taking them there rather than to Fort Smith, which was closer. The man offered the opinion that if a road were opened via El Dorado and Chelsea to Leavenworth, it would be quite profitable to all.[17]

Chisholm was at Leavenworth during the summer of 1867 when Durfee outfitted him with twenty-five thousand dollars worth of goods.[18] During the visit, Chisholm had his only known likeness made. He was badly trail worn at the time and weary. James Mead said the picture did not do Chisholm justice; still it provides history with an image of an important figure of the early West.[19]

Another noteworthy trader to operate in the area of the Little Arkansas was Dutch Bill Greiffenstein, a German immigrant who in 1865 established his trading house on the Cowskin ten miles to the west of the Wichita village. The trader soon began taking his wagons south to the Salt Plains to trade with the numerous bands of Indians that came there regularly to procure salt.[20] Greiffenstein would ultimately play a very large role in the destiny of the city of Wichita.

Other men who now operated as Indian traders at the Little Arkansas included Alonzo Greenway, who came there from Marion Center, Kansas; Charles Whittaker, another Durfee trader; and William Mathewson, who had taken up residence at the juncture of the two rivers.

Mathewson, whose father was a New York stock dealer, had worked his way west to Minnesota as a boy, there joining the Northwest Fur Company at the age of nineteen in 1849. As a member of a hunting and trapping party, he had traveled up the Missouri River to the Yellowstone and the upper Rocky Mountain region. In March 1852, he joined a party of famous mountain men, which included Kit Carson, and traversed the unexplored regions of the Rockies from the Big Horn River to the Arkansas.[21]

Following this sojourn, Mathewson took employ with William Bent at his new fort on the Arkansas near present Lamar, Colorado. He remained with Bent as a hunter and trapper until 1857 when he opened his own trading post at the Little Arkansas crossing of the Santa Fe Trail. After operating there for a year, he constructed a new post at Big Cow Creek only to move again to Great Bend in 1860. When the Indian war broke out in 1864, he returned again to Cow Creek.[22]

Mathewson won himself a high reputation as a hunter and Indian trader. He was a close friend of Mead, who said that Mathewson's Cow Creek ranch was often "headquarters for army officers and all the noted characters who passed back and forth on the Santa Fe Trail."[23] One visitor was a newspaper special (correspondent) named Henry M. Stanley—the man who would soon gain world fame by discovering Livingstone in Africa.

Mathewson gained his nickname of Buffalo Bill in 1860 when a severe drought left many settlers on the Kansas frontier without enough to eat. Organizing a wagon train of buffalo hunters, Mathewson led the group to the buffalo grounds where as many as eighty buffalo per day were killed. This meat was transported back to famished settlers who bestowed the sobriquet of "Buffalo Bill" upon Mathewson. Later William F. Cody would adopt the famous pseudonym to use in connection with his Wild West show.

Having helped bring the Indian tribes of the Territory to the Little Arkansas Treaty council, Mathewson was called on in October 1867 to once again coax the Indians in to talk with peace commissioners at the Treaty of Medicine Lodge. On May 9, 1867, he arrived at the mouth of the Little Arkansas and settled his family there while, like Chisholm, he spent much of the summer contacting the tribes for agent Leavenworth.

After delivering the two boys who had been Comanche captives to Fort Arbuckle in August 1867, Mathewson accepted the Taylor herd of 425 cattle that had been driven up from Texas. At Arbuckle he turned them over to George Ransom, a black man whom Jesse Leavenworth had brought to the frontier. Ransom also worked for Jesse Chisholm, who had such confidence in the man

HO, FOR TEXAS!

Cowboys wave good-bye after delivering a herd of Texas longhorns to Wichita. *Harper's Weekly*, May 2, 1874.

that he once placed him in charge of a wagonload of furs for delivery to Fort Leavenworth.[24]

Circumstances would cause Ransom to hold the Texas herd along the Canadian River through the following winter. In returning to Kansas, Mathewson guided the first herd of fifteen hundred Texas longhorns ever to be driven up the route that became known as the Chisholm Cattle Trail. According to Mead, the herd was under James M. Daugherty of Denton County, Texas, while Joseph G. McCoy credits Col. O. W. Wheeler and his two partners with that distinction.[25] Leavenworth made note of the herd's arrival at the mouth of the Little Arkansas on September 2.[26]

Following the Treaty of Medicine Lodge, Mathewson led a fourteen-wagon caravan loaded with equipment and supplies to the Indian

Territory site of old Fort Cobb for the reestablishment of the agency for the refugee tribes. He crossed the Little Arkansas at its mouth and headed south down Chisholm's route accompanied by his wife Lizzie and her friend Fanny Cox, the first white women to travel over the trail. At the Cimarron, Mathewson cut to the west of Kingfisher Creek and blazed a new trail through to Fort Cobb.[27]

In early December 1867, Dutch Bill, who had established a new trading post on the Washita,[28] joined a Chisholm trading camp on the North Canadian at the head of Salt Creek. Not long afterward James Mead came down with still another train of trade goods. Through the rest of the winter these traders along with Chisholm conducted a heavy business with the Indians. Twice Mead made trips back to the Little Arkansas for more goods and supplies.

When Mead returned to Salt Creek on his final trip, he was amazed to find the trading grounds deserted, the only occupants being a flock of wild geese. Signs indicated that the camp had been abandoned in great haste and in all directions. Mystified, Mead turned his wagons downriver toward Chisholm's post at Council Grove, and after a short drive came to a large mound-like hill that the Indians knew as Little Mountain.[29]

Here, at the foot of the hill where the river bent sharply east then south, Mead discovered a newly constructed log fence that enclosed a grave mound and a headboard with the epitaph of Jesse Chisholm. He later learned that Chisholm had died from eating contaminated bear grease from a brass kettle. Chisholm's good friend Comanche chief Ten Bears, who was present at the time of his death, had taken from his own neck a peace medal given to him by President Harrison and placed it on Chisholm's neck in death and had it buried with him.[30]

Following this sad discovery, Mead drove on to Council Grove, where he found Dutch Bill and A. F. Greenway in camp. The traders decided that their old comrade would have appreciated a wake in his honor, so Greiffenstein dug a small keg of Kentucky's best from a barrel of sugar and acted as master of ceremonies in toasting the memory of their departed friend for the remainder of the day. It was, indeed, a fitting farewell for Jesse Chisholm who had spent so much of his life in the wilds of the frontier and had opened the trail that would render his name immortal to western fame.

Events were under way in southern Kansas that caused Chisholm's route, as well as the mouth of the Little Arkansas, to have special significance. The Osages had ceded some 2 million acres of land across southern Kansas to be sold for them at $1.25 an acre. To prepare for the 1869 opening of these Osage Trust Lands, a government survey east of the Arkansas River was conducted during 1867 even as the refugee tribes were being removed and the Treaty of Medicine Lodge was under way.

Colonel Samuel S. Smoot and Capt. E. N. Darling led a surveying party that made its headquarters at the Little Arkansas juncture. Despite threats by the Cheyennes, who held a strong distaste for surveyors, the fifty-man party was back in Lawrence by February 1868, their task completed.[31]

Another important development had led to the Texas trail herds being driven north by way of the Chisholm Trail. The Kansas legislature had considered a number of solutions to the problem of Kansas stock being contaminated by the deadly Texas fever brought there by the southern herds. Finally the lawmakers settled on a measure that permitted the entry of Texas cattle only to the west of Saline County. This gave great importance to a route directly across the middle of the Indian Territory, which would follow in part Jesse Chisholm's wagon road to the mouth of the Little Arkansas.[32]

The 1867 Kansas legislature passed still another significant measure. The bill approved the establishment of a "national road" from Fort Riley past the mouth of the Little Arkansas to the mouth of Walnut Creek, at present Arkansas City, and on via Fort Cobb to Fort Belknap, Texas.[33] The road would become a prime route for the movement of military equipment, supplies, and troops as well as Indian annuity goods.

But this did not mean that the frontier had yet departed the Arkansas River country. In June 1867 a Dr. Scott and party were sent to lay out the new route. Scott and two others were on their way back to the mouth of the Little Arkansas from the mouth of Walnut Creek and stopped for lunch along the river. While eating they heard shots fired on a small tributary. One of the men, a Captain Thrarsber, rode up the rivulet to investigate, and in doing so came suddenly face to face with from seventy-five to eighty Osage warriors gathered under a bank.

The Indians were as surprised as Thrarsber, but they recovered quickly and took him captive. Immediately fifteen to twenty others mounted their horses and headed pell-mell after Scott and his companion. Hooting and yelling they surrounded the two men and brought them back to their camp in triumph. The badly frightened men were roughed up some and their provisions were taken to be divided among the leaders of the party. But after questioning them for an hour or so, the Osages reluctantly permitted the men to ride on, all more than happy to give up their provisions and retain their scalps.[34]

The years of 1867 and 1868 saw a great flood of Texas cattle up the Chisholm route, initiating the era of trail driving across the Indian Territory to Kansas railheads and spawning rest and replenishing stops—usually called "ranches"—along the way. It is estimated that the head count of Texas beef arriving at Abilene that first year was 35,000, the figure jumping to 75,000 in 1868 and 150,000 in 1869. The herds normally began arriving even before the first of May and continued well into the fall.[35]

During the first years of the cattle drives, the herds followed a route through the Territory that ran close to the Council Grove area on the North Canadian. Trader Charles Whittaker operated a station there for a time.[36] In 1869 the Cheyenne and Arapaho agency was relocated some thirty miles to the west on the river by agent Brinton Darlington.

The drovers then began swinging their herds to the west beyond the South Canadian River and using the agency trading post as a replenishing stop. The original route is identified as the "Abilene Trail" on many maps. Another route that crossed the North Canadian east of present Oklahoma City and headed northwestward to the Cimarron River Crossing was known as the "Arbuckle Branch."

Ranch stops soon sprouted up along the trail, generally at river intersections. Inside Indian Territory, these included locations at Kingfisher Creek, Red Fork Ranch on the Cimarron, Baker's Ranch, Buffalo Springs, Skeleton Creek, and Round Pond Creek. Just across the Kansas border the small settlement of Caldwell began to emerge by 1870, and from there it was on to McClain's Ranch and trading post on the Ninnescah. McClain's was located near present Clearwater before reaching the Arkansas River crossing just below the mouth of the Little Arkansas.

By November 1867, when Philip McCusker referred to "the Chisholm Trail" in his report on the exodus of the Wichitas, the name had caught on.[37] Jesse Chisholm's name had been added to the lore of the area. His good friend Dutch Bill Greiffenstein was also destined to leave a strong imprint on this land of the Little Arkansas.

Chapter Six

Dutch Bill, Knight Errant

The Indians trusted him implicitly, sought his
advice, counted on his aid, anticipated his liberality.
So did the white men. His sole possession was once
an ox, a two-wheeled cart and a pipe.... He was many
a time one of a smoky circle of tribal chiefs,
speaking their language, thinking their thoughts,
voicing their Indian sentiments.
— *Wichita Eagle*, September 29, 1899

He was an improbable western notable at best, this stubby,
mild-mannered little German refugee who wore his dilapidated, floppy-brimmed hat down low over his face and constantly
puffed a large cloud of smoke out of the curved-stem meerschaum
that soiled the goatee of his lower jaw. His small, red-rimmed eyes
were forever blinking inside the metal-rimmed spectacles, and he
spoke his English with a thick-tongued Teutonic accent. "W's"
were persistently turned into "v's"; "ands" into "un's." This and
other such syllabication was uniquely mixed with the rough jargon
of the frontier.

His normal attire was an old black suit, the legs of which were
tucked into his overrun, flat-heeled boots. The distance from the boot
tops to his belt being scant, his figure appeared even more squat than
the five-foot-five he was. The soiled, once-white shirt beneath the

His contemporaries hailed "Dutch Bill" Greiffenstein as the "Father of Wichita." Wichita-Sedgwick County Museum.

black coat was collarless, but his neck was so nearly nonexistent that his beard served in lieu of a cravat.

In his earlier days he had trod weaponless behind his two-wheeled, one-ox cart of trade goods across the roadless, grass-carpeted hills and meadows of the prairie. His protection lay in the security that the Indian tribes normally afforded the traders who brought to them the precious goods of the white man: sugar, coffee, vermilion, tobacco, bolts of colored cloths, knives, axes, and a world of items cherished by the nomadic denizens of the plains.

The bravado of the Anglo-American would have been a dangerous thing for him, and he had learned quickly to adapt himself to the wearisome formality of the Indian council—the lengthy passing of the calumet, the gifting of presents to tribal leaders, accepting the hospitality of food and lodge, and the protocol involved in spreading his goods on a blanket and bargaining with hand signs and whatever Indian words he had learned.

Indeed, there was nothing formidable in the appearance of this man who one day would be mayor of Wichita and overlord to such a legendary western character as Wyatt Earp. Yet beneath his drab exterior there was a strong sense of fairness and regard for all, which combined with a dogged determination to persevere. Instead of six-gun or rifle with which to win his laurels in the untamed West, William Greiffenstein—known widely on the frontier as "Dutch Bill" and to friends as the "Father of Wichita"—possessed a keen, opportunistic mind that employed the assets of a formal German education and an instinct for survival. He generally thought well ahead of others, and never was he known to turn away from a sound calculated risk. Indisputable testimony of his character was the loyalty and admiration that he drew from all who associated with him, white man and Indian alike.

Greiffenstein had come to America in 1848 when he was only nineteen, having been born on July 28, 1829, at Gross-Gerau near Dramstadt, Germany. His father Charles Greiffenstein, an educated and refined gentleman, held the position of revenue collector and, along with his wife Beate, was a member of the Lutheran Church. At the age of fourteen, William was enrolled at the Dramstadt Gymnasium. He was a student there until 1848, later working with a Mainz insurance firm.[1]

Germany at this time was undergoing a political upheaval following a war with Denmark, the thrones of Austria and Prussia feeling the threat of revolution from radical republican groups. After a railroad riot at Mainz, young Greiffenstein was suspected of having been a participant. Though he was later cleared of the charge, it caused him to leave his homeland and seek his fortune elsewhere. While he opted for North America, his brother chose Columbia, South America, eventually becoming a rich and prominent citizen of Baranquilla.

On arriving in the United States, William made his way to the German-established vineyards of Hermann, Missouri, where an uncle resided. Working for a time as a clerk, Greiffenstein saw the cargoes of animal pelts and buffalo hides that were brought down the Missouri River by the trappers and traders, a valuable part of the commerce of the day. He later moved to St. Louis, where he continued his clerking occupation. In 1850, Greiffenstein boarded a steamboat and traveled up the Missouri to the Santa Fe Trail terminus of Westport, then the jumping-off point to the western wilderness. Here he began work in a trader's store.

But Greiffenstein was not content to remain a clerk for long, and soon he moved west to the Shawnee reservation near Lawrence, Kansas, on the Wakarusa River. There he entered into an Indian-trading partnership with Joe Bournett, a half-blood Indian. After a couple of years of trading with the Shawnee and Potawatomi Indians, Dutch Bill plunged into the dangerous Kiowa/Comanche country of southwest Indian Territory and as far south as Texas. There he traveled from one camp to another, carrying his cargoes by pack-mule and conducting his trade.[2]

During the following year he crossed the Plains to New Mexico on a trading expedition, returning in 1855 to take up residence in the new settlement of Topeka. In 1858, on learning that his father was in very poor health, Greiffenstein sold his Wakarusa trading post and returned to Germany. After his father's death, Dutch Bill returned to Topeka for a short time before once again taking up his Indian trade, this time in the wilds of western Kansas.

James Mead recollected that he first met Greiffenstein in the Saline and Smoky Hill country in 1860–61. Dutch Bill and a partner named Horneck were then trading with the Cheyennes and Arapahos with a light wagon and a team of ponies.[3] It was during this period that the German trader was caught in a blizzard while traveling along the Smoky Hill River in western Kansas. Taking shelter under the riverbank, Greiffenstein was held there by the storm for four days. He survived by lying next to his mules through the frigid nights and rationing the jerked buffalo meat he had with him. Eventually the snow subsided, and he made his way to an Indian camp where he received care. Some felt it was being snow-blinded on this occasion that caused his eyes to be red and squinty.[4]

On another occasion when coming into Salina from his Walnut Creek ranch, Greiffenstein was held up by a party of about forty guerrillas, who had just cleaned out the town of Salina of horses and guns. They took the trader's wagons, horses, and goods and left him afoot on the plains forty miles from the nearest settlement.[5]

During this period, Greiffenstein married a Cheyenne woman, the sister of a Cheyenne chief, who became known to whites as "Cheyenne Jennie." Though crippled, Jennie was a commanding figure. She was remembered by early settlers as being both beautiful and graceful.

Instead of wearing the traditional leggings and red blanket,
she wore a gown which was a combination of the mother hubbard and the Grecian robe, which was confined at the waist by
a long red sash of silk. The sash had a profusion of fringe at the
end and it gave her a picturesque appearance, especially when
she was mounted on a prancing steed and the wind was blow-
ing a breeze. On her head she wore a reboza, which, with her
stately mein, gave her a queenly air. . . . She was tall and slight
of stature, with long black hair and even features.[6]

Because of her infirmity, Dutch Bill furnished her a wagon for
transportation. She traveled with him and was an important asset in
his trade. Mead, who spoke of Jennie as a "woman of great ability,"
told of conducting trade with her in her husband's absence.[7]

Greiffenstein now established a trading post at Walnut Creek on
the Santa Fe Trail and tended a stage station for the Southwestern
Stage Company. He continued to trade with the Cheyennes and
Arapahos until the outbreak of war with the Plains tribes during the
summer of 1864 when the Kansas plains became highly volatile and
dangerous to whites. The Cheyenne Dog Soldiers, Arapahos, and
Sioux, as well as the Comanches and Kiowas from the south, were
striking with vengeance along the Platte and Arkansas river roads and
against frontier settlements.

Even Greiffenstein did not feel safe. On losing a large herd of cattle and other stock to Indian thieves, he gave up his ranch and moved
to Salina. For a time he served as a scout for the military at Council
Grove and Fort Larned.

One day the German appeared at Mead's Towanda trading post
with Cheyenne Jennie, two pony teams, a few trailing ponies, saddles,
and camp equipage. He asked Mead to outfit him, saying that the hostile Indians had cleaned him out. Mead did so, and Dutch Bill
returned later that winter with horses, wagons, goods, and money
and repaid the debt.[8]

When the turmoil on the frontier had quieted in 1865,
Greiffenstein purchased a ranch on the Cowskin several miles south
of Wichita. There he again built a successful trade with the Plains
tribes. On occasion he would take his wagons to the Salt Plains of the
Indian Territory to trade.

R. P. Murdock, who first met Dutch Bill in 1866 at Emporia, told
how the trader would come into the store where Murdock was a

clerk. Greiffenstein often brought in half a dozen four-mule-team wagons loaded with buffalo robes. While in town for a week or so, he would come to Murdock's store and sit on the counter, tailor fashion with his legs crossed, wearing a blue wool shirt unbuttoned at the neck, buckskin pants, moccasins, and a broad-brimmed hat—the entirety of his wardrobe.

Dutch Bill would deposit his robes on a valuation base of $4.50 each, four or five hundred at a time, and trade out a percentage of their worth in Indian trade items. He never took or gave receipts or made any accounting notes whatsoever. He would merely say that in the lot of robes so many were Comanche, so many were Cheyenne (these generally being the best dressed and the most valuable), so many were first class, and so many were merely fair in quality, naming the particular tribe by which they had been taken and tanned. There was never any doubt about the number he claimed. Murdock would place by his side a box of smoking tobacco and matches, and the little German would puff a cloud of smoke and converse in his Teutonic-accented English.[9]

His close association with the Cheyennes made Dutch Bill a valuable asset to the government at the Treaty of the Little Arkansas and at Medicine Lodge. The move of the Cheyennes into the Indian Territory during this period caused him to reenter the area for trading purposes along with other traders. He established a new trading post on the Washita just east of the Leased District agency.

On September 14, 1868, Greiffenstein wrote to Commissioner of Indian Affairs N. G. Taylor from Fort Cobb, sending receipts for flour delivered to the Comanches and Kiowas during the preceding June, July, and August. He offered the commissioner some free advice: "You've got to work on the young generation [of Indians] to change the old one, and the sooner the better."[10]

Major General William B. Hazen, who had been appointed as the new Indian agent at Fort Cobb following the Treaty of Medicine Lodge, hired Greiffenstein to break some twenty-five-hundred acres of prairie for the Kiowa Indians. For this purpose, Dutch Bill rode across the Indian Territory to Denison, Texas, where he purchased twenty-five sod-breaking plows.[11]

Not only was Cheyenne Jennie a great asset to Dutch Bill in his trading activities but, according to George Bent, "she did more good work in fostering peaceful relations between the Indians and whites than many an officer or high commissioner sent out by the government."[12] She was especially active in rescuing white prisoners who had been captured by the Indians. Agent S. T. Walkley wrote of her in a report:

> Too much cannot be said in praise of "Cheyenne Jennie,"
> for the interest she took and exertion she made in recovering the captive children from the Comanches, visiting
> them in their camps, invalid as she was, riding in her
> ambulance when she was not able to sit up, giving her
> own horses for the McElroy children that they might go
> home with their father. She also had great influence with
> all the wild Indians which she used in trying to have them
> keep on the straight road.[13]

Meanwhile, a series of events had been unfolding that would affect the fate of Greiffenstein and the course of affairs in the Indian Territory and at the Little Arkansas. The Nineteenth Kansas Volunteer Cavalry had been formed to assist generals Sheridan and Custer in an Indian Territory campaign against the Indians.

Led by Kansas governor Samuel J. Crawford, who resigned his office to command the unit, the regiment marched from Topeka and arrived at Camp Beecher at the mouth of the Little Arkansas on November 12, 1868. Camp Beecher had only recently been established. Not only was it the site's first tangible settlement by whites, but its few infantry troops provided the first military presence by the United States. From there, the regiment camped at Dutch Bill's former ranch on the Cowskin—the term "ranch" then merely implying a stockade stage depot and corral for stock.[14]

For the inexperienced men of the Nineteenth, the Arkansas River marked the jumping-off place to the mysterious and dangerous land of the Indian beyond. But after a short rest, the green command forded the river and plunged headlong toward the Indian Territory.

The march of the Nineteenth Kansas was a near disaster. Led by guides who did not know the country and smitten by a howling blizzard, the command became lost and confused in the severely broken country of the Cimarron River. Eventually, after much suffering and loss of horses, the volunteer regiment reached the newly established Camp Supply at the juncture of Beaver and Wolf creeks. They arrived only to find that Lt. Col. George A. Custer and the Seventh Regiment of U.S. Cavalry had already departed on a campaign to the south.[15]

Custer and his Seventh Cavalry had ridden out of Camp Supply on the morning of November 23 in the same driving snowstorm that had struck the Nineteenth Regiment. Marching down Wolf Creek and turning due south to the Antelope Hills, Custer's scout located a fresh Indian trail. Leaving his baggage train behind, Custer set off in hot pursuit. He pushed ahead relentlessly until during the early morning of November 27 he came onto an Indian encampment of some fifty lodges nestled in a bend of the Washita River.

Surrounding the small village with his troops, Custer waited until daybreak and launched his attack on the sleeping village, which later proved to be that of Cheyenne chief Black Kettle. The attack resulted in the death of Black Kettle, his wife, and many others, the capture of fifty-three Cheyenne women and children, and the destruction of the Cheyennes' lodges, robes, and horse herd.

A number of other Cheyenne and Arapaho encampments were scattered along the Washita to the east. When Custer's attack on Black Kettle's village was learned of, the warriors from those camps came swarming upriver. But Custer, feigning an attack against the other villages at dusk, reversed his march when darkness fell and retreated back toward the Antelope Hills. He left the battlefield without knowing the fate of Maj. Joel Elliott and a number of men who were missing. The Nineteenth Kansas was on hand December 1 to watch as Custer paraded into Camp Supply with his captive women and children.

Sheridan was by no means done with his winter campaign in the Indian Territory, however. With only a few days' rest, the Seventh Cavalry and the Nineteenth Volunteers were again ordered into their saddles for an expedition southward to Fort Cobb. Sheridan also wished to visit the Washita battlefield to learn the fate of Major Elliott and his seventeen men who had not returned from a chase after Indians during the Washita fight.

A visit to the battle site brought the discovery of the cold, mutilated bodies of Elliott and the other troopers. Also found on the battlefield were the bodies of Mrs. Clara Blinn and her baby son. The Blinns had been captured by Cheyenne raiders along the Santa Fe road in Colorado. Burying the dead troopers and the Blinns, the command moved on down the Washita to Fort Cobb.[16]

Even as Sheridan and Custer were marching south from Kansas, Greiffenstein had been involved in an attempt to rescue the Blinns. Greiffenstein dispatched a man known as Cheyenne Jack to make contact with the woman and help effect a ransom. Cheyenne Jack met with the unfortunate Mrs. Blinn and provided her with a paper on which she penned a letter addressed in reply. The message, a pathetic cry for help, was later reprinted in newspapers throughout the country.

> KIND FRIEND—Whoever you may be, I thank you for your kindness to me and my child. You want me to let you know my wishes. If you could only buy us of the Indians with ponies or anything, and let me come stay with you until I could get word to my friends, they would pay you, and I would work and do all I could for you. If it is not too far to their camp, and you are not afraid to come, I pray you will try. They tell me, as near as I can understand, they expect traders to come and they will sell us to them. If it is Mexicans, I am afraid they would sell us into slavery in Mexico. If you can do nothing write to W. T. Harrington, Ottawa, Franklin County, Kansas—my father. Tell him we are with the Cheyennes and they say when the white men make peace we can go home. Tell him to write to the Governor of Kansas about it and for them to make peace. Send this to him. We were taken on the 9th of October on the Arkansas, below Fort Lyon. Cannot tell whether they killed my husband or not. My name is Mrs. Clara Blinn. My little boy, Willie Blinn, is two years old. Do all you can for me; write to the Peace Commissioners to make peace this fall. For our sakes do all you can, and God will bless you. If you can let me hear from you again let me know what you think about it. Write my father; send him this. Goodby.
>
> Mrs. R. F. Blinn
>
> I am as well as can be expected, but my baby is very weak.[17]

When he learned that Mrs. Blinn and her son were dead, Greiffenstein returned to his Washita post.[18] He had his own misfortune to grieve. This was the death of Cheyenne Jennie. Just how this came about is not known for certain. An unsubstantiated (and perhaps unlikely) story is told that she was killed while protecting Dutch Bill from renegade Indians.[19]

Greiffenstein was soon confronted by other troubles. In January 1869, after having moved from Fort Cobb to Medicine Bluff Creek where Fort Sill was established, Sheridan had been persuaded by rival traders that Dutch Bill was selling arms and ammunition to the Indians as well as buying contraband cattle. The hot-tempered Sheridan called Dutch Bill in and gave him twenty-four hours to get out of the Territory or face being hanged. Sheridan caused the issuance of a field order that read:

> 1. William Greiffenstein, *alias* "Dutch Bill," heretofore located as a Trader on the Washita River, I. T., twelve miles southeast of Fort Cobb, for having furnished powder, lead and food to Indians engaged in murdering the frontier settlers of Kansas, Texas and Colorado, is ordered beyond the limits of Indian Territory. All commanders of Posts and detachments of United States Troops, and all law-abiding Indians and citizens, are directed and requested, respectively, to arrest him should he be found within the limits of the Indian Territory after the 15th day of February, 1869, and deliver him at Fort Arbuckle or Gibson.[20]

Greiffenstein always insisted the charges were not true.[21] A Wichita citizen once gave an interesting but perhaps fanciful account of how Dutch Bill pleaded his case with Sheridan one night when the two played a friendly game of poker. The trader was unable to persuade the general to drop the charge of selling munitions to the Indians.[22] However it happened, Greiffenstein was forced to high-tail it back to Kansas, leaving his mules, wagons, and camp goods for Mathewson to bring out. He would later travel to Washington, D.C., to demand an investigation and compensation for his cattle that Sheridan had impounded.[23]

Greiffenstein returned to Topeka where in 1869 he was contacted by Enoch Hoag, newly appointed Indian superintendent for the Indian Territory. Hoag asked him to serve as pilot for a group of Quaker agents that had been assigned to various agency posts inside the Territory. The trader agreed to do so despite Sheridan's threat of hanging.[24]

In August Greiffenstein left Topeka with the Quakers in tow. He took them first to the mouth of the Little Arkansas, where there were now four stores, a saloon, blacksmith shop, post office, and two boardinghouses. Several droves of Texas cattle were passing by on their way to Abilene. A messenger from General Hazen at Fort Cobb met Greiffenstein there. He carried a letter requesting that Dutch Bill take the Quakers by way of Round Pond Creek, where agent Brinton Darlington was attempting to establish his Cheyenne and Arapaho agency.[25]

The aging Darlington and his son-in-law had toiled in the heat of summer to build a warehouse in which to store annuity goods. They had also planted a small patch of corn. But the Cheyennes and Arapahos, partly because of the brackish water there but mainly because of the presence of Osage and Kaw horse thieves in the area, refused to come to the Round Pond Creek location. Hazen, with whom Greiffenstein became good friends, requested that the trader escort Darlington to Camp Supply, from which point the Quaker could search out a new agency location. Dutch Bill did so, then accompanied the other Quakers to Fort Sill, remaining in the Territory until the end of August.[26]

Soon after returning to Topeka, Greiffenstein married Catherine Burnett, the adopted daughter of Potawatomi chief Abraham Burnett, on November 21, 1869. Catherine was born in Germany and brought to America as a small child. She had been orphaned by the death of her mother in Indiana and taken into the Burnett family, who provided her with a good education.[27]

Shortly after the marriage, Dutch Bill loaded his personal effects and trade goods aboard his wagons and headed back to the mouth of the Ne Shutsa Shinka. He felt there was a great future ahead for the small settlement that was now being called "Wichita."

Chapter Seven

Outpost on the Arkansas

No doubt you've heard of Wichita
A city, long the Arkansas
She fears not God nor Kansas law
But worships fiendish whisky, O!
— *Wichita Eagle*, "Fiendish Whisky," February 2, 1882

In July 1869 a traveling correspondent for the Lawrence *Daily Tribune*, riding in a team-drawn buggy, ventured far beyond Emporia, the last substantial community in south-central Kansas. He passed over the barren Flint Hills and visited the frontier locations of El Dorado, Towanda, and ultimately the tiny new settlement called Wichita. He found that the prairie between the Whitewater and the Walnut was virtually unsettled. Though there were a few farms along the Walnut, the place noted so prominently on his map as Towanda was really no town at all. It was merely a still formless cluster of buildings consisting of a farmer's house, which contained the post office, a trading store operated by James Mead, and a schoolhouse.[1]

The map also indicated that it was from twenty to twenty-five miles from Towanda to Wichita, but on this burning summer day, without water for himself or his team, the correspondent painfully reckoned the distance to be at least the full twenty-five. Despite the dryness of the season, the browned grasses rippled to the hot breezes as the team and buggy bumped along a twin-rutted avenue of green-stalked sunflowers whose black buttons and golden halos marked the land the entire distance.

At the place now called Wichita, located where the Little Arkansas—still pronounced Ar'-kan-saw[2] but commonly known as Little River to early residents—flowed into the big Arkansas, the journalist found a small but energetic hamlet of five stores and about one hundred inhabitants. There was a trading post, a mercantile store, two rather primitive boardinghouses, and a saloon. The site could even make the extraordinary boast of having a physician in residence. An impromptu dance, gotten up to celebrate the completion of a new building in town, found the women equal in number to the men.

The wide, sand-bedded Arkansas River with its meandering, shallow channel, the visitor noted, was soon to be crossed by a ferry—a valuable counter to the treacherous quicksand and flood stages of the stream. Tall cottonwoods lined both banks, their leafy bowers flickering in the bright sun and providing shady nooks along the river for human inhabitants and wildlife alike.

Already the buffalo herds, which had grazed here for years uncounted, were abdicating their haunts to the men with the long guns. These grazing pastures were pitted by bowl-shaped buffalo wallows that dented the prairie for miles around and produced puddles after each rain. Now they were trampled by the Texas longhorns that had for the past two years splashed and bawled their way across the ford of the Arkansas and rumbled in a huge cloud of dust on northward toward the railhead at Abilene.

With them came the Texas drovers under their wide-brimmed sombreros—young, rowdy-natured cowboys, a cultural mixture of Texas and Mexico, who fell upon the infant settlement as their first oasis after the long drive across the Indian Territory, ready to drink and gamble and give celebration to their ordeal.

At the same time, industrious, literate citizens were here, the correspondent opined, producing the first signs of creeping civilization at this point on the frontier. Fields of wheat and oats were even then being harvested, while stands of sod corn gave further promise to the agricultural potential of the area and made a lie of the charge that this was an unarable part of the Great American Desert.

For nearly three years, from 1867 to 1870, Wichita existed as a distant outpost, operating pretty much outside the rule of civil law. Though the "border terror" from the Indian Territory was a frequent visitor, most of the early residents were lawful—if unrestrained—men

HALTING-PLACE ON THE NINNESCAH RIVER.

This "ranch stop" at the Ninnescah River on the Chisholm Trail was located just south of present Wichita. *Harper's Weekly*, May 2, 1874.

whose free style of living reflected the self-dependence and rough humor of the frontier. They drank hard, held strong opinions, and lived by their own personal moral codes. They generally expressed themselves with vigorous language that was seasoned heavily with their own brand of profanity. Many of them carried guns in the mode of the old West. Though only an occasional hard case laid claim to gunfighter status, most relied on their pistol, shotgun, or rifle for their daily security.

William Greiffenstein had established his post on Cowskin Creek in 1865, and he was followed in the spring of 1866 by Charles Whittaker, who had earlier located a claim eight miles above the mouth of the Little Arkansas. Whittaker, at that time, was a partner in the Sunset Ranch at the Great Bend of the Arkansas River along with Phares C. Hubbard and Henry Sedrick. The ranch was described by the *Leavenworth Times* as "a most complete and furnished establishment . . . kept by a company of the very best men, well posted on the

Indian trade."[3] Following the Treaty of the Little Arkansas, Hubbard became a Durfee Company trader and relocated his fur trading operation to the south.

During 1867, Henry W. Vigus, a harness maker by trade, came to join Hubbard, taking up his abode in a deserted Indian lodge until he could build a cabin for himself and his wife. That same year, partners Lewellen and Davis arrived to operate a mercantile store, while Jim Gifford opened the first saloon in a log house. During the winter of 1868–69, Gifford became the first white man to die a natural death there. It was later commented wryly that while no one could prove that watered whiskey was dealt out in his saloon, it was a known historical fact that the Arkansas River was very low that season.[4]

An ever increasing traffic in wagon trains freighting in Indian annuity goods and trader caravans had established the white presence here. This fact was emphasized in July 1867 when teamsters Tom Wells and John Lawton, who operated a trading post for James Mead at Round Pond Creek in the Territory, became involved in a dispute at the Lewellen-Davis store. The trouble arose when Lawton, sitting on the counter of the store, remarked with great passion that if he ever ran into an army deserter he would turn in the so-and-so (or s.o.b., more likely). Evidently Wells was a deserter himself, for in a fit of anger he pulled his revolver and shot Lawton twice, committing the first known murder at Wichita.[5]

Eli P. Waterman, who had first visited the town in 1867, returned the following February and situated his family on the east bank of the Arkansas River where downtown Wichita is located today. In December, Durfee freighted in the building materials for construction of a large trading house. This first frame building was on the east bank of the Little Arkansas a short distance above its conflux with the Arkansas.[6]

Philip Ledrick arrived in January 1868 to represent the Durfee firm, which proudly announced completion of its post at a cost of twenty-five hundred dollars.[7] Ledrick soon withdrew from the firm, however, to undertake other matters. He planted one of the first corn crops to be raised in the area by a white settler. Ledrick was replaced by Milo Kellogg, a bookkeeper for the Durfee Company, and Charlie Hunter, who brought his mother and sister with him.

A circular, printed at Emporia for the Durfee concern that spring, advised trail drovers and dealers in cattle that the town of "Wichita" offered facilities plus the protection of a military post. This is thought to have been the first time the name of Wichita appeared in print as a designation for the new settlement.[8]

Henry Vigus soon became connected with the Durfee post, exercising his skills as an expert harness maker in decorating saddles and bridles with ornamental brass tacks and red flannel, which made them invaluable to the Indian trade. Vigus and his wife enterprisingly opened their own home as a combination hotel, eating house, and saloon. This establishment quickly became known as the Buckhorn, where "every class of frontiersman, as well as border terror, had a home."[9]

In May 1868, D. S. Munger appeared on the scene to represent a Topeka townsite group that consisted of ex-Kansas governor Samuel Crawford, W. H. H. Lawrence, James Mead, E. P. Bancroft, A. F. Horner, and Munger. A survey was run and an original town plat prepared by Mead, who had once been a county surveyor. Both Mead and Munger staked claims there in 1868, though the filing on them was not accomplished until later. Munger constructed a cottonwood-log house that has survived the ages and is today on display at Wichita's Old Cowtown Museum.

Some wanted to call the new town "Hamilton" and some "Beecher," after Lt. Fred Beecher who had recently been killed by Cheyennes on the Arikaree in Colorado Territory. Mead, however, held out for the name of "Wichita," giving just recognition to the first-known native inhabitants of the region.[10] Lots were laid out northeast of the juncture of the rivers, but somehow the venture did not catch on and the townsite failed to prosper.

The establishment of a U.S. military camp at the site had been prompted by an incident that took place on May 17, 1868, on Walnut Creek. Two settlers were setting a property cornerstone when they suddenly found themselves surrounded by fourteen Osage warriors. The Osages, passionately defensive of the Kansas trust lands their tribe still held under their Treaty of 1865, saw the men as intruders. They attacked, killing one of the men, Sam Dunn, instantly. The other, James Anderson, was disabled with a tomahawk and then shot and killed. Both men were scalped and decapitated in the usual warring style of the Osages, and the fingers were cut off of one of the men. A party of white pursuers failed to catch the Osages. United States commissioners who were then engaged in signing a new treaty with the tribe demanded the surrender of the guilty parties, and the Osages eventually gave up two young perpetrators to U.S. marshals.[11]

Governor Samuel
Crawford promoted
the founding of Camp
Beecher and joined in
establishing Wichita.
Kansas State
Historical Society.

Increasing concern over the hostile tribes in the Indian Territory and western Kansas had already caused General Sheridan to respond to a request by Sam Crawford to provide the protection of U.S. troops for the frontier. In April 1868 Sheridan issued orders for the location of a military post at the mouth of the Little Arkansas to protect settlers of the area. The frontier-wise citizens were left to ponder, however, just why Sheridan garrisoned it with infantry soldiers whose effectiveness was limited to a few hundred yards of their post and had little chance of ever catching an Indian.[12]

The first troops of Company H, Fifth Infantry arrived on May 11, 1868, and established what was temporarily known as "Camp Butterfield," in honor of D. A. Butterfield of the Butterfield Overland Line between Leavenworth and Denver. The soldiers were put to work building a fifty-by-fifty-foot dugout for their quarters. Located a half a mile north of what would become the initial city of Wichita, the mostly underground structure had a fireplace and dormer windows on the south.

Several of the men of the Nineteenth Kansas who marched past the settlement in the fall of 1868 wrote of it in their letters and journals. A. L. Runyon described the location as being composed "of a few log buildings, and a small fort and stockade." Some of the dwellings, he noted, were built like Indian tepees, and some were built underground with a barrel for a chimney.[13] Captain George Jenness mentioned "one rudely constructed log building, used for Army supplies, another similar, though small, structure inhabited by the post sutler...and one or two adobes."[14] There were about four or five bark and grass woven wickiups, Jenness said, which resembled dirty Sibley tents from a distance. They were uninhabited.

David L. Spotts of the Nineteenth wrote of a long adobe with a wood lean-to and described the wide, sand-bottomed Arkansas where a large number of cottonwood trees had been felled in all directions. They had been cut so that horses could feed off the bark when the ground was covered with snow.[15]

For a time the post was designated as Camp Davidson by Col. Robert M. West, who took charge in June.[16] The first official commander of the post was Capt. Samuel L. Barr, Fifth U.S. Infantry.[17] Other than the capture of six black soldiers who had deserted from Fort Larned, however, the troops at Camp Beecher saw little action. But the military camp was significant to the growth of Wichita both in establishing new, shorter wagon roads to other military sites and in the economic effect it exerted on the local community. "The first dance halls and saloons in the city," historian H. Craig Miner notes, "were not supported by cowboys as much as by soldiers."[18]

By the end of 1868 Wichita was still not an incorporated city, though Sedgwick County had been created out of the old Butler County on February 26, 1867. The county name was chosen to honor Maj. Gen. John Sedgwick, whose military career had involved Indian-fighting service in Kansas before he was killed during the Civil War. The county held its first election in November 1868, helping to choose Ulysses S. Grant as president of the United States.[19]

A steady migration to Wichita continued during 1869. The establishment of a military road from Fort Harker, Kansas, to Fort Sill in the Territory resulted in Wichita's becoming a way station and replenishing point for military troops as well as for Indian department goods and the blossoming Texas cattle trade. Even more significant was the public homesteading of the Osage Trust Lands, whose opening Congress had approved on April 9, 1869.[20]

When the news of this government action reached Wichita, D. S. Munger hurried to Humboldt and filed the papers for his claim along with those of fifty-two others.[21] Efforts were made to organize Sedgwick County, and an election was held to name county officers. However, this attempt was declared void by the governor of Kansas because of certain irregularities.

A census was taken, and the results forwarded to Topeka. A commission was then appointed to complete the organization of the county. An election was called for the following spring, and in it Wichita would beat out nearby Park City for the county seat. Reportedly both of the competitors indulged in rampant ballot box stuffing. Even passing bull whackers and trail-herd drovers had been persuaded to cast ballots. The boys at Wichita simply did a better job of it.[22]

Among those now taking up residence at Wichita were some men who would play important roles in the town's history: Phares C. Hubbard; William Mathewson; James Mead, who moved his residence to Wichita; lawyer Henry C. Sluss, who was destined to become a judge and Kansas political figure; realtor and town-pusher Big John Steele; attorney N. A. English; and others.

In October 1869 the first religious sermon was preached in Wichita by Brother Saxby at the Munger house. The Reverend Dr. W. R. Boggs also came over from Emporia to hold Sunday school meetings in the now-deserted army dugout.[23]

A bridge across the Arkansas River was badly needed; and the Arkansas River Bridge and Ferry Company was organized with a capital stock of twenty thousand dollars, divided into shares of a hundred dollars each. The company, of which Mead was a principal, first put a ferry into operation in May 1871. Osage trader Alonzo Greenway, who had come to Wichita from Marion Center to offer a general stock of supply goods for the Texas cattle trade, operated the ferry.[24]

The Arkansas ferry raft ran between two wooden towers on opposite sides of the river near the mouth of the Little Arkansas. A trolley rope connected the two towers, and the raft was attached to it by two wheel-operated ropes, allowing the otherwise powerless ferry to utilize the river current to move from bank to bank. Mainly, the ferry functioned during flooding periods of the river, the fare being ten cents for foot passengers, fifty cents for one team and an unloaded wagon, and a dollar for one team and loaded wagon.

The ferry operation lasted only until the Arkansas River bridge was built during the spring of 1872. During that time, however, a youngster named L. C. Fouquet worked as Greenway's helper in running the ferry. Fouquet later told how the heavy-drinking Greenway would entertain the boys at Shattner's saloon by performing Osage war and scalping songs and dances with a ferocious demeanor and a butcher knife in hand. At other times he would ride the river in his canoe, drinking and singing Indian songs.[25]

It was a simple fact of demand and supply that caused early Wichita to have three times as many saloons as grocery stores. By the end of 1869, the fledgling town had become a place for replenishment for trail-herd drovers, drifters, travelers, hunters, Indians, buffalo hunters, wanted men, and others.

More than a few of Wichita's male citizens were men who lived beyond the pale of the law. They followed a code of their own making in the absence of legal enforcement of Kansas statutes written by "them fellers" in distant Topeka. There was as yet no marshal or lawman of any sort to mollify the sometimes bellicose behavior of the rough men who appeared and then as quickly disappeared at Wichita.

A mixture of log cabin residences and unpainted lumber or log places of business sat in somewhat of a row running north and south adjacent to the Little Arkansas along what is now Waco Street. These included Doc Lewellen's dry goods, Waterman's grocery, George Clark's saloon, an eating place operated by Mexican M. R. "Charlie" Cordiero, Hubbard and Mason's mercantile store, and Henry Vigus's Buckhorn hotel and saloon. To the west along the Arkansas was Durfee's trading post, which was purchased by Greiffenstein in the fall of 1869; and to the north were the old army dugout and a couple of Wichita Indian lodges that still stood as reminders of the location's namesakes.[26]

The most famous of city landmarks was the Buckhorn. A long structure built of logs, it featured walls plastered with adobe mud, floors of barren earth that quickly turned to dust under the heels of patrons, and a roof of twigs and dirt that sprouted saplings, wild flowers, and weeds during the spring and summer. The home became a public stopping place when Vigus one day accepted monetary reward for the hospitality of his house. It wasn't long before Mrs. Vigus was cooking meals regularly and Vigus was tending bar for the hungry, thirsty passers-by.[27]

A battery of stories grew up around the Buckhorn, promoting it to almost legendary status. One such tale concerned a visit by two strangers, both booted and armed. They claimed to be government men from Topeka and insisted that since Vigus accepted money for accommodations, he was running a hotel. The state hotel license was fifty dollars, they said, and they were there to collect it.

Vigus attempted to argue that, even though people kept dropping in and staying all night or longer, the Buckhorn was not really a hotel. When this argument failed to deter the Topeka men, Vigus quite suddenly remembered that he had only recently dispatched his fifty dollars to the state treasury and was expecting the license back any day. The men were unpersuaded by Vigus's sudden recollection and demanded that he fork over the fee. Vigus dug deep and did so.

Now satisfied with their victory, the Topeka men ordered a meal before going on their way. They ate and then went to Vigus to settle up. He told them the price of the two meals was exactly fifty dollars! The men howled with outrage, declaring that such a price was highway robbery and they would never pay it.

"You'll pay it," Vigus supposedly told them, "or you'll never leave that front door alive."

The two paid their bill and rode off in a huff, though they must have felt pleased that they were a free meal ahead in the deal.[28]

Another much-recited Buckhorn incident concerned its music box, a unique feature whose lively tunes entertained and enlivened the tavern's motley attendance. On occasion the mixture of music and whiskey would bring forth an impromptu, dust-raising dance on the dirt floor. For some reason, however, the music one day had a negative effect on Jack Ledford, a rambunctious border character whose reputation for wildness had flowered considerably around Wichita. Jerking forth a navy pistol from his belt, Ledford emptied it into the otherwise innocent music box, silencing it forever and dampening Wichita's social life.[29]

The affair that capped Wichita's notoriety as a tough frontier settlement, however, took place in another saloon on December 27, 1869. This involved the killing of O. J. Whitman by Charlie Cordiero. Cordiero had come to Wichita as a scout for the army and stayed to operate his saloon and eating place at the north end of town. He was a smallish man with long, snaky black hair and a mouthful of pearly teeth overflown by an oversized handlebar mustache.[30]

Though not an overbearing man, Cordiero was not particularly liked because of his affected manner of dress that emulated that of the Mexican cowboys who came up the cattle trail from Texas. He wore a large white sombrero with a wide brim and a tall crown that was covered over with silver binding and rosettes that sparkled in the sun. His shirt was a pale blue, being joined at the waist by a crimson sash with tassels hanging from it against his purple velvet trousers. A cartridge belt was strapped over the sash, giving support to an ivory-handled six-gun.

Whitman, a wild-natured buddy of Jack Ledford, especially did not like Cordiero. During a heavy drinking spree, he decided it was his civic duty to run the saloonkeeper out of town. The conflict began at Doc Lewellen's store some two or three hundred yards from Cordiero's place. Whitman and a friend were there when Cordiero came in. They proceeded to call him a few names "without smiling." When this did not provoke Cordiero, Whitman began to shove him around. A fist-fight and wrestling match ensued before Cordiero freed himself. He departed with a warning that he would not allow himself to be pushed around by a drunk. If Whitman came to his place, Cordiero said, he would kill him.

Whitman continued on his drinking spree, at one time shooting off a gun in Greiffenstein's store. Eventually he headed for Cordiero's place, rapping loudly at the door before entering. His hand was hidden inside his coat. Cordiero immediately pulled his pistol and jerked the trigger twice, the caps snapping both times without firing. Whitman continued on to the bar, resisting a friend who tried to lead him away. When he refused to go, Cordiero grabbed a carbine and shot him through the body. Whitman, mortally wounded, crawled out of the saloon to the street where he died as a crowd gathered around.

On the advice of friends, Cordiero left town. However, he was found and brought back by John Wade and three other men who, in the absence of a law officer, were deputized for the occasion. Cordiero was placed in jail at Emporia, but he was soon released on bond. In June 1870, a jury heard testimony from witnesses to the affray, including Doc Lewellen, and took only ten minutes to acquit Cordiero.[31] The saloonkeeper remained in Wichita until 1874, when he joined the Black Hills gold rush. It was said around that he later drove stagecoaches in Wyoming and Montana.

There was an abundance of characters around Wichita in those days, and by no means were they all bad men or dangerous. Mostly they were just strong-minded and free-willed men whose personalities matched the roughness of the frontier social order. One of these was Uncle Jack Peyton, a saddler and character of some distinction, who became noted for a lecture he delivered on "Theology and Theocracy." The oration became celebrated among early Wichita lore.[32]

It wasn't the usual Sunday morning sermon. The location of Peyton's great moral pronouncement was Doc Lewellen's log house grocery store at the north end. Sometimes known as "Lewellen's Hall," the building served as a social gathering place for Wichita residents. Peyton had the unique physical distinction of being shorter in one leg by a considerable distance than in the other, the difference being estimated by some at nearly four or five inches.

Thus, when he was standing on the one leg, Peyton was a good deal shorter than when he chose the longer one, which elevated him to about six feet in height. This ability to change his physical stature quite suddenly was striking enough, but Peyton was also blessed with a stentorian voice and an unending supply of descriptive expletives.

Peyton's address was preannounced to the public by means of handbills printed by a single font of wood type and distributed liberally around town. Peyton provided Lewellen's Hall with six tallow candles to supplement the limited lighting provided by the small windows. He also refurbished the room for the occasion with dry goods boxes and planks supported by nail kegs for seating. The absence of any competing social functions whatsoever in the area helped to bring out the citizenry in full attendance to hear Uncle Jack's views on theological theory. The orator prepared himself internally with an ample dosage of bottled warmth before taking his place in front of the expectant audience. Standing at full height on his longer leg, he began in a voice that rose fully to the occasion.

"Ladies and gentlemen," he boomed. "Theology is religion as taught by the ministerial profession. Theocracy is ... is the ... well, by damn, anyhow..." Becoming confused and mentally untracked, Peyton had a sudden loss of confidence and, plop, down he shifted from his longer leg to his shorter one, abruptly lowering the viewing level of his audience considerably. "Theocracy is the ... well, one defines the moral law..." Back up he went. "...and the other is..." Plop, down he went again.[33]

Completely void of sympathy for the struggling orator, Henry Vigus jumped to his feet and shouted: "Jack Peyton doesn't know what he's talking about! Now, I want to tell you why people get themselves drunk."

But Peyton was not about to give up his place before the assembly.

"Sit down," he bellowed at full height. "Who paid for these candles? Who rented this hall?"[34]

Whereupon he continued his lecture amid the hilarity of his whooping, laughing audience. Every time his mind jumped the track, he shifted from one leg to the other, down, then up, then down, then up; and with each shift of leg, the hilarity of the audience grew. Occasionally the commotion was punctuated by the firing of a pistol. Though no one learned much about either theology or theocracy or why people get drunk, the event was a smashing social success. The citizens of Wichita had a grand time.

By 1870, several men who had been with the Nineteenth Kansas when it passed by Wichita in the fall of 1868 had come back to reside in the area. One of these was Capt. David L. Payne, who settled on a ranch between Towanda and Wichita on Dry Creek. Eventually it became a way station for the Southwestern Stage Line and a gathering place for frontier hard cases who were friends of Payne. The place soon gained a bad reputation, and at one time it was charged that Payne and some of his buddies were stealing corn from the stage company stock feed and making bootleg whiskey with it.[35]

Another Nineteenth Volunteer officer to return to the area was A. J. Pliley. Pliley, who had been with Maj. George A. Forsyth, Ninth Calvary, and Lt. Frederick Beecher, Third Infantry, at the Arikaree fight in the fall of 1868, had proved himself to be a hard-minded, eye-for-an-eye man during the Sheridan Indian Territory campaign. When three men had deserted from Fort Sill, taking Pliley's horse with them, he and another officer borrowed mounts from Custer's Osage scouts and went after the deserters. They returned several days later with the horses and guns of the men but with no prisoners. When asked as to the fate of the men they went after, they said only that the last time they saw them they were lying "looking at the sun."[36]

Pliley and a partner named Jesse Vandervort established the Cowskin Ranch at a bridge crossing that river six miles below Wichita, offering outfitting goods and "all sorts of truck" to passing drovers.[37] When Vandervort was killed by a man from Montana named George P. Murray, Pliley captured him and turned him over to law officials. When Murray escaped the following day, Pliley saddled his horse and followed the murderer into the Indian Territory all the way to the Creek Nation. He came upon Murray sitting by his campfire and charged him on horseback. The two men traded lead with one another until Pliley won the day. He buried Murray there and returned to Kansas with the man's pony and revolver, which he kept as "pay for his travel expenses."[38]

Still another man who, like Pliley and Payne, had been with Custer in the Indian Territory, was former scout Jack Corbin. It had been he who had brought Custer the report of an Indian trail near the Antelope Hills, the trail that led to Black Kettle's village on the Washita. In November 1870, Corbin became the victim of a necktie party by a vigilante group that believed him to be a member of a horse-stealing gang.

These were lawless days for Sedgwick County. Earlier that spring two emigrants had been murdered near Wichita, reportedly by a gang of thieves, for their team and money. The perpetrators left a note on the bodies of the victims labeling them as "Horse Thieves." It was subsequently learned that the two victims were really honest, law-abiding citizens.[39]

Later a band of about fourteen vigilantes surrounded four men in the vicinity of Douglass south of Wichita, Corbin being among the four suspected horse thieves. In an assault on the house where they were holed up, one man was shot through the head and breast four times. Two others were shot as they tried to escape. A note was left on the chest of one, reading "Shot for a horse thief."[40]

Corbin was taken prisoner and, though he claimed to be a government scout and had on him a warrant for the arrest of a man, he was hanged from a sycamore tree, supposedly after confessing the names of fifty accomplices and telling where stolen stock could be found.[41]

Following this, a leading merchant of Douglass named Quimby, his partner Mike Dray, a Dr. Morris, and the doctor's son were arrested and charged with horse stealing. They were being held under guard that night when a group of seventy men came and took them a mile and a half south of Douglass and hanged them all without pretense of trial.[42]

Another sordid case involved the murder by a Wichita man of an Illinois boy whom he had met on the way to Kansas. Alexander Jester fell in with the boy, murdered him with an ax while he was asleep, and then stole the boy's team and wagon, trunk, silver watch, and some money. The boy's father reported Jester's crime and had him arrested, but Jester escaped. He was eventually killed, it was said, in an attempted robbery near Dodge City.[43]

Despite such mayhem, by late 1869 Wichita had been firmly established as a new Kansas settlement. Soon it would no longer be a mere outpost—enterprising William Greiffenstein would see to that.

Chapter Eight

For a Span of Mules

A fairer town is seldom seen,
Of all other Kansas towns, the Queen;
Her Pa was Dutchbillgreiffenstein
But ah! she was raised on whisky O!
— *Wichita Eagle*, "Fiendish Whisky," February 2, 1882

For five years Wichita existed as a stopping place on the cattle trail to Abilene. She was rough, rowdy, and reckless during those years; but, still, because of dynamic leadership, she developed into a small but energetic town that outcompeted neighboring communities for trade, population, and physical growth. Though there were certainly others, one being James Mead, who shine forth in Wichita's history, there is no disputing that one of the most progressive citizens of Wichita during that period and beyond was William Greiffenstein.

Titles such as "The Father of Wichita" and "The George Washington of Wichita" were bestowed on him by his contemporaries, and his list of accomplishments seems almost endless.[1] Indeed, the pipe-smoking ex-Indian trader—now dressed in a rumpled black suit and collarless white shirt with a gold watch chain connecting an unbuttoned vest—was involved in almost every civic improvement of Wichita's early years. At the same time he won the admiration and affection of all who knew him.

When Greiffenstein arrived with his new wife in late 1869, he moved into the old Durfee trading post just west of the Munger townsite.[2] Here he did business in dry goods and general merchandise through the winter. During the spring of 1870, he disposed of his store and purchased eighty acres of land from Eli Waterman. This then-vacant acreage located on the east bank of the Arkansas due south of the Munger plat would, through Greiffenstein's promotion, become the central downtown area of Wichita. Dutch Bill paid ten dollars an acre for the land, some say more.[3] One way or another, he made a bargain out of it.

Hiring William Finn to survey the eighty acres and draw out a plat on the back of an old flour sack, Greiffenstein drove to the land office at Augusta and filed his townsite on March 25, 1870.[4] He then announced that he would give away lots free to those who would build on them, selling others at a price low enough to encourage people to invest in the Wichita land.[5] Some of the settlers who had built on the Munger townsite now mounted their houses on wagon wheels and moved them to the Greiffenstein development.[6]

Meanwhile, Dutch Bill was making other investments in the locality. For one, he purchased A. A. "Lank" Moore's 160-acre claim just south of his eighty acres at the price of a pair of dilapidated mules, a wagon, harness, and three hundred pounds of flour. He paid the government $117.50 for a deed to the property.[7] In July 1870, he bought Phares C. Hubbard's 160 acres lying inside a bend of the Little Arkansas to the north of the old Durfee post, the purchase being made in the name of his wife Catherine. This plot would become known as "Greiffenstein's farm."[8]

Another move was made to compete with the Munger townsite that summer. Dutch Bill revised his original plat so that lots along a wide avenue running eastward from the ford of the Arkansas River would face onto the street. He named it Douglas in honor of Steven A. Douglas of Illinois.[9] This avenue, which followed the course of the cattle trail to Abilene, soon became the dominant street of the town in competition with Main Street, which ran perpendicular to it through the Munger area. The *Wichita Vidette* of August 13, 1870, reported:

He [Munger] had several buildings put up, which gave it the appearance of a town. Little else was done until about three months ago when William Greiffenstein laid off a town south of the old town, since which the buildings have been going

The Munger House became the first rooming and boarding house on the site of Wichita. Wichita-Sedgwick County Museum.

up as fast as mechanics can do the work and building materials furnished.

Greiffenstein set about to erect the first lumber house of the new town, a commodious structure located on South Water Street at what became known to his friends as "Strawberry Hill." The residence was completed on April 23, 1870.[10]

Now the growth of Wichita began, a virtual explosion of new houses and business structures sprouting up from the town's vortex at the juncture of Douglas and Main. Wagonloads of freshly cut pine rattled in over the long, ninety-five-mile wagon road from Emporia, setting to tune the sharp commands and expletives of teamsters, the rasp of carpenter saws, and the tattoo of hammers where not so long before Indian women had constructed their lodges of matted grass and twigs.

Hotels, boarding houses, cafes, saloons, real estate and professional offices, general merchandise stores, blacksmiths, drug stores, hardwares, liveries, bakeries, newspapers, boot shops, saddleries, banks, and other enterprises flourished in the double rows of unpainted buildings that stretched forth, fronted by boardwalks and hitching rails, on Douglas and Main. New houses rose beyond in the Greiffenstein, Waterman, and Mead additions.

Setting the standard for this new community on the prairie was the two-story Empire House hotel at the corner of Third and Main, built by Greiffenstein. It would soon be renamed the Wichita House.[11] A visitor to Wichita noted that when she had seen the town only a year before in May 1869, it had been a frontier village with only half a dozen sod-roofed huts. Now, within the last two months, the writer reported, Wichita had almost miraculously sprouted forty-six buildings with thirty-two more under contract to begin as soon as materials arrived.

She counted a hotel, five good-sized boardinghouses, five groceries, three restaurants, two lumberyards, two butcher shops, one combination dry goods, grocery, boot-and-hat shop, agricultural implement and everything else store, one drug store, one livery and feed stable, a barbershop, two real estate offices, two physicians, one dentist, five carpenter shops, a public hall, a hardware store, a millinery shop, two clothing stores, two bakeries, one flour and feed store, and a number of others.[12]

The visitor also witnessed a sight then common at Wichita—a herd of thirty-one hundred bawling Texas longhorns fording the Arkansas River. Equally as common were oxen bull trains plodding the trails leading to Fort Harker and Fort Sill or one of the Indian Territory agencies. At the same time, wagons loaded with everything from stacks of raw lumber to crated pianos plied the streets of Wichita.[13]

Intermingled with all this civic and business progress, however, was the hurly-burly of Texas drovers who celebrated in the several saloons of the town before pushing on to Abilene. The omnipresence of the frontier in Wichita still shaped the town's reputation, which had already felt the negative effects of the Lawton killing and the Cordiero affair.

Added proof of Wichita as a wild frontier town came in May 1870 when a well-known Texas cattle thief named Hurricane Bill Martin was caught in the act of driving off some cattle he did not own. When he tried to escape after being arrested, he was shot and seriously wounded. The incident gave rise to the story that when Hurricane Bill and his gang were arrested in Wichita, they dropped their weapons in the weeds on the northwest corner of Water Street and Douglas, causing the location to be dubbed "Horse Thief Corner."[14]

In an effort to change Wichita's image and overcome her negative reputation, Greiffenstein and others decided to utilize the town's first Fourth of July celebration to persuade others that the town was not so bad as it was painted. Accordingly, a notice appeared in the July 1, 1870, edition of the *Emporia News* declaring:

THE GLORIOUS FOURTH
The good people of Wichita extend the invitation to everybody "and the rest of mankind" to participate with them in celebrating the Fourth of July at Wichita.[15]

There would be a parade and speeches and the reading of the Declaration of Independence, these preceded by a buffalo hunt on the second and third of July to supply the attending crowd with barbecued buffalo. In concluding, the notice declared: "Hurrah for Lexington, Boston, Bunker Hill and Wichita!"[16]

The ad may well have been penned by the grand marshal of the event, a strapping man of thirty-three who stood six-foot-four and possessed a handsome face along with a jovial, likeable personality. He was David L. Payne, whose rugged frontier style had quickly made him a favorite when he moved into Wichita from Dry Creek.

Payne, who had been known to his company of Nineteenth Kansas volunteers as "Old Oxheart," had become a well-known fixture in the saloons of Wichita. He won a popular following that would eventually encourage him to try his hand at politics and win a seat in the Kansas legislature for one term. Ultimately he would become leader of the Oklahoma Boomer movement that pushed for settlement of Indian Territory. Some would dub him the "Father of Oklahoma."

As Grand Marshal of the Independence Day fete, he was at the lead of the buffalo hunting party of eight men that rode west from Wichita early on the morning of July 2. The retinue was later joined by a group of visitors from Emporia, including three or four women and the Rev. W. R. Boggs. Boggs had only recently moved from Emporia to Wichita to organize a Presbyterian church there. One of the women guests penned a description of what would be one of the last buffalo hunts to be conducted on the prairie surrounding Wichita.

After eating a hasty breakfast, we started up the Great Arkansas River and nearly *parallel* with it. At Park City we were met by an immense delegation of Buffalo *gnats*. Like the sword Gazul, they "pierced through hide and hair." We found a few new varieties of flowers, beautiful crimson mallows, spiderwort of a dazzling blue, and the delicate, rose-colored, sensitive brier. Lead plant and buffalo clover abounded. We crossed the Arkansas twenty five miles from Wichita. The first team floundered considerably in the quicksand, causing no small commotion in the minds of the girls, but no more trouble was experienced. We were now beyond all civilization. One of the horsemen rode to the top of the hill and rushed back with the cry of Buffalo!

Sure enough, there was a buffalo, about three miles away. The Dr. [Boggs] took the spyglass—"Yes that is a buffalo!" The Captain [Payne] took the glass, "Yes, that is a three-year old buffalo!" "Why, Cap'in, how can you tell so far off?" "By the wrinkles on his horns,"quoth he. "I can see him wink," said Dan. "Yes," said, the Rev. Dr. "I can see him switch his tail!" "Well boys," said the Captain, "just say so, and I'll bring him in for dinner." They said so, and three of the most valiant rode after him, while we proceeded to make ready for the buffalo steak. In half an hour the hunters returned saying, in disgust, *it was a hole in the ground!*

It was supposed that the buffalo, seeing no escape possible, sunk to some U.G.R.R. [underground railroad], and left the hole where he went in. The heat was intense—130 deg. in sun, we guessed—faces burned almost blistered. We were fairly on the plains; everything looked desolate; no timber; short grass and endless hills.

The next morning, the Dr. announced buffalo! This time he was right. We could see dark lines away to the southwest. We were soon going in that direction—horsemen far ahead. We soon came up to one of them and found him somewhat demoralized. He had led a favorite horse all the way, so as to have a good chance, and while galloping over the prairie his horse stepped in a hole, throwing him, breaking his gun in two places and his saddle, and nearly killing him, as the others thought. He afterwards remarked, "that he didn't see how a man could stick both eyes in the ground at once and not scratch his nose!" We could, his eyes were "bugged out" looking for buffalo.

We bivouacked near the timberless Ninnescah. One of the teamsters, hastily unharnessing his team and taking his gun, started off, remarking that "he would have some of them buffalo if he had to walk clear to Santa Fe." We corralled our wagons near a sharp bluff, so that in case of a stampede we would be safe, as buffalo always avoid abrupt places. We girls, the Dr. with his broken arm, and Mr. L. with his broken eyes, climbed the hill and "viewed the landscape o'er."

Thousands of buffalo met our astonished vision. They were pouring over the ridges like an immense army, heading towards the Arkansas. We were heartily repaid for our weary journey. We confess to an uneasy sensation as we saw the dark forms moving over the far off hills, and remembered that we were fifty miles from Wichita, the last outpost of civilization, miles farther out than any party had been this summer, and on Cheyenne hunting ground. We returned to the wagons and in their meager shade awaited the coming events.

Noon passed without any dinner. We could see the hunters crawling on hands and knees, and occasionally see the smoke of their guns. About 1 P.M. they came back with no buffalo, and very tired and thirsty, all save Santa Fe. They again started in pursuit of the shy though ponderous game. In an hour our Santa Fe friend appeared, walking like a man that had done his very best and failed.

"How close did you get to them?" "Close enough to tie their hind legs together with a toe string." "How far did you travel?" "I walked sixty eight miles and crawled five hundred!" With a long sigh, he gave the concluding remark that "if crawling would make a man a baby he was about two years old." He had seen barefoot tracks in the sands with toes turned in, which again suggested Indians. About four P.M., Mr. L. came back and said Dan had actually killed a buffalo!! The wagons started at once for Dan. Yes, there the huge animal lay larger than an ox. Head and fore quarters covered with long shaggy hair and hind quarters nearly bare much like an elephant's hide. It was quickly dressed and placed in the wagons.[17]

The weary hunters returned to Wichita with their lone kill, reaching the village at sundown on July 3. According to Payne's carefully laid plans, the Independence Day celebration got under way early on the morning of the Fourth with the firing of thirty-seven shots—one for each state then existing in the Union. During the morning, farm families began arriving in town in their wagons, many dressed in old-country holiday costumes. At eleven o'clock the parade began, moving from the Wichita House up Main to Waterman's Grove.

The procession was led by a four-horse wagon containing the ten-man Wichita Cornet Band, followed by another thirty-foot wagon containing Greiffenstein, Payne, and other city officials. Behind them was another long, eight-horse wagon carrying thirty-seven young girls dressed in white, each wearing a sash bearing the name of a state. At the center of the girls was a young woman who wore red, white, and blue and held aloft a U.S. flag. She personified the Goddess of Liberty.

Other wagons and carriages followed, and behind them were the younger men and boys on horseback. At Waterman's Grove, long tables had been set up to hold cold boiled hams, some seventy roasted chickens, pies, cakes, confectionery, nuts, raisins, figs, canned fruit, and, even in the Wichita of 1870, ice cream. The buffalo brought in by the hunters had been duly barbecued; but the "poor bull" was far too tough for human consumption, and it was tossed into the waters of the Arkansas River.[18]

Big John Steele, who had arrived that spring to operate a real estate firm and become Greiffenstein's right hand man, read the Declaration of Independence. Steele, who stood six-foot-six and wore boots and spurs "with a trace of border carelessness," still carried a Civil War Minié ball inside his skull. His presentation was followed by orators, including Payne, and by a vocal presentation from eight-year-old Mary Grey.

That night a ball was held at the Wichita House, eighty-four tickets being sold at three dollars each. Though bowie knives and revolvers were visible and Cordiero, who had just been acquitted of his murder charge, was present in the crowd, there was no rowdiness or fighting. Wishing to make a sober impression on the visitors, the city fathers had decreed that no beer or liquor could be sold in Wichita during the Fourth.[19]

There may well have been in the crowd that day an unnoticed eleven-year-old boy who was destined to become a legend of the

American West. A clue to his presence lies in a petition signed by Wichita citizens on July 21, 1870, requesting town status for Wichita. The one woman to sign the petition was Mrs. Catherine McCarty, who operated a laundry in town and owned a quarter section of land at Twenty-first and Oliver.[20]

Catherine McCarty had two sons. The oldest boy, Henry, eventually changed his name to William Bonney and became known to western fame as Billy the Kid. The presence of Billy the Kid in Wichita remained virtually unrecognized for many years. The migration of Catherine McCarty and her lover William H. Antrim from Indianapolis to Wichita was eventually brought to light. Taking the boys with them, Catherine and Antrim later moved to New Mexico where they married. Antrim's brother Jim served as an assistant marshal in Wichita.[21]

Wichita was incorporated as a town of the "third class" during the summer of 1870. In August the first newspaper of the entire Arkansas valley, the *Wichita Vidette*, began publication under the editorships of F. A. Sowers and W. B. "Hutch" Hutchison.[22] Hutchison, an "angular, muscle-mouthed fellow," was an outspoken Wichita civic leader and an active Presbyterian.[23]

On one occasion Mead, who had donated some land to the church, proposed to swap it for another lot farther away. Hutchison rose up in righteous wrath at church and declared to the vestry that he would be damned before he would stand by and let anyone "cheat Jesus out a foot of ground."[24]

Hutchison became extremely indignant when newspapers at Emporia and elsewhere erroneously printed a story that the Kansas outlaw Jim Curry, alias Kid Curry, had killed two women in Wichita. The supposed victims were Ida May, a well-known Emporia madam, and one of her girls. Hutch branded the story "a miserable and malicious lie" that had been perpetrated by Emporia men who were jealous of Wichita's growth.[25]

Ironically, life was made so unpleasant for Ida May by persistent appearances before the police judge at Emporia that she picked up and moved to Wichita, where her house gained prominence in years to come.[26] In June 1871, Ida May was charged with keeping a house of ill fame in Wichita. The trial caused considerable commotion among the citizens of Wichita before Ida May was found "not guilty" by the all-male jury.[27]

Time and again it was William Greiffenstein who took the lead in civic and commercial projects for the betterment of Wichita. A bridge across the Arkansas was deemed vital to the commercial future of the town and for development westward. Log cabins were already dotting the west bank of the Arkansas. Dutch Bill helped to organize the Wichita Bridge Company in August 1870 and served on the board of directors along with Payne and Mead.[28] The bridge bond issue—free travel versus toll bridge—became snarled in local politics, however, with Payne and the *Vidette* leading the Democratic opposition to the project.[29]

Payne's ranch had been designated as a polling place, and he managed to bring in enough of his friends to soundly defeat the bond proposal 171–40.[30] Because of this, Greiffenstein and others financed the building of a toll bridge with private investment. A wooden, one-thousand-foot, ten-span bridge, resting on iron piles driven twenty feet into the bed of the river, was constructed and opened for use on June 11, 1872—the only bridge spanning the Arkansas River in Kansas at the time. It crossed the river at Douglas Avenue.[31]

Receipts from the bridge from June to December 1, 1872, were upwards of ten thousand dollars, and stockholders felt confident of reaping a good profit from their investment. There was, however, strong opposition among the public to a toll of fifty cents to cross with a load of corn, plus twenty-five to return. Farmers complained that this dug deeply into their profits. Farmers threatened to take their business to another town. Pressure was brought against the toll charge by a group of "northenders" who began a new bridge near the juncture of the two rivers. As a result, the original bridge was sold to the county, which then abolished the tolls.[32]

An intense rivalry had developed between the commercial elements of North Main Street and those of Douglas Avenue. Greiffenstein's home on South Water Street became a gathering place for "Uncle Billy" and his friends on Sunday afternoons. Among these were John Steele, N. A. English, M. W. Levy, Sol Kohn, and W. P. McClure, all important Wichita men who sat and listened to Greiffenstein as he developed strategy for the bridge, a depot, a bank, a courthouse, and other city attributes affecting Douglas Avenue development. One of his adherents wrote later:

> To my mind there was one main figure in Wichita, and that was Wm. Greiffenstein; others had no avocation. "Uncle Billy" played rounce, the devil among tailors, and smoked an admixture of tobacco and perique—and deliberated.

Douglas avenue was his business. It was his "first born," the apple of his eye, and all the ends at which he aimed were Douglas avenue. The iron gray German was a wizard who rubbed his "snow blind eyes," touched his enchanted Meerschaum wand, and in the dissolving circling clouds of ascending smoke beheld visions of a future Douglas avenue akin to the streets that the genii of Aladdin's lamp created at his call. He was not a talker, but a thinker.[33]

At the same time that the Arkansas River bridge plans were being developed, Greiffenstein, Mead, and friends were working hard to bring a railroad to Wichita. They knew the importance of railway service—that new western towns often lived or died according to whether or not they had one. But for Wichita, the matter was even more imperative. If it could become a shipping point for Texas cattle instead of a mere way station, the town's future seemed assured.

On October 13, 1870, a proposition was passed by a vote of the county to issue $200,000 in bonds to subscribe to the capital stock of whichever of four railroads was the first to complete a line to Wichita. When this failed to produce the desired results, the Wichita & Southwestern Railroad Company was formed in June 1871 with Mead as president and Greiffenstein as treasurer.[34]

Another countywide bond election on August 11, 1871, provided $200,000 to aid in construction of the Wichita & Southwestern spur from Newton. This line was completed the following spring, and on May 11, 1872, the first railroad engine puffed and steamed into Wichita, followed on the sixteenth by the first train, which arrived after dark in a heavy rainstorm.[35] Despite the foul weather, jubilant Wichita citizens with umbrellas stood in their wagons, which were hub-deep in water, and cheered lustily as a brass band heralded the town's first train.

Later it was told how Greiffenstein and N. A. English had made a hurried trip to Emporia to secure a promise from the Atchison, Topeka, and Santa Fe Railroad to tie its line in with the Wichita & Southwestern.[36] Accordingly, the AT&SF leased the Wichita line on its completion and later purchased it. The first eighteen carloads of cattle were shipped from Wichita on June 8, 1872, marking a drastic change in the commerce and character of Wichita.[37]

Stockyards were rushed to completion to accommodate the influx of Texas cattle. Greiffenstein donated twenty acres of land for the construction of a packinghouse. Having already ventured into the brick-making business, he began an important new addition to the town during November 1872 with the erection of the Douglas Avenue Hotel at Douglas and Water streets.[38]

This three-story structure, costing twenty-five thousand dollars and boasting fifty rooms, quickly became the centerpiece of the town. Stagecoaches arrived and departed from the hotel daily, while at noontime following Sunday morning services the hotel was overrun with dinner guests. Once again Greiffenstein was lauded as a "man of enterprise and liberality. No scheme or proposition that promises substantial advancement to the place escapes his attention, and no worthy object goes begging around where he is."[39]

Yet, even as Greiffenstein and others were doing their best to modernize and improve the character of Wichita, the accelerating cattle trade from Texas was stamping its own brand of "wildwestness" on the town. Wichita was still being reared on whisky, o!

Chapter Nine

Gateway to Adventure

Well, come along, boys,
And listen to my tale;
I'll tell you of my troubles
On the Old Chisholm Trail.
Ti yi youpy, youpy ya, youpy ya!
— From the trail-driving song, "The Old Chisholm Trail"

As much as anything else, Wichita was a hub for frontier adventures during the 1870s. Not only was it an entrepôt to the Indian Territory, but it served as a landing and jumping-off place for travel and commerce by military units, government surveyors, trading caravans, buffalo hunters, Indian agents, overland travelers to and from points within the Territory as well as to Texas and places west, and of course, for the swarms of Texas cattle on their way to Kansas railheads at Abilene, Newton, or Wichita itself. Not to be overlooked either were the Indians of the Territory who came through Wichita en route to or from Washington, D.C., or simply as visitors to shop for goods not available south of the Kansas border.

Despite occasional flare-ups of Indian conflict, Wichita's commerce with the Indian Territory grew unabated. This fact was visible daily on the city's streets where long ox-and-mule-drawn wagon trains could be seen headed south with their caravans of trader's merchandise, government supplies, or Indian annuities. These or

A DROVE OF TEXAS CATTLE CROSSING A STREAM.—Sketched by A. R. Waud.—[See Page 166.]

Herds of Texas cattle once forded the Arkansas River at the head of Wichita's Douglas Avenue. *Harper's Weekly*, October 19, 1867.

similar trains came back into Wichita loaded high with buffalo hides held in place with boom poles and covered over with wagon sheets to keep the rain off.[1]

Others unloaded piles of buffalo and cattle bones alongside the railroad tracks for shipment to the East. Cavalry troops, carbines slung across their backs, galloped out of town in formation, headed for adventures with the hostile tribes; and, on occasion, small parties of surveyors waved farewells from the backs of canvas-covered army ambulances.

There is no question that the trail herds coming north across Indian Territory from Texas played a significant role in Wichita history. The 150,000 head to come up the trail in 1869 doubled to 300,000 in 1870, then doubled again in 1871 to 600,000. The year 1872 was a banner year for the cattlemen and trail drovers, but in 1873 a financial panic swept the East, causing a great disaster for the western cattle industry. Even so, it was estimated that some 450,000 head of cattle entered Kansas from Texas that year to be shipped from Wichita and Ellsworth, while another 50,000 went out of Coffeyville.[2]

Kansas farmers, meanwhile, were still putting up strong resistance to the influx of Texas longhorns, which potentially carried the infectious Texas fever. Evidence of the fever as a hazard is illustrated in a letter written from Fort Sill on August 23, 1869. The letter tells of an ox train that was freighting along the trail to Fort Arbuckle. The animals became infected with the Texas fever from a trail herd and nearly all of the 150 head of oxen in the train died. The teamsters were forced to get mules from the fort to haul their goods the rest of the way.[3]

The Indians of the Territory sometimes presented a formidable barrier to the Texas herds. Though most bands were willing to extract a passage fee of either money or beef, sometimes their reaction to the herds crossing their lands was more belligerent. An example of this took place in August 1869 when a herd owned by Charles Apitz was attacked on the Salt Fork of the Arkansas. Apitz, a citizen of Lawrence, Kansas, had gone to Texas to push his line of harnesses, saddles, and other supplies. While there he purchased a large number of cattle and hired a dozen or so Texas men to drive them to Kansas for him.

While the drovers were camped on the Salt Fork, a band of Comanches and a few Kiowas made a sudden attack. The Indians were successful in running off nearly all of the drovers' horses, then turned on the Texans, who were armed only with revolvers. The raiders were finally driven off after a fight; but two of the drovers where killed, and seven more were badly wounded.[4]

The drovers who brought herds to Wichita were of a mixed culture from the ranches and small towns of Texas, some raw youths, mostly white of Southern extraction who still swore fiercely to the Confederacy, some ranch cowboys, some of Mexican descent, some Negro—all hired as cheap labor to push the cattle across Indian Territory to market. Personal and racial conflicts sometimes erupted into violence and death among these men. A traveler on his way to the Darlington Agency in July 1871 stopped briefly in Wichita. While there he learned of two brutal incidents among drovers, which he described in a letter:

> Wichita is on the Arkansas river, and here I first struck
> the trail of the Texas cattle driven north for shipment to
> Chicago and other eastern markets. Here, too, I found a
> marked difference in the settlers compared with those of
> Augusta. Drinking saloons were numerous and seemed well

patronized, while the faces of many showed they had not
recovered from the effects of their patriotic efforts on the
Fourth. A brawny-looking drover [who] just arrived related
an incident of the trail still further south, and as it illustrates well the ideas of morality current among these frontiersmen I will give it here. Two men, previously acquainted,
had been drinking together, and one became quarrelsome
and began to use abusive language. This, according to the
narrator, was received with a remarkable degree of patience
until his mother was alluded to in disrespectful terms,
when the aggrieved man turned and shot the other, wounding him in the right side. The wounded man fell over on his
side, exclaiming, "Oh, Charlie, you have killed me!" when
the shooting man, stepping up, placed the muzzle of his
revolver at the left side of the fallen man and shot him
through the heart, of course killing him instantly. "I justified
him," said the drover who told the story and so did the others who were about and "Charlie" was not molested.[5]

The traveler told of still another incident farther up the trail. A
Mexican herdsman had exchanged some angry words with the trail
boss when he was not allowed to ride a certain horse. The insulted
herdsman came up behind the head drover and shot him through the
neck, wounding him fatally. The herdsman then jumped aboard his
horse and fled back down the trail toward Texas.

Friends of the murdered man rode after him in hot pursuit,
overtaking the man in an eating house. One of the pursuers walked
up behind the man as he sat with a cup of coffee in his hand and
shot him dead. The avenger then gave five dollars to the proprietor
for his trouble in disposing of the body and returned with the others
to the herd.[6]

Hundreds of other trail incidents, not all of them so violent,
remain unchronicled, though occasionally they were reported to the
public. An 1873 report from Fort Sill told of a band of Apache Indians
who brought in a mulatto boy whom they had found wandering
about on the prairie. The boy, about seventeen years of age, said his
name was George Stone. He had been employed with a cattle herd
owned by a man named Rector who resided at Waco, as did the boy.
The youngster carried two Henry rifles, a pistol, and a heavy silver
watch and chain.

He said he had accompanied a trail herd to Wichita, leaving it there to return across the Territory in July. But somehow he had become lost, and the Indians found him forty miles away from the cattle trail. At first it was thought the boy had stolen the guns and watch and run away, but it was eventually concluded that he was telling the truth regarding his ordeal.[7]

In 1872, during its first year as a railroad town, Wichita shipped four thousand carloads of cattle, a feat duplicated in 1873.[8] Becoming a cattle shipping point brought enormous change to Wichita, transforming it from a frontier settlement into a gathering place for cattlemen, drovers, cattle buyers, drummers, railroaders, and men of attendant professions. There was a great demand for more business accommodations, storage room, banks, hotels, and other facilities.

One significant addition to the town during this period was the Occidental Hotel, a three-story brick structure with sixty-two guest rooms, a billiard parlor, ladies' parlor, gentlemen's sitting or smoking room, and a barroom. Also, the Wichita stockyards were completed north of town.

Wichita was by no means without competition for the Texas cattle trade—or for wildness. Already the Kansas Pacific Railroad had reached Ellsworth, and the Leavenworth, Lawrence, and Galveston Railway was shipping beef from Coffeyville. Ellsworth proved to be a tough competitor once the stockyards had been constructed there. The fathers of that town immediately hired Maj. Henry Shanklin, the former Wichita Indian agent, to locate a new trail along the river to their location. Shanklin was provided with a wagon, a team of mules, and a driver and sent southward to intercept the Texas trail herds. He was to direct them to Ellsworth instead of Wichita.

It was reported in Wichita that Shanklin was telling the Texas drovers that Kansas farmers, fearing Texas fever, had closed off the old trail through Wichita and that the grass had all been burned off leaving stubble that would injure the feet of the cattle. With four Texas herds in tow, Shanklin began moving up the Ninnescah toward Ellsworth, stopping at each creek and camping ground to nail up posters giving information about the new route.

Word of this reached Wichita, and a meeting was quickly called among the town leaders to consider this threat to the future of their city. It was decided to send a committee down the trail to counter Shanklin's efforts. The men assigned to this task were James Mead, Big John Steele, N. A. English, and Wichita marshal Mike Meagher.[9]

These four horsemen galloped out of Wichita late that same evening, riding through the night until they found Shanklin's camp. After a brief word with Shanklin, the men rode on until they located the Texas herds. The Wichita men were attempting to persuade the Texans of their error in going to Ellsworth when Shanklin came rushing up. The former Indian agent repeated his argument that the burned grass would injure the feet of the cattle and added that Chisholm Creek was then a quagmire. Though the Wichita four offered to guarantee that the herds would have safe escort and protection, the Texas men were not persuaded.

Finally, it was up to English to save the day. Taking the leader of the Texans to one side, he offered the man a "handsome consideration" to change his mind. The bribe was effective, and the order was given for the herds to swing about and head for Wichita. The four Wichita men rode with the herds to Wichita and saw to it that the drovers were given the run of the town. A meeting was later held north of Wichita between the drovers and the Wichita boosters. The Texans were persuaded to sign a paper testifying that via Wichita was the shortest, best, safest, and most practical route and that the town was the first, best, and only supply point on the trail.[10]

The rivalry between the two towns remained hot and heavy. Wichita hired James Bryden to ride south and sell Texas drovers on coming to Wichita. Private businessmen raised money to encourage Joseph McCoy, the well-known promoter of Abilene as a cattle town, to come to work for them.[11] Officials of the Santa Fe Railroad hired cattleman A. H. "Shanghai" Pierce to aid their interests in promoting Wichita.

Pierce, a transplanted Rhode Islander, possessed a booming voice and a wealth of stories that set him in good stead with the trail herders. He and two others rode south from Wichita to help guide herds in that direction.[12] They were successful, and by the middle of May 1872 several large herds had arrived from Texas and were put to grazing on Wichita's outskirts along the Ninnescah and Cowskin.

Cattle buyers began arriving to join the Texas drovers in crowding the Wichita hotels. Many slept in and around the Blue Front Store, known by some as the Drover's Headquarters, where a register was maintained telling buyers where they could find the sort of cattle they were looking for. Herds were kept from becoming intermingled by a rigidly followed agreement of grazing area.[13]

In May 1873 the *Wichita Eagle* reported that herds on the trail to Ellsworth had been turned back when buffalo stampeded them. An

Ellsworth representative was then at Hull's Ranch on Round Pond Creek in the Territory drumming up business for Ellsworth. However, the *Eagle* claimed, the Kansas Pacific drummers had given up hope on the new trail and departed.[14]

During this time, James Mead and William Mathewson continued their trading operations inside the Territory. In April 1872, Mead reported the arrival of robes valued at over twelve thousand dollars from his trading post at Fort Sill. The robes had been garnered in just one month of trading with the Comanches, Kiowas, Wichitas, and other tribes of the Leased District.[15] During the following January a Mathewson train arrived from Fort Sill with more hides and furs assigned to Mead, and in April a Mead train brought in a load of robes estimated in value at about five thousand dollars.[16]

Other traders were also reaping similar harvests of robes and pelts from the Indian Territory and using Wichita as their base of operations. An average of two carloads of buffalo robes per day (about a thousand) as well as shipments of buffalo tongues, were being sent from Wichita. Some of them went overseas to Liverpool, England.[17]

Concerned over the demise of the buffalo, Marsh Murdock, publisher of the *Wichita Eagle*, opined that the U.S. Congress should act to prevent the "wanton destruction of the monarchs of the plains."[18] But Congress did nothing, and the slaughter escalated daily. Professional buffalo killers from Wichita, Dodge City, and other frontier locations went off into western Kansas, the Indian Territory, and the Texas Panhandle in droves to conduct kills among the rapidly diminishing herds. On occasion the hunters paid the price for their gluttony. In January 1873, hunters brought in the body of a comrade who had frozen to death on the plains. In February, five more buffalo hunters who had perished in much the same fashion were taken to Dodge City.[19]

Freighting operations up and down Chisholm's road grew constantly. Typical was a Beard and Vance train of fourteen wagons that left for the Cheyenne-Arapaho and Wichita agencies in July 1873 loaded with eighty-four thousand pounds of flour. Another was the Lafflin train of thirty-four prairie schooners that arrived back in Wichita from the Territory and was reloaded with coffee, sugar, and other annuity goods for the tribes.[20]

On February 12, 1873, a stage line and mail route began operation between Wichita and Fort Sill via the Darlington Cheyenne-Arapaho agency and the Wichita agency at Anadarko.[21] The Southwestern

Marsh Murdock, editor and publisher of the *Wichita Eagle,* played a significant role in the town's early history. Wichita Public Library.

Stage Line established relay stations along the route every twelve to fifteen miles and stocked them with good horses. The 240-mile trip took two days and one night of continuous stagecoach travel at a fare of twenty-five dollars.[22]

A doctor who made the trip in mid April described his experience in making the journey, which still involved some peril due to sporadic Indian troubles.[23] As the stage crossed the border below Caldwell, passengers viewed a sign on the Kansas side reading "Last Chance" and on the Indian Territory side, "First Chance." The stage driver, Billy Brooks, explained that these messages meant the last chance in Kansas and the first chance in the Territory to buy a drink.

The stage entered the Territory on the cattle trail, which was already very wide and well beaten. Stops were made at Round Pond Creek, Polecat Creek, and Skeleton Creek during the night, making only brief pauses before dashing on. With daylight the occupants of the coach saw their first buffalo, hundreds of them, grazing lazily on the endless prairie. They also spotted an occasional wolf and prairie dog town. At Baker's Ranch they met the northbound stage. From there, it was on to Red Fork Ranch on the north bank of the Cimarron River.

The first Indians were seen at the Darlington Agency, which was reached at nine o'clock that night; and it left the travelers a bit shaky, they having heard of attacks that the Cheyennes had made on surveying parties inside the Territory. However, there was no trouble from the Indians, and the stage continued on to the Wichita agency, where horses were changed and breakfast partaken before heading on to Fort Sill.

During this early period of Wichita history, Indian conflict flared up frequently along the trail. In April a fight between the Cheyennes and Arapahos on the Cimarron was reported, and during that same month the head chief of the Wichitas, Sadawah, was murdered by Osages on the Cimarron. A cowboy looking for stray cattle for the Sewell Ranch was reportedly shot in the back of the head by Osages, who left his gun, watch, and some money but took his scalp.[24]

It was the surveying parties that were of particular incense to the Cheyennes, who knew from western Kansas days that surveys foreboded them no good. Thus, the Barrett-Stanley survey of central Indian Territory during 1871–73 stirred the Cheyennes to hostile reaction. In April 1873, E. H. Barrett returned to Wichita with his party to report that four members of his surveying crew had been killed in Cheyenne attacks.[25]

By 1874, a number of factors were working to create trouble inside the Territory. The wholesale slaughter of buffalo by white hunters was severely antagonizing the hungry, sometimes starving tribes. Particularly upset were the Cheyennes, who now hunted the western ranges between the North Canadian and main Canadian rivers. Whiskey peddlers from New Mexico were plying their wares among the Indians, exciting the hostile inclinations of the young warriors. Horse thieves, both Indian and gangs of white renegades, persistently raided the valuable pony herds of the tribes. U.S. troops could do little to stop it.

The hostility of the tribes was unleashed during 1874. A party of some 250–300 Cheyennes, Arapahos, Comanches, and Kiowas surrounded the small buffalo hunter's post at Adobe Walls in the Texas Panhandle on June 27 and besieged it. The accurate fire of Billy Dixon and others with their buffalo rifles held off the Indians.

Mead-Mathewson trains continued to be active, one making the trip down the Chisholm Trail in April with twenty thousand pounds of flour and other stores.[26] In June, Wichita marshal Mike Meagher went to Fort Sill over the route and returned with a prisoner without incident. However, during that same month, Indians killed and scalped a man near Mulberry Creek between the Cimarron and Kingfisher Creek. Another war party attacked and wounded four soldiers near Camp Supply, and two buffalo hunters were wounded near the Canadian.[27]

Despite this highly volatile state of danger, freighting operations between Kansas and Indian Territory continued. On June 30, a Mathewson-employed freighter named Patrick Hennessey left Wichita for Fort Sill with three wagons carrying sugar and coffee. With him were teamsters George Fand, Thomas Calloway, and Ed Cook. On July 3, Hennessey camped his wagons at Burr Mosier's Ranch at Buffalo Springs. While they were there, news arrived that Indians had killed a man named William Watkins just south of the Cimarron and chased another man into Red Fork Ranch. Though cautioned against it, Hennessey headed on south on the morning of July 4.[28]

Darlington agent Maj. John D. Miles had already realized that he had a small Indian war on his hands and decided that more troops were needed to control matters. After sending an urgent call to Fort Sill for reinforcements, he decided to risk a dash up the trail to Kansas. He took with him a small group of Darlington employees and residents. Thirty miles above Darlington they found the body of Watkins, left where he had been killed. At Kingfisher Station, stage attendants joined the Miles group in their flight.[29]

When Miles reached Baker's Ranch, he found it deserted and proceeded on. Four miles to the north of the location, he made a gruesome discovery. The charred remains of Hennessey's wagons sat smoldering along the trail with the horses all missing. Beside the wagon lay the bodies of the Wichita teamsters, all of them dead and all scalped. Hennessey himself had been tied to a wagon wheel and burned along with the wagon. The culprits, it was later learned, were Cheyennes; though it was believed that some Osages had arrived on the scene during the fight, fired the wagons, and made off with most of the plunder.

Miles and his party gave the dead men a hasty burial by the side of the trail and hurried on to Mosier's Ranch. There they found other teamsters, stagecoach drivers, travelers, and ranchmen taking haven. Miles took the women who were there with him and dashed on to Kansas, meeting a Lafflin ox-team train southbound at Round Pond

Creek. The train was loaded with subsistence stores for the agencies and had only three guns among its drivers. Miles had great fear it would be captured.

Despite these interruptions, commerce and travel on the road south from Wichita continued. The Indian troubles of 1874 were brought under control by early 1875, the Cheyennes eventually surrendering to military pressure. In January of that year, Johnny Meagher, brother to Mike, arrived in Wichita with three wagonloads of hides and furs for Hays Brothers Company. He reported that three men had been found frozen to death three miles south of Skeleton Creek.[30]

In April a new disturbance took place when young Cheyennes rebelled against being placed in chains at Fort Reno, which had been established near Darlington. The resulting fight in the Sand Hills near the fort led to the eventual deportation of thirty-one Cheyenne men and one woman to Fort Marion, Florida, where they were imprisoned. These prisoners would eventually have a Wichita connection.

Chapter Ten

Near Brimstone

The greatest town I ever saw
Is this town of Wichita.
Fun is plenty and so is law
And everybody plays Keno.
— Wichita Scrapbook, Wichita Public Library

The wild and woolly reputation that Wichita had attempted to shed in 1870 had by no means disappeared. If it had faded any at all, it was reestablished by a violent gun battle that took place in downtown Wichita in the spring of 1871. The matter was further confirmed in full when the town became a cattle-shipping Mecca in the years following. During the mid 1870s, Wichita would hold the reputation of being the most uproarious town between the two oceans and a place where "everything went."[1] During that period, few towns were more typical of the old Wild West than was Wichita.

One of the most violent cases in Wichita's history involved Jack Ledford, the rambunctious early-day citizen who had doused the music box at the Buckhorn with his six-shooter. It had appeared that Ledford was changing from his wild and reckless ways when he took a bride. He also purchased an interest in a mercantile store as well as the Empire House Hotel, which he renamed "Harris House," after his wife's maiden name.[2]

But Ledford may have been involved in other enterprises not so legitimate. In January 1871 he was arrested by Sedgwick County sheriff W. N. Walker, who was also a deputy U.S. marshal. The charge had to do with complicity in a transaction following a raid on a government freighting train. The fifty-wagon train had been plundered, the stock driven off, and several of the freighters killed. Ledford gave bail for his appearance at the next term of the U.S. court at Topeka, but he never made it.[3]

During the summer while working on the line of the Kansas Pacific Railroad, Ledford had bested another man in a fight. In doing so, he made a dangerous enemy. The man he had soundly thrashed was Jack Bridges, a deputy U.S. marshal at Hays City. On the afternoon of February 26, 1871, Bridges galloped into Wichita accompanied by a squad of twenty-five U.S. Fifth Cavalry troops under the command of Capt. G. W. Randall and a scout named Lee Stewart.

They were after Ledford. Evidently Ledford knew it for he took refuge in an outhouse behind George DeMoore's saloon. The violence that followed would leave witnesses of the day divided as to whether it was prompted by a judicious desire to arrest Ledford or if it was merely a cloak for the premeditated intent to kill him.[4]

The troops surrounded the Harris House, and a detachment entered the hotel to make a search of the premises. The soldiers ignored Ledford's young wife, who tried to persuade them that he was not there. When Ledford's presence in the outhouse was somehow discovered, Bridges, Stewart, and a lieutenant advanced on the structure with pistols in hand. Ledford, who saw them coming through a crack in the outhouse door, was armed only with a pair of old rusty pistols he had grabbed up at the saloon. Throwing the door open, he faced the trio with the pistols in hand. Immediately all parties began to fire.

Ledford was expert with a pistol, and he drove the others back to cover. Stewart loosed a shot that struck Ledford in the wrist, knocking one pistol to the ground. Ledford wheeled to return the fire with his good arm, and as he did so he was hit in the back by a bullet from Bridges's gun. He remained on his feet despite this, leveling a shot at Bridges. His ball struck the deputy marshal in the arm and knocked him to the ground. Immediately Ledford rushed to Bridges's prone figure, jammed his pistol to the man's chest, and pulled the trigger, but the old weapon would not fire.

Throwing the pistol away, Ledford attempted to escape; but as he ran he was struck in the spine by a shot from either Stewart or Bridges, along with other hits. Still Ledford managed to remain erect, staggering to the front of Dagner's cigar store a hundred yards away. There he plopped down on a barrel, sitting there bleeding and dying.

Soon he toppled off the barrel and was carried to the parlor of his hotel where he died within an hour. Bridges, though he had taken four of Ledford's bullets, survived to become marshal at Dodge City during the early 1880s.

This bloody gun battle served almost as a prelude to the wild years to follow during Wichita's reign as a cattle-shipping town. The arrival of the railroad in 1872 brought with it not only the big-spending Texas cattlemen, well-heeled cattle buyers, and the hell-for-leather Texas cowboys but much of the hard elements of Abilene and Newton as well: saloonkeepers, gamblers, prostitutes, and other flotsam of the frontier. Whiskey houses, gambling dens, variety shows, and "houses of ill repute" flourished in the virtual day-and-night continuum of drinking, dancing, gambling, and celebrating.[5] A scribe of the day wrote:

> At that time the streets were thronged with Texan cow boys, with huge spurs on their heels, and howitzers strapped upon their backs. Every other door opened into a saloon. The first thing heard in the morning and the last at night was that unceasing music at the saloons and gambling houses. The town was headquarters for harlots for two hundred miles around. Fighting, shooting and even killing were not infrequent. The streets were patrolled by a half dozen policemen. Gamblers were more numerous than respectable men.[6]

Men of all callings crowded in and out of the establishments along North Main where spirits were poured forth by the gallons and the call of keno numbers was heard above the incessant din. There were Indian visitors, too, strolling the streets and stoically observing the white man's debauchery even though they were barred by federal law and public attitude from buying liquor or joining in with the white man's fun.

A constant carnival atmosphere prevailed in Wichita during these heydays of the Texas cattle drover. A part of this was Professor S. Gessley, an armless marvel who not only drove a team and wrote with a pen but he could load, prime, and fire a gun with his toes. Also on display for a price was the child wonder, extravagantly advertised as "born alive but now dead, with two heads, four arms, two feet, and a perfect body; plus a pig with two bodies and eight legs." All this was exhibited to gasping audiences while a hand organ ground out its rasping tunes, punctuated by the sharp report of the professor's shooting performance and his Dutch-accented exclamation: "Dere she goes again; kick like a mool."[7]

A visitor to Wichita found a musical conglomeration enlivening the activities:

> There is a town situated at the confluence of the Little and Great Arkansas rivers, which has three brass bands, four orchestra bands, an Italian street band, and two concert saloons, all of which not only torture the zephyrs by night but the air by day. In addition, this three-year-old town has a grinding organ which plays the mocking bird most deliciously for a "six legged and no armed show," over on the corner, forty fiddles, several pianos, and innumerable organs, all operated upon independently as the whim seizes the proprietors, from one month's end to another, until the music of the spheres becomes a mere squeak in the estimation of the enraptured listener. And then the auction bells, the whack and crack of the drovers' whip and pistol, and the low cadence of the cow-boy as he with the speel of music holds to the trail the wild herd.[8]

Across from the Occidental Hotel, Madame Sage ran a billiard parlor that was very popular with the drovers, while frontier personality Ida May operated her bawdy house at the corner of Eighth and Main. The house was also a cowboy favorite. But on one occasion some forty trail herders found cause to encircle the place on horseback, whooping and firing their guns at random. Inside, Ida May and her girls hit the floor and muttered temporary prayers of faith, begging forgiveness for their sins.[9]

Still another visitor described the Wichita scene:

> The streets clanged with the noisy spurs of Texas cow boys and Mexican ranchmen, while the crowds that marched along the resounding sidewalks, were as motley as could be seen at any one spot in America. Texan sombreros and leather leggings; brigandish-looking velvet jackets, with bright buttons, close together, of the Mexicans, buckskin garments of the frontiersmen, and the highly colored blanket; representatives from a half dozen different tribes of Indians, were familiar sights on the streets. A brass band played from

morning until far into the night, on a two story platform raised over the sidewalk, against the large frame building, still standing, opposite the New York store. This music was to attract customers to gambling dens.[10]

Large signs were posted conspicuously at the four entrances to town, reading: "Leave your revolvers at police headquarters and get a check. Carrying concealed weapons strictly forbidden."[11] This warning was supported by an enlarged police force under Marshal Mike Meagher, whose deputies (one of them Wyatt Earp) roamed the streets at night and during the day made daily checks on the operations of the saloons. They cleared away the leftover drunks and controlled the border-hardened men who clogged the saloons and bawdy houses.

At the same time that the Wichita jail was being erected, the *Wichita Tribune* punned that "Our saloon keepers sell the drinks, and next week Marshal Meagher will be ready to cell the drinker—in the new calaboose."[12] A newspaper editor in a neighboring town chastised Wichita for permitting notices to be plastered about town advertising the opening of new keno rooms, commenting that he would not be surprised to see houses of prostitution advertised in the morning papers.[13]

When longtime Wichita businessman and "street waterer" O. C. Daisey arrived in 1872, he found that the town "belonged to the cowboys." During the trail herd driving months, some fifty to eighty drovers were likely to be staying at the Texas House, operated by Charlie Cordiero at 92 Main Street. The Texans left their horses standing in front with bridle reins hanging to the ground, scorning the hitching rail that the grangers and town folks used. Daisey found that the cowboys were prone to pull their guns and fire them at the least excuse. One of their favorite pastimes in their rooms was shooting flies on the walls with their pistols.[14]

Some of the Texans, particularly the cowboys of Mexican descent, were fancy dressers when in town. A well-heeled drover of the day might wear a large white hat, light shirt, bright red sash, red-topped boots, and silver spurs decorated with small bells that tinkled like those on Christmas sleighs. All the cowboys carried from one to three six-shooters, which they would fire in the air as they rode whooping and shouting across the Arkansas River bridge to West Wichita where they would celebrate at Rowdy Joe's or Red Beard's place. When these

Saloonkeeper Rowdy Joe Lowe contributed much to Wichita's Wild West reputation. Wichita Public Library. Courtesy of Kansas Historical Society.

dance houses were in their "zenith of immoral splendor," guns and knives were not prohibited there as they were in Wichita proper.[15]

In July 1873 a St. Louis journalist visited Wichita and penned a colorful description of the frontier cowtown, the article appearing in the *St. Louis Globe* under the heading of "NEAR BRIMSTONE."[16] The visitor was impressed initially as he looked westward across the Arkansas River and viewed the immense herds of Texas longhorns that grazed on the vast expanse of green prairie.

The men who brought them, he noted, were "a class of young men who are lost to the restraints of home and good society...they arm themselves with revolver and bowie knife, and carry their lives in their hands."[17] These youthful Texans knew no law but the law of self-preservation, the writer observed, amusing themselves with gambling away their hard-earned wages or losing them in the company of the "soiled doves" who swarmed there from Kansas City, Leavenworth, Topeka, and other places on virtually every incoming train.

Wichita's resident population was almost doubled by the small army of prostitutes and gamblers who fell on them from June to

December. The paint and powder business flourished almost as much as did the whiskey business. Money was in great supply. It came easy and went more easily, circulating freely among the gamblers and dance hall girls. Gambling houses, billiard halls, and saloons operated the night through, offering every sort of card and dice game to the tune of cards being shuffled, dice rattling in cages, and gamblers chanting forth their gambling lingo. "Much of the profits of the Texas cattle trade," the writer noted, "changes hands here."[18]

It was all there, a carnival of western cowtown life of 1873: the armless professor performing his feats, the brass band pouring forth its musical airs, the discordant hand organ screeching for attention, the keno callers, the entrepreneurial painted women, the reveling crowds moving along the boardwalks from one place to another in search of entertainment. A new theatrical show that opened as the "Alamo Varieties" was a favorite for the "lovers of vulgar jest." Here the "poor unfortunate girls who perform have outgrown all their clothes except their stockings."[19]

But it was across the river in West Wichita where "hades begins" that the St. Louis journalist discovered the "most pandemonical institutions this side of Brimstone."[20] A little to the right of the bridge, down among the brush, were two dance houses where the regular call was "All hands round and promenade to the bar." West Wichita, or Delano as it was also known, was the wildest and roughest part of town by far, mainly because of the place operated by Rowdy Joe Lowe and his wife, Rowdy Kate.[21]

Rowdy Joe's was a combination saloon, dance hall, and house of prostitution and a favorite spot of the tough element in Wichita. Joe and Kate had come to town from Ellsworth, where they had also operated a bawdy house. In 1869, Joe and a cohort had drugged and robbed a man there. A posse rounded up the pair, retrieved $750 of the money, and graciously permitted them to leave the county. The pair got as far as Wichita, where Lowe had no sooner arrived than he was accused of stealing a mule. The accuser did not show up in court to press charges, however, and the case was dismissed.

Rowdy Joe was heavyset at five feet nine inches, with black hair and a dark complexion. He wore a heavy black mustache and bore a scar on his neck from a pistol wound. Though only twenty-six years of age in 1872, Joe quickly won a reputation suitable to his nickname, and his dance house became the most notorious on that part of the frontier. Nonetheless, he possessed a gruff but likeable demeanor that won him a better press than he perhaps deserved. When a correspondent of the *Daily Kansas Commercial* visited Joe's establishment in October 1872, he concluded that "while I would not recommend Rowdy Joe as a model for Sunday school scholars, yet I am constrained to say there are many men passing in society as gentlemen whose hearts are black in comparison with his."[22]

The writer described Joe's dance house as being patronized largely by cattle drovers with broad-brimmed hats and mammoth spurs. There was no charge for dancing, but customers were expected to buy drinks for themselves and Rowdy Kate's girls after each dance. The scribe observed gamblers holding forth at poker in a corner of the room, while well-dressed gentlemen and cattle drovers alike danced with heavily painted and bejeweled courtesans.[23]

Rowdy Joe served as his own bouncer; and no one, the writer claimed, dared to break his rules or pick a quarrel with him. Earlier that year Joe had pistol-whipped a customer, leaving the man in critical condition. Despite this, the *Wichita Eagle* gave him credit for having "a most peaceful disposition" and for being a man who valued his spoken word in a commercial transaction "more highly than many more reputable men do their oaths."[24]

A similar dance house was operated next door to Rowdy Joe's by E. T. "Red" Beard, whose wealthy father had founded Beardstown, Illinois. Beard had long, red hair that fell in curls to his shoulders, an enormous mustache of the same color, and a large nose to match both. It was at his place that a shooting occurred in June 1873, setting off a chain of events disastrous to both Red and Joe.[25]

A Sixth Cavalry soldier entertaining himself at Red's place became angry with a dance hall girl who, he charged, had bilked him out of five dollars. He threatened to shoot her if she did not keep "her side of the bargain." But the girl responded with a show of contempt for the soldier, enraging him to the point that he did, indeed, pull out his revolver and blast away, the ball striking his victim in the buttocks.[26]

Instantly Red came forth with his revolver, apparently firing indiscriminately, for his bullet struck two other soldiers who had no part in the argument. One man was hit in the neck, and the other had his right shinbone splintered. The soldier who shot the girl escaped unharmed. The troopers all belonged to a unit that was passing through Wichita en route to Fort Hays, and many of its members were highly incensed over the shooting.

A group of the soldiers decided to gain revenge by burning Red's place to the ground. Some thought they might as well get Rowdy Joe's while they were at it. Their threats were not idle ones. Waiting until the deep hours of the following morning, a squad of some thirty soldiers conducted a well-planned operation against their targets. They posted a guard around the house of Marshal Meagher, another at the bridge, and still another with their horses on a back street.

The marauders then crossed over into West Wichita and set fire to Red's place. A gunfight ensued wherein one civilian was wounded. The fire was doused, however, and the dance hall saved. Rowdy Joe's place was also saved from destruction when a large number of citizens arrived on the scene and caused the soldiers to disperse.

Perhaps it was inevitable that one day Rowdy Joe and Red Beard would clash, as such they did in October 1873. Red, the records reveal, became involved in a drunken frolic with friends at his place one night when it was decided to pay Rowdy Joe's a visit. Red evidently announced his arrival by firing a shot that struck one of Kate's girls, Annie Franklin, in the stomach.

Rowdy Joe immediately brought forth a shotgun and shot Red through the hip and arm. Pistols began blazing throughout the room; and when they had finally ceased, a friend of Red's had been hit with a bullet that passed behind his eyes, blinding him. The man was Bill Anderson, a Texan who had "accidentally" killed a man that spring while scuffling over a pistol in a Wichita blacksmith shop. He had killed another man not so accidentally the year before during a drunken quarrel in a Delano saloon. Red himself was mortally wounded, lingering for a few days before his festering wounds brought his end.[27]

Rowdy Joe gave himself up to the law and was released on two-thousand-dollars bail. He was tried in Sedgwick County District Court in December and found not guilty of the murder charge. However, another writ was issued immediately afterward in regard to the shooting of Anderson. Joe now disappeared. A posse was sent out for him, but it failed to find the saloonkeeper. A hundred-dollar reward was offered for his arrest, but it was generally conceded that he was, in the expression of the old West, "GTT"—Gone to Texas.

This ended Joe's connection with Wichita, his existence drifting off into a series of reported adventures and demises. One account told how he had been killed by Indians in the Black Hills in 1874; another that he lived a long life and was finally killed in a Denver saloon in 1899.[28]

Prostitution was rampant in Wichita with harlots coming, or being recruited, from miles around. A glimpse of the behind-the-scenes operation came to light when a thirteen-year-old girl was rescued from a Wichita dance hall and bawdy house. The girl, originally from Kansas City, told how she had been recruited by a man who claimed to be in search of dancing girls. She had been put on a train with several other girls bound for Wichita, where her employment involved more than just dancing.[29]

Horse racing was a much-favored sport in Wichita, and a racetrack operated just north of town. There on the fifth of July 1872, a contest of great interest was held between a Texas racer and a Wichita mare. Thousands attended the event, including five carriage loads of demi-mondaines, leaving the streets of Wichita temporarily deserted. A great deal of money was wagered on the race, which was won by the Wichita mare.[30]

The cattle business was seasonal, however, and so was much of the entertainment business that fed at its trough. "The shade of the cow-boy's sombrero has fled," mused the *Wichita Eagle* in November 1873, "and the jingle of his spurs are no longer heard upon our streets. With the fading of the one and the silence of the other, the flight of soiled doves for other and more wicked towns has been precipitous."[31]

Though the cattle trade would continue for many years in Wichita, the end of the town as a drover's headquarters was in sight. Within two years the *Eagle* would publish a comment by a citizen regarding the long train of empty cattle cars going out of Wichita even as hundreds of wag-ons loaded with grain were coming in. It was the end of the reign of the "*cowboy*," the writer noted, and the day of the "*plowboy*" fairly begun.[32]

Two important factors contributed to this. One was the extension of railway service on farther west along the Arkansas River from Newton to Dodge City, which now began to take over as the trail herder-cowboy Mecca. The other was the introduction by Mennonite settlers from Russia of a hardy winter wheat known as "Turkey Red." The strain proved to be highly adaptable to the Kansas climate, and soon long lines of wagons loaded with grain were dominating the streets around the elevator of the Wichita Wheat Market.[33] The Alamo Varieties had closed its doors, and already citizens were making plans to build a church in West Wichita.

Chapter Eleven

"Someday They'll Get Me!"

With nothing of the dare-devil or reckless bravado in
his composition, nevertheless Mike Meagher did not know
the meaning of personal fear. As marshal of this city in
the day when one-half of our residents were the worst
desperados between the Missouri and the Rio Grande...
Mike Meagher, by his consummate coolness and wonderful
bravery, preserved the lives and property of our people.
— *Wichita Eagle*, December 22, 1881

Though Wichita held the potential for sudden violence and death at any moment, much of the time the town was what the city fathers wished it to be—a placid, progressive city going about its business of trade and commerce. But its penchant for trouble would last well beyond its rowdy years. Always there was need for tough-minded, determined men who would step forward to face down the hard elements that clung to the Kansas border, rode in with the trail herds, or drifted by. Perhaps the most notorious of the Wichita lawmen was Wyatt Earp, who for a short period was employed as a policeman by the city.

But there were other men whose acquaintance with the six-gun, rifle, or shotgun gave them high repute on the frontier. Some of them were men whose footsteps sometimes crossed back and forth over the line that divided law and outlawry. A good example was Jack Ledford,

Mike Meagher (left), the man who tamed Wichita, died in a blaze of gunfire at Caldwell. Wichita Public Library.

who prior to his demise, had run for the post of sheriff in Sedgwick County's first election during the fall of 1870. Representing the People's ticket against Republican W. N. Walker and Independent William Smith, he made a strong showing despite his reputation for being wild and reckless. Perhaps because of Ledford's reputation, Walker won the post.[1]

It was Ledford's death that made the citizens of Wichita realize their need for a strong law enforcer. Prior to this there had been three men who served briefly as city marshal, all resigning or leaving for one reason or another.[2] In April 1871 following the Ledford affair, the Wichita city fathers made a fortuitous move by appointing Irishman Mike Meagher as city marshal. He would hold that position on and off for the next ten years. Ultimately he, too, would perish in a wild gun battle at Caldwell that would outdo most "B" western movies.

Born in Ireland about 1844, Mike Meagher was a member of a pioneer family of Sedgwick County and of Wichita. "One of the first on the ground" in the spring of 1869, his father Timothy Meagher brought his wife and three children to their homestead on the east bank of Chisholm Creek near Wichita. Mike was the oldest of the children at twenty-five or twenty-six then, while his brother John was a couple of years younger. Their younger sister Molly married Big John Steele in the fall of 1870.[3] Mike was soon to build his own cabin on the Munger townsite in Wichita proper.

He received his appointment on April 10, 1871, following the resignation of William Smith. His brother John was named as his assistant.[4] Keeping the Wichita of 1871 in line was no simple chore, but Mike soon let everyone know that he wasn't running a Sunday school operation. He set out to prove this by entering a saloon with two deputies and arresting a soldier who was sleeping off a drunk on one of the tables. Later, the three lawmen returned, and one of the deputies read off the saloonkeeper for letting his customer get drunk.

The saloonkeeper replied that he had paid for a license to sell liquor, and his fee went to help pay the salaries of the officers. Mike was not impressed with the man's line of reasoning and joined his deputies in slapping him around with their pistols. Then the three lawmen hustled the saloonkeeper off to jail, roughing him up considerably in the process, or so the victim later claimed in a petition to the city council. Meagher padlocked the saloon, and the owner was forced to pay eight dollars to square himself with the law. The city council supported Meagher and refused to act on the petition.[5]

The pages of the *Wichita Eagle* and the *Wichita Beacon* during the 1872–74 period contain occasional mentions of Meagher quieting disturbances, taking knives and guns from saloon toughs, arresting wanted criminals, and riding long distances to capture horse or wagon thieves. One *Eagle* item noted: "Our efficient city marshal, with his usual promptness and unflinching bravery, on Tuesday last, quelled a disturbance that was fast assuming dangerous proportions by promptly arresting and lodging the leaders in the calaboose."[6]

During 1874, Mike gave up his Wichita badge to serve as a deputy U.S. marshal in the Indian Territory, but in April 1875 he ran for the Wichita office again and easily defeated William Smith. Serving with him during this term of office was twenty-six-year-old Wyatt Earp.

Earp had already caught the attention of the public the previous fall when he and John Behrens followed some men who were attempting to skip the country without paying for a new wagon and some other goods. Earp and Behrens took out on the trail of the men, riding "from sun to sun" without stopping, and caught up with them near the Territory line. Leveling a shotgun and six-shooter at the perpetrators, the officers ordered them to pay up, which they did without much hesitation.[7] The *Wichita Beacon* described Earp as "a man of nerve and brave to recklessness, yet one of the quietest of men."[8]

Earp's career as a lawman at Wichita was comprised of the usual arrests of horse thieves, celebrating cowboys, and, in one case, three men who had stolen eight yoke of oxen and a wagon at Fort Sill and brought them to Wichita. On another occasion, Earp's honesty was evidenced when he found a stranger lying passed out by the Arkansas River bridge one night. The man had on his person a five hundred dollar roll. In other places, the *Beacon* noted, the money would never have been seen again; but Wyatt duly reported it.[9]

It was a case of overzealousness, perhaps, which brought Earp's career as a Wichita lawman to an end, even though he was still recognized as a very capable officer. It was during the city election of April 1876 that Earp committed a transgression that cost him his job. The election was a heated one, with William Smith again opposing Mike Meagher for the city marshal's post. During the campaign, Smith accused Meagher of sending for Wyatt Earp's brothers to help bolster up the police force during the election. Wyatt was incensed by the remark. According to later testimony, Meagher instructed Wyatt to stay away from Smith and avoid any personal collision with him.

Wyatt, however, had "fight on his brain."[10] On the Sunday night before the election, he invaded Smith's hotel room and went after the man, striking him before Meagher interjected himself into the fracas and ordered his deputy to clear out. Earp was arrested and fined thirty dollars and costs, being simultaneously relieved of his position on the police force. Rumors floated about town that the whole thing had been a put-up job by Mike Meagher.

Meagher was reelected, but Wyatt Earp's day at Wichita was done. When the city council refused to rehire him, he left Wichita and moved on to Dodge City, where he served on the police force for a time before trailing on to Tombstone, Arizona. It was at Tombstone that he emerged as a legendary figure of the West.[11]

Uniquely, in all the time that Mike Meagher had served as marshal of Wichita and had on many occasions been placed in dangerous situations in dealing with armed outlaws and murderers, he had always been able to handle the problem coolly without gunplay. But on New Year's Eve 1876, Meagher was forced to shoot and kill his first man in the line of duty.

The victim was Sylvester Powell, commonly known as "Sill." Yet a young man, Powell had once been a stage driver for the Southwestern Stage Company. Now, however, he was employed as a driver of the four-horse city bus that carried passengers between the railroad station and the city hotels. A quiet man when sober, Powell was a demon when in his cups. He was known particularly well around the brothels of Wichita, where he had caused trouble on numerous occasions. His brag was that he had killed two men, one with brass knuckles. On this particular occasion, Powell and his friend Al Singleton had been taking part in the daylong celebration that Wichita then held on New Year's Eve.

A brass band had paraded through town, followed by floats, cowboys, Indians on horseback, and people wearing costumes. Powell had masqueraded as a clown that day, and he had also been drinking heavily. During that evening Powell and Singleton took over a horse that had been standing in front of Hope's saloon. The horse belonged to E. B. Dennison, who approached Powell and made a friendly, bantering remark.

The bus driver was in a drunken, antagonistic mood. He picked up a neck yoke that was available and struck Dennison such a hard blow that it broke the man's arm. Powell then threatened Dennison with dire harm if he dared report the matter. Dennison did, however, report the incident to Mike Meagher, who arrested Powell and took him to the city jail.

Because Powell was needed on duty to drive the bus, his employer paid his fine so he could be released. Meagher let him go only after Powell had promised not to drink any more that night. But the man was no sooner released than he began making threats against Meagher. Approaching a policeman in front of Hope's saloon, Powell demanded to know the whereabouts of the marshal. He declared that Meagher had spent his last day on earth.

A short time later Powell discovered that Meagher had gone to use the toilet behind Hope's saloon. With a pistol in hand, he hid behind a coal bin until Mike came out. He then stepped forth and fired at Meagher point blank. One shot creased Meagher's knee while another passed through the officer's heavy ulster coat, barely missing Mike's chest and leaving a large egg of cotton protruding from the back of the coat.

The overcoat prevented Mike from drawing his own gun quickly enough, so instead he grabbed Powell's pistol by the barrel. The gun discharged another time, the ball grazing Mike's hand and the powder burning his left thumb, causing it to swell and turn black. The bullet went through a window and struck a door casing inside the saloon.

Powell now broke away and ran down the alley, while Meagher circled around to the street in front of the saloon and intercepted his attacker as he emerged in front of Hill's Drug Store. Meagher pursued

Powell to the corner of Main and Douglas. There he raised his pistol and fired one time, hitting Powell dead center in the heart and killing him instantly.[12]

A sequel to this affair was told later by an ally of Meagher, who said that one day Meagher came face to face with Wash Walker, formerly a close friend of Powell, in the stage line office. The two exchanged looks without speaking. But when Walker left the office, Meagher commented to the others present: "That's the only man on top of the ground that I fear. They'll get me some day; they *will* get me some day."[13]

His remark was all too prophetic. Mike left Wichita and moved to Caldwell. He served stints both as mayor of the border cowtown and, briefly, as city marshal. But he had a stormy career, making enemies on both sides of the law.[14] His end came in a wild gun battle that rivaled one in which his former deputy, Wyatt Earp, was involved at the OK Corral at Tombstone, Arizona, at about the same time.

An account of the Tombstone fracas had appeared in the *Wichita Eagle* in early November 1881, telling how Wyatt and his two brothers "got into a row with a crowd of drunken cowboys who they were trying to arrest."[15] The Earps and their friend Doc Holliday killed two of the Clanton gang and mortally wounded another during the fracas.

Meagher's trouble began early on the morning of December 17, 1881, a Saturday, and the main instigator was a hard case named Jim Talbot. Talbot, who had a wife and two children living in town, had only recently helped bring a herd of cattle up the Chisholm Trail. Since returning he had been gambling, drinking, and bullying people around in Caldwell. Talbot made threats against "Hutch" Hutchison, who now edited the *Caldwell Post*. He was even more incensed against Meagher over some old grudges.[16]

On this particular day he was joined in his spree by Jim Martin, Doug Hill, Bob Bigtree, Tom Love, Bob Munsen, Dick Eddleman, and George Speers. The trouble began at the saloon that Meagher now operated. Talbot and his friends were drinking heavily and getting more and more out of hand by the moment. When Meagher decided they had had enough whiskey, he cut them off. This angered Tom Love to the point that he tried to draw a gun on Meagher, but a man known as Comanche Bill wrested the firearm away from Love.

Now Talbot began making loud talk about killing Meagher. Mike responded by going to the home of city marshal John Wilson and asking him to come to town and help stop the trouble he felt was about to occur. Wilson went to the Moores Brothers' saloon and arrested Love for firing off his gun there.

Meanwhile, Talbot and his followers had hurried to Talbot's home and, on finding the door locked against their entry by Talbot's wife, kicked their way in and armed themselves with revolvers, rifles, and shotguns. They then returned to town where Comanche Bill quieted them down some and encouraged them to have some breakfast.[17]

Comanche Bill had also persuaded them to lay down their guns, but Talbot refused either to disarm or go inside to eat. When someone told him that Tom Love had been arrested, he dashed into the cafe yelling: "They've arrested one of the boys. Let's take him away from them!"

The others grabbed their weapons and headed up the street behind Talbot, intercepting Wilson who was then on the way to the jail with Love. Seeing his friends coming to his rescue, Love broke free from Wilson, who called to Meagher for help. When Mike came forward, Talbot's gang aimed their guns at him, threatening to kill him then and there. Meagher retreated up the outside stairs of the Opera House. Wilson was forced to take up a position at the bottom of the stairs from where he vowed he would shoot the first man who made a move against Meagher.

Talbot backed down and led his gang away. Still he declared that "Meagher is the man we want, and Meagher is the man we will have." Talbot and his followers went back to his house where one or two went to sleep, the time now being eight o'clock in the morning. However, Talbot and the rest of his men returned to town, where they continued their drinking spree during the morning.

Shortly after noon Wilson arrested Jim Martin for carrying a concealed weapon and took him before a judge who levied a fine. As Wilson and his deputy W. D. Fossett were taking the prisoner to get the money for his fine, Talbot, Love, Munsen, Hill, and Eddleman intercepted them to rescue their friend. Mike Meagher came forward again to lend his assistance to his fellow lawmen.

It was then that the gun battle exploded. Talbot took off at a run, turning to fire two shots at Wilson. He missed. Meagher and Wilson followed Talbot in hot pursuit down the sidewalk and into an alley. Here they ran into fire from Talbot, who had taken up a position with a rifle. Wilson saw him taking aim at Meagher and yelled for his friend to beware. The report of a rifle sounded, and Meagher staggered. He had been hit in the chest. Ed Rathbun came up to help as Mike began to sink to the ground.

"I am hit and hit hard," Meagher said, still with his six-shooter in one hand and rifle under the other arm. "Tell my wife I have got it at last."

He then crumpled to the ground. Rathbun dragged him to a place of refuge behind a store. Later Meagher was carried into a barbershop where he died half an hour later from a bullet that had passed through his right arm and lungs.

Talbot and his gang now ran to the livery stable. At gunpoint they forced the attendant to saddle some horses for them. The group included Talbot, Martin, Bigtree, Munsen, Hill, and Speers. Speers, who had done none of the shooting, was still saddling his horse when he was shot and killed. The remaining five headed east out of town across the railroad tracks with a hail of bullets following them. One of their horses was hit and killed, but the rider crawled up behind another of the group.

A short distance down the road they met a farmer who was bringing hay to town with a spare horse in tow. The escaping men cut the horse loose and took it, then stole two more at a farmhouse to replace mounts that had been wounded by the gunfire. They galloped on from there across the border into Indian Territory, where supposedly the local law officials could not pursue them.

But the incensed posse that had formed behind them was pressing close by the time they reached the Deutcher Brothers Ranch on Deer Creek, and gunfire was being exchanged. Not having time to get the fresh horses they had hoped to get there, Talbot and his men instead took up positions in the bluff and canyon area nearby where there was the remnant of an old stone dugout. From there the gang traded shots with the posse, hitting one of them in the wrist.

A standoff continued until dark, when the group managed to slip away. A search of the area was made the next day, but a freighting outfit coming up the Chisholm Trail reported that it had encountered the fugitives, who had taken five of the freighters' horses. Another bullwhacker reported seeing the five men headed south near Pond Creek.

Hill was arrested in 1887, tried, and given six months in the county jail. Talbot was eventually brought to trial in 1895 and acquitted. He was killed the next year by an unknown party, who some thought was his wife's lover.[18]

Meagher's body was carried to Wichita by his brother-in-law Big John Steele and buried in the town where he had maintained the peace for over a decade.[19] There were other officers of the law who contributed to the demise of the border toughs at Wichita and its environs. But it was Mike Meagher more than any other who, in the jargon of the West, "rode the wild bronc" at Wichita.

Chapter Twelve

Guests in Town

These Indians have not forgotten their old friend
and trader, William Graiffenstein [*sic*], of our city.
As soon as they reached the city they flocked to his
residence with presents, among which were ten fine
buffalo robes and a large bear robe. During the day
they made many purchases, noticeably fifteen or
twenty baby dolls of G. H. Herrington. They were
delighted with the dolls ornamented with real hair,
and would have no other kind.
— *Wichita Eagle*, August 2, 1877

The Indians had lost the Little Arkansas as a home and as a hunting ground, but during the decade of the 1870s they would return on numerous occasions as friendly visitors. Holding as it did a strategic location close to Indian Territory, Wichita provided a place for the Indians to come on occasion, purchase goods, and swap horses, mules, and furs for the products of white civilization. Also, they had a firm and lasting friend there in William Greiffenstein, who always received them warmly and treated them in grand style during their stay.

To the south of Wichita, the drama of the Indian wars was being played out as the U.S. Army sought to conquer the last of the hostile bands, pursuing them into the depths of the Texas Panhandle and ultimately defeating them. Yet even during these dark days of warfare, Wichita was on many occasions host to Indian visitors from Indian

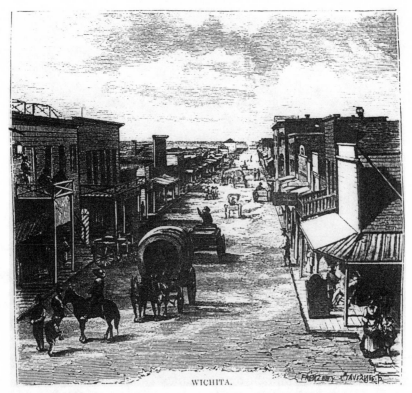

Wichita had become a model western town in 1874. *Harper's Weekly,*
May 2, 1874.

Territory, some of them noted war chiefs who had only recently done
battle with the U.S. Army.

In November 1872, a delegation of Arapaho chiefs returned home
by way of Wichita. The chiefs were taken to the newly erected home of
William Greiffenstein on Water Street, each giving their old friend a
hearty hug and a grunt of friendship. They held a talk and described
the "heap of things" they had seen in Washington, including the tall
"up, up houses" (tenements), and the many fine presents they had
received there. The Arapahos spent two days in Wichita before their
guide and interpreter Phil McCusker led them off to their homes in
Indian Territory.[1]

In June 1873 the Kansa Indians, replete with camp equipage,
ponies, and dogs, passed through Wichita on the way to their new
reservation in northern Indian Territory.[2] The Kansa were a part of the

government's move to relocate the Indian tribes of Kansas and other areas within the Indian Territory. They would become neighbors to the Sac and Fox, Osage, Otoe, Missouri, Pawnee, Iowa, Potawatomi, Kickapoo, and for a short time, the Nez Perce Indians from Oregon— all of whom were moved into the Territory during the 1870s. Parties from these tribes visited Wichita to trade at one time or another.

An attempt was made in 1876 to move a portion of the large Sioux Nation to the Territory; and in November of that year Wichita was visited by a group of ninety-six Sioux leaders. The group was headed by their famous chief Spotted Tail, along with chiefs Red Dog, Man Afraid of His Horses (more correctly, "Man Who Is So Brave That His Enemies Fear Even His Horses"), and other principal men in addition to twelve Sioux women, all from the Black Hills of South Dakota.

Government officials were hoping to relocate some ten thousand of the tribe in a district east of Darlington Agency. The area, which was unassigned to any tribe, would soon become known popularly as the "Oklahoma Lands." The Sioux were being given a tour to see the country and decide if they wished to reside there or not. Escorting them was Commissioner J. W. Daniels and Albert G. Boone, grandson of Daniel Boone, who had spent many years among the Indians in Colorado, Kansas, and Indian Territory.

The Sioux arrived at Wichita by train on a Saturday, spending the first night at Eagle Hall before going into camp the next day on the banks of the Little Arkansas at the lower end of town. They were shown the city by Greiffenstein, who was then serving as mayor. Dutch Bill drove the head chiefs about in his carriage and showed them the sights of the town.

Marsh Murdock of the *Wichita Eagle* was impressed with the Sioux. He described Spotted Tail as "an intelligent, shrewd man" whose brothers had "got away with the dashing, but rash Custer" only six months earlier. Murdock described the Sioux as being over six feet in height, muscular, and robust.[3] A Wichita man was awarded the contract for transporting the Indians on their tour of the Territory's unassigned region and thence to Muskogee, I. T., where they took the Missouri, Kansas, and Texas Railroad back to their homes.

Greiffenstein became Wichita's unofficial host to most visiting parties of Indians. In September 1877, agent John Miles of Darlington Agency arrived in Wichita at the lead of a group of Cheyennes and Arapahos from the Darlington Agency. He brought them there to help initiate his new policy of having the Indians transport their own annuity goods to Darlington. The Indian delegation was headed by Cheyenne chief Little Robe, whom Greiffenstein had known for many years.[4]

Greiffenstein invited the Indians to put their lodges in his pasture and provided them with a beef to kill and eat. During their stay in Wichita, the Indians made their home in the area between English Street and Kellogg on the west side of Water Street.[5] While in Wichita, Miles purchased the Cheyennes and Arapahos forty new wagons, with teams and sets of harness for each.

Miles's policy for the Indians to transport their own annuity goods resulted in the appearance of befeathered, blanketed figures on the streets of Wichita as a common sight. Wagonloads of families would arrive in town, erect their lodges at Greiffenstein's place, and enjoy a visit at this village of the white man. One newspaper scribe made note of the fact that the Indians were especially fond of chewing gum, a lasting national habit that originated in the Territory.[6] Sometimes a few of the local boys would go to the Indian encampment and take part in their dances, which they humorously referred to as "doing the blanket jig."[7]

During the spring of 1878, Dutch Bill hosted another group of Cheyennes. These were the Indians who had been incarcerated at Fort Marion, Florida, following the Indian outbreak of 1874 and 1875. They had spent the last three years as prisoners under military discipline with daily drilling. Having just been released from imprisonment, they were on their way back to their homes at Darlington; led by Chief Minimic, they were to be met at Wichita by Miles and escorted home. Many of the Cheyennes were old friends of Greiffenstein, and he was at the Occidental Hotel to welcome them back. The *Eagle* reported:

> These sturdy chieftains liked to have eaten our chief executive up in their joy at seeing one they had known in the long years agone. They hugged him and shook him up in such an earnest manner that for a brief space we thought we would not only be compelled to attend a funeral but participate in another "blue ribbon" election for Mayor.[8]

Minimic, who had changed from his prison soldier's uniform to the dress of a white citizen, was escorted by Greiffenstein around town and taken into the offices of the *Eagle*. Murdock found the chief to be a fine looking man with an intelligent and kind face. The Cheyenne spoke humorously of his captivity, saying that he had never really understood why he was taken away from the green, rolling hills of the buffalo to the barren beaches of Florida. Though some of his men had been up to mischief on occasion, he said, he had never violated any treaty promise himself.[9]

An interesting meeting between Greiffenstein and an antagonist of old took place at Wichita in February 1878. The man who had run Dutch Bill out of the Indian Territory, Phil Sheridan, arrived in Wichita by train. The general and his entourage, which included Gen. George Crook, went off to the Territory to make a tour of the military posts. They returned to Wichita again in late February. Among those especially interested in meeting the generals was Capt. Will White, publisher of the *Wichita Beacon* who had served with General Crook during his Indian-fighting days in Wyoming and Montana.[10]

But it was the meeting between Sheridan and Greiffenstein that held the interest of the town. The story of how Little Phil had ordered Dutch Bill out of the Indian Territory and threatened to hang him was well known. On learning of Greiffenstein's presence and stature in town, Sheridan penned a note suggesting that the two meet. Greiffenstein responded by inviting the general to dine with him. The *Eagle* provided its readers with an interesting account of the affair:

> Wm. Greiffenstein took supper with General Sheridan the other afternoon upon which occasion Bill and Phil canvassed their old differences and wiped out the unpleasant memories of certain little episodes connected with border life experiences. It was all about some Indian captives, cattle, etc., and at a time when Phil was not as well known as Bill among the aborigines. Phil "threatened" and Bill "dared," and thus our two worthies had it, the one backed by blue coats and the other by red blankets. It was before Wichita was, but neither gentleman would ever acknowledge himself beaten although Phil did not carry his point. Sheridan's "forty miles away" goes down in history and literature, but Greiffenstein's name will live while stands the metropolis of the Southwest. One is now a Lieutenant General, but the other has been for a long time a Boss General, and as we go for home instructions, titles and men, we were for Bill until Phil came round and like a true Irish

gentleman that he has acknowledged the equality of the
Dutch, and we are satisfied.[11]

Sheridan would return to Wichita again in July 1885 following
another Cheyenne disturbance in the Territory over cattle grazing
rights on Indian land. He arrived by private railroad car, this time
accompanied by Gen. Nelson Miles. The officers, wearing civilian
clothes, were strolling on the railway platform when an *Eagle* reporter
interviewed them.

"Is the old Dutchman here?" Sheridan asked, meaning
Greiffenstein, adding with a laugh, "I made that Dutchman's fortune
for him by compelling him to remain east of the river."[12]

It was one of Little Phil's favorite stories to tell how he had
made Dutch Bill rich by giving him thirty-six hours to get out of the
Indian Territory.[13]

Greiffenstein had only recently been elected mayor of Wichita
when Sheridan first visited in 1878, and he would fill that role for most
of the next eight years. He was a principal mover in the big Sedgwick
County Fair that was held at Wichita in September 1878. In attendance
was a party of 115 Cheyenne and Arapaho Indians brought up from the
Territory by J. G. Seger and J. A. Covington, officials at the Seger
Colony Industrial School for the tribes. The Indians took part in the
opening day parade, which marched from the intersection of Main
and Douglas to the fairgrounds north of town.

One planned event of the fair involved the killing of two beef cows
by the Indians in the fashion by which they hunted buffalo. It became
a contest to see who could dispatch their animal first using bows and
arrows. Following a race between a Wichita horse and a Newton
horse, two cows were driven onto the racetrack. The Cheyennes took
a white cow, while the Arapahos chose a black one. Immediately the
braves galloped forth and surrounded the two animals, firing their
arrows broadside into the cows. The Cheyennes quickly downed their
quarry with only four arrows, all mercifully striking within a small
area near the animal's heart. The Arapahos were not so adept, however. They shot arrow after arrow into their victim without success
until finally it was necessary to end the animal's suffering with a pistol. Observers did not find the event nearly as sporting or entertaining as they had anticipated.[14]

George P. Morehouse, who had come up from the Ponca reservation to take part in the celebration, witnessed the cow-killing contest.

The former resident later recalled scenes of earlier days in Wichita: the streets jammed with visitors, many of them tenderfeet; the hotels and rooming houses overflowing with guests; the horse-drawn buses and hacks carrying loads of people to the fairgrounds; a four-horse Concord stage, which careened down Main with passengers clinging to the roof as it made a breathtaking two-wheel turn onto Douglas without slowing and headed pell-mell up the avenue; and the Indian dog feast at which Mayor Greiffenstein was the lone citizen of the town who would partake of the prairie delicacy. Marsh Murdock and Big John Steele had both said they thought the dog looked well cooked "but unfortunately they had already eaten."[15]

The Indian delegation displayed a large number of Indian artifacts, many produced by Indian craftsmen: a scalp shirt, which had belonged to Cheyenne chief Grey Beard who was killed on his way to Florida when he tried to escape; a war bonnet of Chief Whirlwind; a war shield belonging to warrior leader Medicine Water; plus war lances, baby cases, Indian doll dresses, fancy dresses ornamented with elk teeth, a buckskin lodge lining, an Indian bed, lariats and bridles made of hair, a medicine rattle and case, a swan-foot tobacco pouch, a medicine pipe, a coffee bean necklace, a fancy buckskin dress, a powder horn and bullet pouch, bows and arrows, a mountain lion arrow case, silver belts, elk horn scrapers, eagle feather fans, moccasins, a hair pipe, breast ornaments, owl cases, paint sacks, a polecat tobacco pouch, and wildcat robes.[16]

Seger also exhibited a photographic display that included pictures of the 1875 Sand Hills battlefield, the mission school, the four Germain sisters who had been captives of the Cheyennes, Cheyenne chief Eagle Head, Kiowa chiefs Kicking Bird and Lone Wolf, and others. Log-cabin quilts made by two Indian school girls were displayed along with white and calico shirts, calico dresses, jars of pickles preserved by the students as well as fancy sewing, specimens of penmanship by an Indian boy student, and produce such as peanuts, beans, and corn that had been raised by Cheyenne boys—all designed to illustrate the educational and "civilizing" results of the Indian school.

A letter from a woman named Fanny Kelly told of an interesting sequel to the Indians' visit to Wichita. Fanny had once been held captive by the Indians herself, but she left her Indian captors with strong affection for those with whom she had maintained ties of friendship. While in Lawrence earlier, Fanny was approached by Mrs. Celia C. Short, widow of surveyor O. F. Short. Short's government survey party, which included both Short and his son, had been massacred by Cheyennes under Medicine Water on August 24, 1874, in western Indian Territory. The affair is known today as the "Lone Tree Massacre."[17]

Having had no success in getting the government to make recompense for the loss of her husband and son, or even for the instruments and other property taken by the Cheyennes, Mrs. Short had made a desperate appeal to the Indians, attempting to get them to sign a paper assuming responsibility. The Cheyennes refused. Though they admitted that their warriors had committed the murders, they were shy about signing papers of any kind and feared some sort of trick. Mrs. Short then appealed to Fanny Kelly to use her influence with the Indians to make an appeal in her behalf.

Fanny agreed to do so and caught a train to Wichita, where she joined the thirty-five-wagon Cheyenne and Arapaho caravan heading back to the Territory on October 2. The cavalcade included 150 Indians, 30 schoolmen, and 3 white women teachers. The trip was made without incident except for an attempt by three white men at the border to get some of the Indian boys to take a drink of whiskey.

Once Darlington Agency was reached, the Cheyennes assembled in council at Fanny's request and allowed her to present Mrs. Short's petition. Fanny stressed the inoffensive nature of Short's presence on the plains and the financial plight of Mrs. Short. The Cheyenne council listened and made several speeches, eventually concluding that Fanny would not attempt to betray them. The Cheyennes then signed a paper saying they were willing to have ten thousand dollars taken from their appropriation by Congress to give to the widow. The paper was signed and attested to and presented to Congress for approval.[18]

Victor Murdock, Marsh's son who wrote extensively of Wichita's history, once told of a Texas boy, Lee Temple Friend, who had been captured by the Comanches. During 1872, his grandfather, Rev. Leonard S. Friend, learned that the boy had been rescued and was being held at Fort Sill. The minister went there and attempted to talk with the boy. But the former captive had become "completely Comanche" and understood virtually no English, not even his name. He was brought back to Wichita where he was a "great curiosity," never readapting to white civilization before he passed away while still young.[19]

A great Indian scare swept over Wichita and southern Kansas at virtually the same time the Cheyennes and Arapahos were visiting Wichita. In 1877 the government had forced bands of Northern

Cheyennes to move south to the Indian Territory, much against their will, and join the southern bands. There the northerners were poorly fed and left without medicine or medical assistance when many became ill. Their entreaties to be permitted to return to their beloved northern homes were ignored by government officials. Finally on the night of September 9, 1878, some of them under chiefs Little Wolf and Dull Knife left their camps near Darlington and headed north.

Though the retreating Indians attempted to avoid conflict with whites, several clashes ensued with pursuing troops and buffalo hunters. The press greatly magnified the threat posed by the fleeing Cheyennes, and Kansas was in dire alarm. Dull Knife's band was captured and taken to Fort Robinson, where on January 9, 1879, the Indians made a break for freedom and were massacred in bitter cold by troops. Little Wolf and his band were recaptured later that spring on the Little Missouri River in Montana, they surrendering peacefully.

Seven of the Cheyennes were taken to Fort Leavenworth and thence to Fort Dodge to be tried on charges of killing Kansas settlers. While they were at Dodge, Greiffenstein was summoned as a witness in the case.[20] Chief Minimic wrote a letter expressing his feelings in regard to the Northern Cheyennes:

> Don't give yourself any trouble about the "Sioux-Cheyenne" who ran away; they loved the country up north, and could not be persuaded to remain here. I have told the agent to "throw them away," for they were foolish. I have sat with the agent in council and have helped him to talk to Dull Knife and party, but they would not listen to good talk.[21]

In May 1879, agent Miles was again in Wichita, this time escorting another delegation on its way to visit Washington, D.C.[22] In July the Cheyennes were back again in full force with teams and wagons for supplies.[23] That same month Secretary of the Interior Carl Schurz visited the ten-year-old city on the Arkansas. It was a special pleasure for William Greiffenstein to entertain another German immigrant who, like himself, had fled the political oppression of Germany. Schurz had risen to great public heights as a general in the Union Army during the Civil War, as a newspaper publisher, and now as a cabinet member.[24]

Wichita was also visited during November 1879 by a celebrity who was virtually as famous at the time as Phil Sheridan. He was Chief

Joseph, who had led his Nez Perce Indians on a masterful retreat down the Yellowstone River and had outwitted and outfought the U.S. Army before being forced finally to surrender. The Nez Perce were being relocated from their former homes to a small reservation area in the Territory just south of Hunnewell.

Joseph and his band remained in Wichita for several days, and citizens were highly impressed with them. Murdock described the Nez Perce as "physically magnificent, intelligent and courteous, and above all clean in their person and wardrobe."[25]

The *Wichita Eagle* quoted a speech by Chief Joseph that reveals the depth of the renowned Indian leader:

> Let me be a free man, free to travel, free to shop, free to trade where I choose, free to choose my own teachers, and free to follow the religion of my father and to talk, think and act for myself, and I will obey every law or submit to penalty.[26]

It was small wonder, thus, that Marsh Murdock felt the Nez Perce leader and his people were the closest Indians he had seen to the noble red man of literature.

Chapter Thirteen

Boomer Bastion

But little of interest comes up from the border this week.
It's horrible cold camping out, and the boys are short
on grub. The sixty days rations have petered. The ragged
patriots hump over the flickering flames of an expiring
buffalo chip, eyeing askance the well fed blue coats,
wondering whether they are natural born fools
or dupes of adventurers.
— *Wichita Eagle*, December 23, 1880

During the first half of the 1880s, Wichita became headquarters for the Oklahoma boomer movement. Led by Wichita pioneer settler David L. Payne, the movement sought to colonize a 14-million-acre tract of land at the heart of the Indian Territory that had been left unassigned to any Indian tribe following treaties in 1866. This Unassigned District had come to be known popularly as the "Oklahoma country."

Indeed, for most of the period between 1879 and 1889, Wichita played a central role in the promotion and activity of opening Indian Territory to settlement. Many of the town's citizens took part in the cause, while others watched daily the progression of events surrounding Payne's attempts to invade the Indian Territory in the face of federal opposition.

The Oklahoma boomer movement was an ongoing news event for Wichita newspapers, with Marsh Murdock's pro-Republican *Wichita Eagle* heaping ridicule and scorn on Payne and his free-land crusade.

David L. Payne, an early
settler at Wichita, led the
Oklahoma Boomer move-
ment to settle Indian
Territory. Manuscript
Division, Oklahoma
Historical Society.

Meanwhile, the pro-Democratic *Wichita Beacon,* under Frank Smith
and Will White, offered general approval and support. After Payne's
sudden death in November 1884, Murdock began to see the entrepreneurial potential of opening the Indian Territory to settlement
and became a staunch advocate of the boomer effort.

Actually, as evidenced by the emotional tribute he wrote at
Payne's death, Murdock held a personal liking and admiration for
the boomer leader. Murdock and Payne had served together as
members of the Kansas legislature at Topeka. When Murdock moved
from Osage City to Wichita in 1872 to begin operation of the *Eagle,*
Payne was present to help him unload the press and equipment
from his wagon.[1]

During the years to follow, both men would command the attention and following of many people in the Wichita area, the red-
headed Murdock exuberantly promoting the progress of Wichita in
the *Eagle* even as he stoutly opposed Payne's efforts, the rawboned

Payne speaking to knots of men on the corners of the town and addressing town meetings whenever and wherever he could about the Oklahoma lands.

Payne, a lanky, handsome man with a congenial, likeable nature, had been on the frontiers of Kansas since he first home-steaded in Doniphan County with his brother in 1858. His history, however, had been that of a ne'er-do-well frontiersman, soldier, and part-time politician. Following an undistinguished enlistment as a soldier during the Civil War, he won a seat in the Kansas legislature of 1865, reenlisted briefly until the war's end, and then secured appointments as sergeant-at-arms of the Kansas Senate and as postmaster at Fort Leavenworth.[2]

Payne took leave from the postmaster's duties during the summer of 1867 to accept a captain's commission in the Eighteenth Kansas Volunteer Cavalry, which had been formed especially for the purpose of fighting Indians on the western plains of Kansas. The Eighteenth had little success in finding and combating the Indians and was hit hard by the cholera scourge sweeping Kansas that year. Payne was discharged from the unit that fall, only to find that his post office accounts were badly in arrears; and he was forced to sign his Doniphan County homestead over to Governor Samuel J. Crawford, who had gone his bond.[3]

In the fall of 1868, a new Indian-fighting unit was recruited as the Nineteenth Regiment of Volunteer Cavalry, and Payne was named as a company commander of the group. Again with a captain's rank, he rode with the Crawford-led unit when it marched south from Topeka in November, passing by the future site of Wichita on the way to meet Sheridan and Custer in the Indian Territory.

Payne served several months in the Territory at Fort Cobb and Fort Sill. He also took part in Custer's expedition into the Texas Panhandle whereby two white women were rescued from the Cheyennes. When the unit returned to Kansas shortly thereafter, he was again discharged. After a brief visit back to his original Indiana home, in the spring of 1870 Payne established a homestead on Dry Creek ten miles east of Wichita. The place became known as "Payne's Ranch."[4]

Payne won a hotly contested seat for the state legislature from Sedgwick County and served as a representative at Topeka in January and February of 1872. During that time he became affiliated with the cause of creating Harvey County out of a part of Sedgwick and moved to Newton, where he took up residence. While there in 1872, he ran for the Kansas senate against Marsh Murdock and was defeated. Payne also suffered some serious financial setbacks, losing Payne's Ranch as well as another 160-acre homestead that he had filed on at Newton.[5]

A long-continuing romance between Payne and his Doniphan County sweetheart, Anna Haines, resulted in a male child being born out of wedlock in 1871. Payne evidently made no offer of marriage, and Anna Haines moved with her family to faraway Oregon. Thus in 1875, Payne's prospects in Kansas were dim at best; and he looked with hope to Washington, D.C., where the Democratic Party was enjoying a rejuvenation of power. But the Capitol was overrun with down-and-out position seekers, and Payne was forced to take a job with a sawmill. He later secured a spot with the Washington metropolitan police force for a short time.[6]

Meanwhile, Payne actively cajoled political and military acquaintances to work in his behalf. For a time, he worked for the Office of Invalid Pensions as a messenger and general helper. Eventually he won a place on the House of Representative's much abused payroll as an assistant to its doorkeeper, Col. J. W. Polk. He had charge of one door of the House for a time, allowing him to claim on his return to Kansas that he had served as assistant door-keeper of the House of Representatives. Payne became involved when the Republicans pushed an investigation into Polk's payroll padding. When he was fired, he ignored the action and continued to sweep up and light the fires in the offices.[7]

While in Washington, Payne became acquainted with railroad lobbyist Elias C. Boudinot, who was from a prominent Cherokee family of Indian Territory. Boudinot had published a paper describing the 14 million acres of land in Indian Territory that had been left unassigned to any tribe following treaties with the Creeks and Seminoles.

The Boudinot paper and strong agitation by the *Kansas City Times* led to an abortive attempt to invade the Indian Territory during the spring of 1879. Leading the attempt was a flamboyant frontier figure, Col. C. C. Carpenter, who quickly capitulated when his settlers were ejected from the Territory by U.S. troops and he was personally confronted by an Indian Bureau official.[8]

Soon after this, in August 1879, Payne returned to Wichita with a scheme to launch his own invasion of the Oklahoma country to force settlement. Anna Haines and their son George returned from Oregon to join Payne at Wichita, renting an upstairs room in the home of A. B. Calvert on North Mosely Street. She set up housekeeping with Payne and contributed some modest financial support to his promotion of the Oklahoma crusade.

Payne opened an office in a small shack on Douglas Avenue with a sign reading "Office, D. L. Payne; On to Oklahoma."[9] A persuasive talker on a man-to-man basis, Payne soon found the sympathetic ears of Wichita leaders such as Frank Fisher of the *Wichita Beacon,* Big John Steele, and Dr. D. R. B. Greenlee, a prosperous Wichita physician and farmer. By the last of 1879, Payne had developed a cadre of supporters with whom he formed the Southwest Colony Town and Mining Company. On January 14, he issued a proclamation of intent to invade Oklahoma on March 15 with the questionable claim of five to ten thousand followers.[10]

Through speaking engagements along the border, Payne continued to fan the coals of interest in Oklahoma. At Coffeyville he called for a thousand recruits with which to storm the Unassigned Lands of Oklahoma and bragged of strong support from the *Kansas City Times.* When reminded that the Creek and Seminole treaties contained a clause saying the Unassigned Lands would be settled by *"freedmen or other Indians,"* Payne had a simple answer. He would take along fifty Indians and fifty Negroes as claimants for his group.[11]

Republican figures in Kansas, particularly U.S. District Attorney J. R. Hallowell and Marsh Murdock, were keeping Washington informed of Payne's activities. There the matter was brought to the point of discussion in a cabinet meeting with President Rutherford B. Hayes wherein the president was persuaded to issue a proclamation on the matter of the Oklahoma lands.

Hayes's edict warned that "all persons so intending and preparing to remove on said lands or into said Indian Territory without permission...will be specifically and immediately removed by such agents according to the laws made."[12] Hayes also threatened use of the U.S. Army to restrain or remove violators.

The presidential proclamation cooled the Oklahoma fever in Wichita considerably, and most people thought that this was the end of Payne. They were badly mistaken. He continued to recruit a small but loyal band of followers and developed a new strategy. On March 29, 1880, he addressed a letter to Hallowell informing the attorney of his intention to occupy lands inside the Territory for farming, suggesting that if such an act were illegal Hallowell should have him arrested at once and have the issue tested in court.[13]

Hallowell did not respond, but Payne really had no desire to be arrested at this point. On the night of April 24, he slipped quietly out of Wichita and headed south. He was guided by E. H. Kirk and Harry L. Hill. Hill had been with the Carpenter-inspired intrusion and had spent the previous winter on the South Canadian buying Indian ponies. Three men from New York met them on the border near South Haven. The group then crossed the Kansas–Indian Territory line and joined up with Payne's lieutenant Harry Stafford—another early settler of Wichita—and others.

Waiting on Bitter Creek until nightfall, the party headed out along the trail southeastward toward the Ponca reservation just below the Kansas border. But when Hill, scouting ahead, discovered troops on the trail, Payne changed directions and headed more westerly across the reservation of the Nez Perce Indians, who had recently been moved into the Territory. The Nez Perces were annoyed at the intrusion, but they let the men pass through without incident.[14]

With Hill and Stafford scouting ahead in a wagon and dropping buffalo skulls to mark the way, the Payne-led intruders moved overland under rainy skies to a small rivulet and followed it to the Cimarron River just northeast of present Guthrie, Oklahoma. From there they moved due south to the head of Coffee Creek, swung to the west around it, then turned south to intersect the Arbuckle branch of the Chisholm Cattle Trail.

Following the cattle trail southeastward, they pushed on to the North Canadian River at the site of present Oklahoma City. With Payne chilled from the rain and feeling ill, Hill took him across the river to the deserted Wantland Crutch-O Ranch cabins, where he had wintered while buying horses. On the following day, May 3, Payne and his men selected a treed hilltop south of the North Canadian as the site for their initial Oklahoma settlement. Payne named it Ewing, in honor of General and Senator Tom Ewing, under whom he had served during the Civil War.[15]

Payne's invasion party immediately set about to hew a townsite out of the forest wilderness, exultant over their conquest. Their joy was short-lived, however, for on the morning of May 4 Lt. J. H. Pardee and a company of troops, guided by John Meagher of Wichita, galloped across the North Canadian and up to the camp. The affable Payne was unruffled. He shared a drink and a cigar with Pardee and convinced the officer that his orders were invalid. Pardee's orders called for the ejection of any settlers found on "Indian land." Payne contended that the orders did not apply because the Oklahoma lands were unassigned to any Indian tribe.[16]

Pardee withdrew, leaving Payne and his boomers to their town building. But on May 15, another detachment of troops from Fort Reno arrived at the Ewing site, this time led by Lt. G. H. G. Gale. Gale was not to be persuaded by Payne's technicalities and ordered his men to round up all of the squatters and escort them to Fort Reno. Payne and his men were held there for a time while the array decided what to do with them. Finally it was decreed that the group be escorted back north and held just inside the Territory line at Polecat Creek, out of civil jurisdiction, while their disposition was debated. The group was taken to the Kansas border and released.

The border press, led by Marsh Murdock and the *Eagle*, scorned Payne's attempt at settlement of Oklahoma. But many in Kansas and elsewhere cheered his brash defiance of the government. Once back in Wichita, Payne found a rejuvenated interest in his Oklahoma boomer movement. Once again there were crowds at his little office on Douglas Avenue. Hardly had he been released than he was planning a second intrusion into the Territory, and on July 6 he led another group of twenty-one men southward over his original trail. This time, however, on learning that troops were after him, he turned westward at the Deep Fork to Council Grove, Chisholm's old trading area in present western Oklahoma City.[17]

Having sold townsite lots at the Ewing site, however, Payne was committed to returning there and did so on July 14. No sooner had he arrived than Sgt. Tom Donnell and a squad of Cheyenne-Arapaho scouts from Fort Reno rode up to place him and his party under arrest.[18]

This time Payne put up token resistance, refusing to surrender to "a bunch of redskins." Donnell sent for Pardee, who this time had the honor of arresting Payne. Once again the boomers were taken to Polecat Creek and held. During his detention there, Payne wrote a letter to Maj. Gen. John A. Pope, commanding the Department of the Missouri at Leavenworth, pointing out that it was illegal to hold him and his boomers longer than five days without charging them with an offense.[19]

Now the government decided that all of the prisoners would be released except those who were second offenders, and these would be taken to Fort Smith, Arkansas, to be tried before Judge Isaac C. Parker's court. During August, Payne and five of his men were taken by train to Muskogee, and from there by wagon to Fort Smith. Judge Parker bound them over for a November hearing and released them to return home.

Payne was forced to borrow money from his friend Elias Boudinot for fare home. The boomer leader arrived back in Wichita to an exuberant reception. Bands played, people cheered, and a buggy carried Payne at the head of a parade from the station to Eagle Hall.[20] Murdock again scoffed at Payne and printed the comment of Dutch Bill Greiffenstein, who, like Murdock, saw Payne as a threat to Wichita's progress:

"Stuff un bosh. Vat un who is Cap Payne?" Dutch Bill asked an excited social meeting of Wichita men, "Vat's he ever done that you should make yourselves so ridiculous tonight? Payne un his crowd don't have a red cent of interest in this town. If you want to depopulate this country, yust go on backing this Oklahoma boom. You fellers stood around and hurrahed for your own funeral. Eh, hain't it?"[21]

Having now become a virtual hero to many of the impoverished agrarians of the day, in a somewhat heady move Payne decided to make a military-style invasion of the Territory. He would do so with a large, well-organized army of settlers who would face down the government troops. But when the attempt was finally made in December 1880, Payne refused to cross the border in the face of cavalry units posted there. Instead he led his boomer caravan westward along the border with the troops following close behind.

In the face of his extravagant claims, this was interpreted as a lack of nerve by some of his followers. Bowing to criticism, Payne stepped down as field commander in favor of Wichita bartender H. M. Maidt. But Maidt, too, dared not risk a possible clash with the troops, and he led the rapidly disaffecting settler army to Caldwell. There Mike Meagher, then mayor of that town, invited them to use the town's camping grounds. The boomers spent a cold and miserable season's end at Caldwell. Finally on January 21, Payne called it quits, disbanding what was left of the invasion army.[22]

Many, especially Murdock, again wrote an end to Payne and his Oklahoma boomer movement. But again they were all wrong. Despite the setback, he remained committed to his dream. He made a trip to St. Louis where he talked with business leaders, convincing many of great commercial potential in the development of Oklahoma.

Payne returned to Fort Smith in March 1881 to hear his case argued by a St. Louis attorney, but Parker deferred a decision until

May 2. At that time the judge ruled that Payne was guilty under the Non-Intercourse Act of 1835, a law that levied a thousand dollar fine for a second unauthorized entry into Indian Territory.[23] But the fine was superfluous; Payne had no money or property against which the fine could be levied.

With some degree of sympathy, the *Eagle* gave Payne credit for grit even as it decreed that "the Boom gently but surely went down— it may never to rise again."[24] Once again Murdock had underestimated Payne, who immediately set off for St. Louis again to talk with supporters and to Arkansas to see Boudinot. July found him in Gainesville and Denison, Texas, recruiting followers for an invasion of the Territory's Unassigned Lands from the south. Though he was unsuccessful, he and two friends crossed the Territory from Gainesville. Continuing on to Wichita, he brought with him some 108 pounds of galena and what he claimed was silver ore. Using this, he pumped the possibility of mineral wealth in the Oklahoma country.[25]

By November, he was in Denison once more and from there led a small group of settlers to Payne's Springs at the site of present Oklahoma City. Once again he was arrested by troops and taken to Fort Reno, and once again he was escorted to the Kansas border and released. Payne now instigated a suit against General Pope and Secretary of War Robert T. Lincoln, claiming damages of fifteen thousand dollars for his arrest, detention, and ejection from the public domain of Oklahoma.[26]

Early in January 1882, Payne left Wichita with still another small party, returning to Payne's Springs. There he was again placed under arrest, taken to Fort Reno and escorted back to the Kansas border. Payne now decided to try another tactic. In February he and a friend, Wichita gambler Tom Craddock, made a wagon trip to the Deep Fork near present Arcadia, Oklahoma. The two men built a dugout cabin beside a small rivulet before Craddock returned to Kansas.

There Payne, with only his two dogs for company, spent the next month by himself. Becoming ill, he suffered also from extreme loneliness and worrying about danger from Indians, whom he believed had robbed him of some tobacco and poisoned one of his dogs. When Craddock and boomer W. H. Miller arrived on March 12 to take him back to Kansas, Payne wrote in his diary: "From the very depths of my heart do I thank God for his Goodness in sending them."[27]

By May, Payne had still another invasion organized, leading it from Wichita to the Deep Fork, only to suffer arrest and ejection again. On his return to Wichita, Payne began advertising another invasion for July 20. At this time, however, he decided on a trip to Washington to lobby for his Oklahoma settlement cause.

Though he found little or no support from government officials there, Payne did manage to publicize his initiative. At the same time, his agents at home were selling shares in Payne's Oklahoma Colony to notables such as Buffalo Bill Cody, Dr. Morrison Munford of the *Kansas City Times*, and Indian Territory cattleman Thomas Fenlon.[28]

The July invasion had been postponed because of Payne's absence; but when he returned to Wichita in early August, the small expedition of about twenty members got under way, moving from camp at South Haven to a cattle trail crossing of the Chikaskia in the Territory known as Rock Falls. From there the group traveled down Payne's trail to the Deep Fork, where William Osburn remained to build a cabin.

Payne led the rest of the group on over the dividing ridge to the North Canadian River, stopping at its north bend near present Jones, Oklahoma. When the army appeared this time, Payne and his followers staged a good humored sit-down strike. The troops had to pick him and his men up bodily and place them in wagons.[29]

Once again Payne and his people were taken to Fort Reno where the exasperated military, weary of removing the persistent boomer leader, decided on a new plan of action. Instead of sending him and his people back to Kansas, it was decided, they would escort them to Texas. A company of cavalry troops forced Payne and his followers, which included two women and a child, to make a grueling march to Henrietta, Texas. There the officer in charge, Lt. C. W. Taylor, made the mistake of letting Payne go into town unescorted to purchase supplies. The boomer immediately secured a writ of habeas corpus against the officer and then proceeded to get gloriously drunk in a local saloon.[30] Taylor refused to submit to arrest by a Henrietta deputy and managed to get Payne and his crew aboard a train just ahead of a Henrietta posse that was coming to the boomers' rescue.

At Fort Smith, the Territory invaders were released pending a future hearing. As soon as he was freed, Payne filed suit against Taylor on grounds of assault and false imprisonment. The suit was later dismissed. Payne also made charges against the army over his treatment, winning much public sympathy. Now he launched an attack against the cattle barons of the Territory, whom he claimed were bribing both Indian and government officials for special privileges of using Territory grazing lands.

On January 12, 1883, Payne's boomer organization issued the first edition of its organ, the *Oklahoma War Chief*, for which Wichita postmaster Marsh Murdock refused mailing privileges. Conflict within the Oklahoma Colony, meanwhile, had erupted with a rebellion by two Wichita old-timers, former close friends of Payne—W. B. Hutchison and E. H. Nugent. Payne moved his boomer headquarters to Arkansas City, where another big invasion was being organized. In late February in bone-chilling weather, Payne's largest invasion group yet crossed the border and headed down the Payne trail. His destination this time was the North Canadian at its bend near where he had been camped before.[31]

The boomer leader declared that he would "suffer both of his arms to be pulled off and his throat cut ear to ear" before being removed this time. Still he was quick to acquiesce when U.S. troops appeared and placed him under arrest. The caravan, however, was permitted to continue on to the North Canadian where Camp Alice was established. When more troops arrived under Capt. Henry Carroll, Payne advised the settlers to submit to arrest. Colony secretary William Osburn refused to do so and physically resisted until he was overpowered, hog-tied, and tossed into a wagon by the troops.

The colony straggled back to Kansas while Payne, Osburn, and others were taken to Fort Reno and then returned to the border. This time Payne faced a serious dissention in the Oklahoma Colony ranks that erupted with charges of bad faith and collusion being made against him in public print by Nugent. William L. Couch, a former Wichita merchant and farmer, came to Payne's defense, and the boomer leader was soon back as strong and confident as ever, recruiting new followers for his cause.[32]

Again, Murdock predicted that the Camp Alice expedition would be Payne's last. But on August 7, 1883, a 150-man, 38-wagon boomer caravan crossed the border at Arkansas City and headed southward.[33] This time Payne stayed behind, seeing to his suit against Pope and Lincoln while William Couch served as field leader. Like all the other attempts, the expedition was captured by federal troops, this time at the Cimarron River. During the ordeal of being moved to Fort Reno, a pregnant boomer woman gave premature birth to a child that died, the mother expiring soon after. The boomers were returned to Kansas.

Payne was on a speaking tour of Kansas and Missouri when he learned that a delegation of freedmen—former slaves of the Indian nations who had been freed but without franchise—from the

Territory were in Washington, D.C. Their hope was to have the Unassigned District—as the Creek treaty had specified—made available for settlement by African freedmen.

Payne immediately hurried to the capital to lobby for his cause again. While there, he sent an open letter to a St. Louis newspaper charging Commissioner of Indian Affairs Hiram Price with "crookedness, writhings, twistings and spiralties of that head of a rotten department."[34] He also attacked Kansas senator Preston B. Plumb, charging him with having cattle interests in the Territory with a man named Harry Hibben.

While Payne was thus engaged on the political front, Couch was leading still another expedition into the Oklahoma country. In mid April he took a large colony of settlers to the Council Grove area and then on to what is now downtown Oklahoma City. When troops arrived, Couch's father put up resistance to the point that he was unceremoniously bound, along with boomer Daniel Odell, and dumped into the back of a wagon by troops.

Couch, who was away from camp at the time, escaped arrest by pretending to be a cattleman and quickly made his way back to Kansas, where he immediately recruited another colony of settlers and headed back into the Territory.[35] This time Couch stopped at the Cimarron and was establishing a settlement until Lt. M. W. Day arrived, arrested the boomers, and took them back from whence them came.[36]

Payne returned from Washington to launch what would be his last and most serious effort to plant a colony inside the Indian Territory. He had now persuaded himself that the title to the Cherokee Outlet across northern Indian Territory was held by the United States and that it, too, was public domain.

Accordingly, in May 1884 he began making plans to establish a settlement at Rock Falls at the cattle trail crossing of the Chikaskia River. During August, Payne led a caravan of settlers there and went into camp. The group formed a townsite company, sold lots and homesteads, and erected a small frame building to house the printing press of the *Oklahoma War Chief*.[37]

Colonel Edward Hatch was sent to the Kansas border to remove the intruders. Establishing a headquarters camp ten miles below Rock Falls on the Chikaskia, Hatch maintained a surveillance of Payne's operation. He personally paid a visit to the camp to warn Payne and the others to leave only to receive a barrage of angry verbal abuse from an inebriated Payne.

On August 7, two troops of Ninth Cavalry, tactfully placed under the command and direction of Indian Bureau officials rather than the army, descended on the Rock Falls settlement. They were guided and aided by delighted Caldwell citizens who were in sympathy with the cattle interests and the Cherokee Live Stock Association, which head-quartered in their town.[38]

After seizing the *War Chief* press and torching its building, the troops took Payne and his lieutenants prisoners and sent them off to Hatch's camp. The frightened and now leaderless colonists fled back to the Kansas border. Then, in a move designed to punish Payne and his men without the niceties of legal action, Hatch had them loaded into the back of canvas-covered, springless wagons and sent off on a long, suffocatingly hot, and torturous trip over rough, roadless country to Fort Smith.

On reaching the north bank of the Arkansas River across from Fort Smith, but still on Territory ground, the officer in charge was ordered to take the prisoners to Fort Gibson. After a brief wait at Gibson, orders were changed again, and Payne and his men were put on the trail back to Fort Smith. There they were finally released after nearly a month of being dragged haplessly about the Territory.

It was a miserable ordeal for the boomers, but the army had over-played its hand. Now the frontier press rushed to defend Payne against such abuse by the military. Payne returned to Wichita to a hero's welcome. At a large skating rink rented for the occasion, the featured speaker was Joseph G. McCoy, the cattle entrepreneur. When Payne arrived, he was cheered loudly and long.[39]

Payne's health was in bad shape following the trip to Fort Smith, but when he felt better he undertook a series of speaking engage-ments. On the morning of November 17, 1884, Thanksgiving Day, Payne and Annie Haines drove in a wagon from Hunnewell to Wellington, where he spoke that night to an audience at the court-house. On the following morning he arose from his bed at the DeBarnard Hotel in Wellington and went down to breakfast. He had just finished eating when he suddenly slumped from his chair onto the floor. Mrs. Haines attempted to revive him, but Payne was dead from an embolism of the pulmonary artery—a massive heart attack. He was buried at Wellington, his funeral attended by an overflowing crowd of mourners.[40]

Murdock, who had vigorously opposed Payne's Oklahoma move-ment throughout, was grief-stricken to learn of Payne's death. He penned an emotional tribute to his old political rival, describing him as "a perfect type of frontiersman, being a Hercules in physical strength and prowess and the possessor of a spirit which had never brooked the restraints of civil life...the hope of making a settlement in the Indian Territory governing his every aspiration and impulse."[41]

Following Payne's death, William Couch assumed leadership of the Oklahoma Colony, and in December following he led a large invasion force to the site of present Stillwater, Oklahoma. The group was eventually removed by U.S. troops in January. In October 1885, Couch led still another expedition to the site of Oklahoma City, again being removed by troops.

The Oklahoma boomer movement would then fall into limbo for a time, its impetus being replaced by construction of the Santa Fe Railroad extension from Arkansas City across Indian Territory to Gainesville, Texas. The line would conveniently cut through the very heart of the Unassigned Lands. The Oklahoma boomer movement would find a revival in 1888, and once again Wichita would play a key role in it.

Chapter Fourteen

The Fading Frontier

The departure of Big John Steele and his family for
far-off Tacoma, Washington, caused Marsh Murdock
of the *Eagle* to muse sadly on the "uncontrollable
desire that Western men have to go further west."
— *Wichita Eagle*, October 4, 1883

During the early 1880s, several significant events occurred that
gave clue to the inevitable demise of the old Wild West. On July 14,
1881, Billy the Kid was killed by Sheriff Pat Garrett at Fort Sumner, New
Mexico, causing some settlers of Wichita to recall the eleven-year-old
street gamin who lived among them in 1870–71.[1] A short time later, a
stalwart figure of the old West died a more natural death near
Westport, Missouri. He was Jim Bridger, the noted mountain man.
Then during the following spring, the renowned train robber Jesse
James—whose married sister was said to be living incognito at
Wichita—was killed at St. Joseph, Missouri, by Robert Ford.

The personalities and passions of the old West were rapidly fading away in Wichita, too. Bat Masterson, after a career as a frontier
lawman, was now living a quiet existence in Wichita where he was
receiving treatment for his eyes.[2] In April 1882 Wichita was shocked by
the sudden death of its earliest settler Henry Vigus, who succumbed
to a stroke.[3]

Vigus's son Will, who came back to Wichita for the funeral, could
hardly find a single landmark or characteristic feature of the cowtown
he had known as a boy.[4] Even the old "Star of the West" dance hall,

erected in 1870, had been torn down. While Wichita daily became more and more a modern commercial center, strong vestiges of its wild ways remained.

A journalist visiting Wichita in 1882 noted the presence of western notables such as Dave Payne and Bat Masterson on the streets of the town, along with numerous gamblers, street peddlers, and fast women. A few of the old long-haired frontiersmen could be seen. Saloons were running full blast all over the city. The smell of beer on Douglas Avenue, the scribe calculated, was enough to intoxicate the nonimbibing. In fact, it was proclaimed that there was more whiskey drinking going on in Wichita in 1882 than at any other time in the town's history.[5]

Still the voices of reform had grown loud in Wichita, threatening serious change to the old cowboy orientation of gambling saloons, houses of prostitution, and brassy street spectacles. The cattle herds no longer bawled their way across the Arkansas. Now the drovers headed them for Dodge and other new shipping points. Many of the old-timers of the frontier, even those who followed a more sedate lifestyle, began to find the new Wichita of civilized airs to be downright distasteful. Some looked longingly southward to Indian Territory where the western frontier yet lingered.

Though Wichita could now claim that it had tamed its penchant for violence and that law and order prevailed, it remained at the frontier's edge as a northern entrance to the Territory, where outlaws, hostile Indians, bridgeless streams, wild animals, and other dangers lurked for travelers.

Accounts of incidents on the Chisholm Cattle Trail connecting Wichita with Indian Territory were the common diet of city newspaper readers. In the spring of 1882, cattle buyer Henry T. Stevens accompanied by Charles F. Parsons left Wichita by wagon and headed down the Chisholm Trail for Fort Worth. At Caldwell, Stevens hired two men to go along and help bring back the herd of cattle he intended to buy. The men were Edward Derusha and Jim Morgan. Five days down the trail, Stevens's party was camped in the vicinity of the Cimarron River.

Everything had been agreeable among the four up to the time they arose on March 18, a Sunday, had their breakfast, and were relaxing around the campfire preparing to take to the trail again. It was then that Morgan, a man of about thirty-two years of age who had worked for the Caldwell-Fort Sill stage line and at Fort Reno, grabbed the two six-shooters that Parsons carried and leveled them at the others as he backed up against the wagon.

"I've been with you fellows long enough," he told the surprised trio. "You had better strike out over the hill."

Morgan had the drop on them, and they were unarmed. Thus the three did as they had been told and headed out over a hill. But after going a few steps, Stevens turned around and said something to Morgan. Parsons and Derusha kept on going: and when they heard a shot, they did not turn around to see what had taken place.

The two men became separated, and Parsons shortly met with a detail of Cheyenne scouts led by Sgt. Tom Donnell. Riding quickly to the former campsite, Donnell found Stevens lying dead where he had fallen, a bullet hole in his chest. Morgan had departed with all five of the horses, two saddles, a Winchester, and four revolvers, though in his hurry he had not touched the $67.55 that was still on Stevens's body. A few days after the incident, Morgan coolly appeared at Red Fork Station on the Cimarron, paid to have his beard shaved off, and rode away to the northwest not to be heard from again.[6]

With the establishment of the U.S. District Court at Wichita in 1883, the hotels and rooming houses overflowed with attorneys, jurors, witnesses, and criminals, many of whom were brought in from Indian Territory. The mixture of old and new West could be seen in the mode of dress of Indians who came up from the south. Some tribal members still wore the tribal blanket and feathers, but many were attired in the coat and trousers trappings of the white man's fashion.[7]

Among the breed of Wichita men who were simply more adapted to the frontier than to civilized society, there seemed to be a certain compulsion to move on. Mike Meagher and W. B. Hutchison left Wichita for the border town of Caldwell. Milo Kellogg moved on to Kingman, Kansas, leaving his name behind for a principal Wichita street.

Johnny Meagher, Mike's brother, left Wichita to take up residence at Darlington, while brother-in-law John Steele moved to faraway Tacoma, Washington, in 1883. Even Dutch Bill, now one of Wichita's wealthiest and most prominent men, was developing a renewed connection with the Indian Territory. It would ultimately draw him, too, away from the town he had helped so much to build. His wife held lands in the Potawatomi reservation located just east of the Unassigned Lands.

In October 1883, Greiffenstein with his wife and three children made a trip to the reservation, visiting Chief Burnett and other old friends.[8] The journey over a rough and poorly defined trail quickly reminded the former Indian trader of the perils of frontier travel. A heavy rainstorm struck their mule-drawn wagon and buggy conveyance, soaking all of their clothes, bedding, and belongings. Soon after, the whole family nearly drowned when their wagon became mired in the bed of the Cimarron River. On reaching the North Canadian, the family was forced to take an entire day to build a raft on which to tow their goods across the stream. Then, when the children were being towed across the flooded Little River, the box of their wagon came loose and its occupants were swept downstream screaming for help. They were saved by the action of some Territory cowboys who snagged the wagon box with a rope.

All three children were badly soaked in the cold water, and the youngest son Charles became dangerously ill. He was taken to the Sacred Heart Mission on the Canadian River, and from there runners were sent in all directions to find a doctor. Though one was found fifty miles away, the boy was so ill that Greiffenstein was forced to take him to the nearest Missouri-Kansas-Texas railway station and return him to Wichita by rail.[9]

An event designed in part to show the economic advancement of Wichita and Sedgwick County took place in the spring of 1884. It was initiated by a letter to the *Eagle* from W. C. Woodman, Wichita's pioneer banker, who suggested that help be sent to flood victims of the Ohio Valley. In 1874, when Kansas had been invaded by swarms of crop-destroying locusts, people of the Midwestern states had sent help. Now, Woodman suggested, the people of Sedgwick County should return that favor. He offered the first fifty dollars to raise funds for provisions.[10]

The idea took hold, and from it grew the concept of a "corn train"—thirty-one railroad cars loaded with Sedgwick County corn to be sent to the people of the Ohio Valley. The train departed Wichita on the morning of March 17, 1884, accompanied by Mayor Greiffenstein and three other representatives of the area. A large crowd and a brass band saw the train off, and a picture of it later appeared in *Harper's Illustrated Weekly*.[11]

The sides of the cars were emblazoned with signs and pictures. One car carried the image of a giant ear of corn on wagon wheels being drawn toward the Ohio Valley by a team of grasshoppers with a huge grasshopper wielding the whip. Still another depicted two grasshoppers holding a car-length sign reading:

"Given 1874—Returned with Interest 1884, Compliments of Wichita and Sedgwick County, Kansas, to the Ohio Valley."[12]

Recipients of the gift, however, were nonplussed as to what could be done with the generous gift. When it was suggested that perhaps it could be made into corn whiskey and sold to raise money for the flood victims, some of the citizens back in Sedgwick County were a bit miffed. Nonetheless, the Kansas men were toasted and feted by the Cincinnati Chamber of Commerce. With this done, Greiffenstein went on to Washington, D.C., where he took advantage of his wife's place on the Potawatomi roles to lease thirty square miles of tribal land at two and a half cents an acre for the purpose of grazing cattle.[13] During the recession of 1893, Dutch Bill would leave the town he had done so much to create and move to the Potawatomi reservation where he laid out a new town called Burnett.[14]

Following the death of David Payne, the Oklahoma boomer movement had gone into an eclipse in Wichita despite the efforts of William Couch to keep it alive. This was partially due to the fact that the main thrust of Oklahoma settlement had now been placed in legislative channels in the U.S. Congress. Construction of the Santa Fe Railroad extension across the Territory to Gainesville, Texas, had occupied many of the old boomers who worked on grading and rail-laying crews. As railroad men they could now enter the Unassigned Lands without fear of harassment from the army.

At the same time there was an important behind-the-scenes awakening of capitalistic interest in the Oklahoma country. Men such as Marsh Murdock, who had so strongly opposed settlement of lands in the Territory, now began to realize the market potential of the country to the south. The *Eagle* now spoke of "a new empire soon to be made accessible to us."[15] This new interest by men of money was joined with efforts of the old agrarian boomers during 1888.

The business leaders of Wichita were further stimulated to become involved in the Oklahoma movement when border towns such as Caldwell, Arkansas City, Winfield, and others began to actively seek to become the headquarters and supply centers for boomer activity. In early February enthusiastic boomer meetings were held at Caldwell and Arkansas City in advance of a large conference at Kansas City on February 8. Leading men from Kansas and surrounding states were in attendance as a resolution encouraging Oklahoma settlement was drafted to send to the president and Congress.

Murdock joined with boomer leaders in promoting another interstate Oklahoma conference at Wichita on November 20. Hundreds of delegates arrived in town to fill the Crawford Opera

The Wichita Corn Train of 1884 repaid Ohio farmers who had once sent aid to Kansas. *Harper's Weekly*, April 5, 1884.

House "to suffocation" as such speakers as Representatives William M. Springer of Illinois, Charles H. Mansur of Missouri, and James B. Weaver of Iowa addressed the audience on the Oklahoma question.

Oklahoma Harry Hill, Payne's former guide who was now prominent in Wichita business as stage line operator and owner of the Wichita Horse and Mule Market, and Wichitan H. L. Pierce were placed in charge of raising the fifteen hundred dollars needed to send still another committee—which included Marsh Murdock—to Washington in behalf of Oklahoma settlement.[16]

At the same time, the Wichita Board of Trade made a move to regain Wichita's position as headquarters of the Oklahoma boomer movement that it had held, ruefully, during Payne's day. The board wrote a letter to Maj. Gordon W. Lillie (Pawnee Bill) whose Wild West show was then stranded in Philadelphia, bankrupted by a rain-plagued tour. Lillie, the board felt, was just the sort of flamboyant character, similar to Payne, that they needed.

For Lillie the offer of financial help was a golden opportunity to return his show to Wichita and eventually regroup. In December 1888,

Oklahoma Harry Hill oper-
ated a livery stable in
Wichita and formed a Wild
West Show. *New York Sun.*

he and his show troupe arrived in Wichita by train. They were met by Murdock, Hill, and other members of the Wichita Board of Trade. A brass band paraded Pawnee Bill to his hotel, much as had been done for Payne a few years earlier, and a banquet that evening launched him as the new head colonizer for Oklahoma settlement.

Lillie began his promotional activities immediately. As Payne had done, he issued public challenge to the cattlemen inside the Territory and threatened to invade the country in face of opposition by U.S. troops. In Washington, William Couch saw this move as a serious threat to his political efforts to push the Springer Oklahoma Bill (sponsored by Representative Springer) through Congress. He fired off a wire to the Wichita Board of Trade protesting Pawnee Bill's activity and inflammatory public statements.

As a result, Harry Hill was sent to contact Lillie, who was then at the head of a boomer colony encamped at Hunnewell. Hill had instructions to dissuade Lillie from his threats to invade the Territory and, if he could not, to withdraw the support of the Wichita Board of Trade. Lillie refused to halt his march, though he did graciously give in on the matter of challenging U.S. troops. He accepted an offer from the Caldwell Board of Trade to use that city's fairgrounds as a camping area until the Unassigned Lands were officially opened to settlement.[17]

Through the efforts of the Kansas-Oklahoma boomer lobby and interested congressmen, a rider was attached to the Indian Appropriations Bill then before Congress. It provided that the lands ceded by the Creeks and Seminoles should be considered public domain and opened to public settlement on proclamation of the president of the United States. On March 27, 1889, newly elected President Benjamin Harrison signed such a proclamation.

Lillie and Hill were especially prominent in the exciting period prior to the Oklahoma land rush of April 22, 1889, and many Wichita residents would take part in the preliminaries and the run itself. Lillie eventually led his colony into the settlement area near Kingfisher, Oklahoma, while Harry Hill established the first stage route from Oklahoma Station to Edmond Station, Guthrie Station, and Kingfisher Station.

Hill had been looked to by some of the old boomers as the one to lead them into the Oklahoma lands. While he did make a preopening visit to the region, Hill played only a limited role in the April 22, 1889, land opening itself. He had become deeply involved in another exciting enterprise back in Wichita.

Chapter Fifteen

Show Biz West

He [Oklahoma Harry Hill] gathered together here
those who had been long strangers to these streets—
all the material of a wild west show—the booted and
spurred cowboy, the crack marksman, the blanketed
and feathered Indian, the congeries of men, women,
guns and animals which the sophisticated
East believed the simple West to be.
— Vic Murdock, *Folks*, 1921

Almost as a campfire will sometimes make one last flicker before dying out, so did the image of the Old West have one last moment of glory at Wichita before the former cowtown rushed on to its destiny as a modern American city. For a brief instant in its history, Wichita became the center of a traveling show extravaganza that sought to re-create and dramatize the more colorful aspects of the Wild West for the entertainment of audiences in towns across the country. Shows of this sort were popular at the time, and Wichita's opportunity came about when Pawnee Bill Lillie was recruited by the Board of Trade to put the city at the lead of the Oklahoma settlement movement.

The Pawnee Bill Wild West Show had played Wichita in May 1888 with Pawnee Bill and Miss May Lillie doing trick shooting, steers being lassoed, desperate scenes of the far West being enacted, wild ponies being captured and ridden, stagecoaches undergoing attacks by war-painted Indians, and other melodramatic acts being performed.[1]

Showman "Pawnee Bill"
Lillie was called on by the
Wichita Board of Trade to
take over after the death of
David Payne. *Frank Leslie's
Illustrated Newspaper,*
March 16, 1889.

On one occasion, a stagecoach under chase by the Indians ran amok into the crowd. Another time a local drunk dashed into the fairgrounds arena declaring that he could ride a bucking bronc better than any of the Indians or cowboys in the show. Then between shows, some eight or ten members of the troupe roped an old man and dragged him around the racecourse. He was told he would be killed if he complained; and when he did, the sheriff was warned that blood would be spilled if any arrests were attempted.

When Pawnee Bill returned to Wichita at the town's request in December, he brought with him his defunct show and entourage, dumping it lock, stock, and barrel on the town: the trick ropers and riders, Indians, crack marksmen, acrobats, clowns, sideshow performers, canvas men, horses, mules, cattle, and all the other elements of a traveling circus. Most of the members were destitute, too broke to pay the fifty dollars required to return east.[2] Without even the price of hotel fare and bound by calling and disposition to the habitat of the livestock, they gravitated to the environment of Oklahoma Harry Hill's Wichita Horse and Mule Market, located between the Douglas Avenue Hotel and the Arkansas River bridge.[3]

Harry Hill had settled in Wichita originally as a horse and mule trader, developing his enterprise with stock from Indian Territory and

Texas. These he sold to Eastern markets and to the U.S. cavalry as well as locally. During the heyday of the horse and mule business, Hill's barn and livery stables became a makeshift social center for much of the male population of Wichita.[4]

The place was occasionally the scene of rowdy western humor and pranks. One such occasion occurred when Hill sold a man an unbroken horse for sixty-five dollars, telling the customer that he would have to break the horse. The animal was saddled, and the man climbed aboard. The result was a real-life rodeo-style performance that drew a large crowd of cheering onlookers.[5]

Hill himself did not play the role of the wild westerner. He kept his hair short and dressed as a businessman, refusing to participate in any pretense of flamboyancy. But in 1889 the horse-and-mule business was in a serious decline, as was the stagecoach business into which Hill had ventured. Meanwhile, Pawnee Bill's show people, who lolled around his livery stables, painted glowing pictures of how much money a traveling show could make, as supposedly the Buffalo Bill Cody show was doing in Europe at the time.

The idea began to grow on Hill that he had at hand, perhaps, the makings of a good business venture. Undoubtedly his business judgment was affected by show business glamour. He talked the matter over with a friend, wealthy Wichita businessman Joe Rich, intriguing him with the notion of forming a Wild West show. Rich was willing to invest his capital in it.[6]

Even as Harry Hill was making a trip to the Oklahoma country in March 1889 to see about establishing a stage line there, plans were under way to organize "one of the most attractive Wild West exhibitions in the world."[7] It was to be called the "Oklahoma Historical Wild West Show," though the "Historical" was soon dropped from the title. This undertaking had enough financial backing that a whole train of specially built railroad cars was put into manufacture by the Burton Car Works of Wichita.

In April, an *Eagle* reporter accompanied financier Rich to visit the railroad car plant and check the progress. Seven cars were then completed or under construction. Two of them were flatcars for carrying the stages, tents, bandwagons, electric light apparatus, and other heavy equipment. Both were forty-four feet long and ten feet wide; and they were painted and lettered in a colorful, "circusy" manner.[8]

Two cars were of extra length to carry the large amount of livestock that would be required by the exhibition, each with feeding and watering equipment. All in all, there would be over a hundred head of livestock: thirty spotted ponies, a herd of Texas longhorns, twelve mountain burros, trick horses, bucking horses, and riding horses. Two other extra-long cars provided sleeping quarters, one to be occupied by the performers. On the sides of these cars were scenes of buffalo hunting and Indian battles that were supposed to have taken place in the Indian Territory.

The other car would be occupied by the Indians and the buffalo, and the side of the car would be emblazoned, "Buffaloes and Indians from Oklahoma."[9] The car would have bunks for the Indians at the front. An "Indian collector" for the company had already secured a permit from the government to recruit fifty Indian men, women, and children—though the vernacular of the day used the terms "bucks, squaws, and papooses," indicating the less-than-considerate attitude of the times regarding Indian people. Fifteen buffalo had been secured for the show.

Additionally, the train would carry an electric dynamo capable of producing its own lighting and thus avoid dependence on the communities it visited for nighttime showings. Beneath the cars were storage chests for transporting provisions, arms, ammunition, and other show necessities such as the glass balls that Sam Cody Jr. and his wife would shoot in midair and from the heads, hands, and mouths of one another.

It was intended that this show would offer much of the normal diet of Wild West shows. Added, however, would be a special exhibition depicting scenes that had been much in the news about the Oklahoma country during recent years—cowboy life such as branding cattle, horse stealing and other such outlawry, and frontier law enforcement in capturing renegades hiding out in the Territory. There would be Plains warfare, complete with scenes of Indian depredations—especially an enactment of the macabre massacre of Pat Hennessey. The capture and imprisonment of David Payne and his Oklahoma boomers would be played out for audiences. In one scene, Harry Hill would act out the role of a stage driver during a holdup.[10]

The Indians recruited for the show assumed the role of Cheyenne warriors, though they were really Potawatomis, reflecting a Greiffenstein connection. They would give displays of their riding and shooting from horseback. And there would be a parade of Spanish beauties who would demonstrate their graceful horsemanship atop elegant white horses. The very best talent had been procured for the riding and shooting.

Already contacted were the renowned Capt. A. G. Bogardus, a native Wichitan, and his two sons who had performed throughout America and in Europe. One of the sons, young Pete, had displayed his shooting skills in England before Queen Victoria, receiving from her both a kiss on the cheek and a beautiful medal, which he wore about his neck with great pride.

Bogardus had stated that while waiting to get under way, he and others of the company intended to go down to Oklahoma and stake claims. Yellowstone Vic, a superb specimen of western manhood, would ride anything from a bucking horse to a Texas steer. He offered to undertake a special feat at each show; he would ride a wild buffalo!

Texas Charley, the great lasso thrower, would perform his skills, while Capt. Harry Horne would exercise his famous talents as a lecturer by describing the intriguing features and characteristics of the Wild West exhibits. And, if that were not enough to amaze and amuse the crowds, the aeronaut Professor Lanford would go up in a hot air balloon to a height of one mile and leap from it, descending by parachute.

At one time during the show there would be loosed in the arena, simultaneously, a herd of wild ponies, the buffalo, and some longhorn steers, all with riders. It would be, the planners hoped, a melee of bucking, kicking, prancing animals that would arouse the audience to great passion.

Music for the performances was to be provided by select members of the Wichita Board of Trade band with Professor Woods as the musical director. The band would be carried in a special wagon, then being constructed at a cost of five thousand dollars. It was to be drawn by six white mules, the animals richly caparisoned to make a striking appearance in preperformance street parades.

Also scheduled for parade use were two old stagecoaches that bore marks of their action in carrying mail and passengers across the Plains and through the blazing gunplay of border fights. These parade exhibits would be joined by the Indians in costume, the cowboys in ranch gear, the Spanish beauties, the buffalo, the longhorn steers, the horses, the mules, and all the rest of the company in their special outfits.

On May 5, 1889, the Oklahoma Wild West Show left Wichita with Emporia as its first road stop. Everyone was filled with excitement and high enthusiasm to be on the road at last. The show's Emporia debut was not a great success, however, and Hill was initiated into the unforeseen difficulties that such a traveling show could, and often would, encounter.

First, there was the weather. As the cavalcade of western life paraded through the streets of Emporia, high, swirling winds blew dust and biting sand into the faces of onlookers and paraders alike. The winds continued that night, inhibiting the shooting performances and other acts. Because the fairgrounds were some distance from town, many Emporians stayed home, and the crowd turnout was a great disappointment.

Then, during the act where the cowboys charged to prevent the capture of the Black Hills stagecoach by Indians, a horse fell and broke its leg. The animal had to be shot there before the dismayed audience.[11]

The show plunged hopefully onward to other sites, but at Kansas City another difficulty presented itself. The manager of the ball park for which the show had a usage contract, refused to permit the menagerie of horses, mules, longhorns, buffalo, stagecoaches, wagons, and whatnot to enter. The man even hired a force of Pinkerton men to prevent entry.

Oklahoma Harry Hill confronted the manager at the gate of the park. Pulling out his watch, he said he would give the man just three minutes to get out of his way or he would clean out the place just like he had "cleaned out Oklahoma." The bluff worked, and the manager gave in, puffing off and threatening to swear out a warrant for Hill's arrest.[12]

But Hill could not bluff away the bad weather. Rainstorms dogged the show wherever it went. In Chicago, the group managed only two performances in a week. And there were other unforeseen incidents. On one occasion Texas Charley, now billed as Buffalo Charley, tried to climb aboard Harry Hill's old buffalo. The annoyed animal took off, charging about the amphitheater and sending the crowd flying in all directions. Then, during a scene in which road agents attacked a Wichita stagecoach, the vehicle overturned preventing the timely escape that had been planned for it.[13]

The show continued bravely on eastward to Andersonville, Illinois; Louisville, Kentucky; Cincinnati, Ohio; and other towns along the Ohio River. The incessant wet weather followed persistently. Though the final stands improved in attendance, overall the tour was considered by experienced troupers to be a bad show season. Not only had it been hampered by rain but by the large number of competing shows encountered on the road. In late July the Oklahoma

Harry Hill Wild West Show made a final jump from Springfield, Illinois, back to Wichita.[14]

When the show pulled into the depot at Wichita, twenty-five Indians in full regalia were perched atop the boxcars while cowboys, performers, roustabouts, and other members of the entourage waved and cheered from the car windows. When Hill appeared at the door of his sleeper, he was given a big ovation and was quickly surrounded by friends.[15] Already an advertisement had appeared in the paper announcing a short engagement for the show in Wichita before heading off westward to southern California.

The billing now listed such attractions as California Fran, an expert rider and roper; champion roper Mexican Rafael; Negro steer-rider Santa Cruz; the "Wichita Kid" who rode bucking burros; Texas Tom, the finest roper of Texas; and Malto, the Spanish Queen, who along with Buffalo Bessie rode wild horses and a wild buffalo to boot.[16]

To promote attendance, Harry Hill loaded a stagecoach with reporters and others and took them to the Wichita fairgrounds where they witnessed his camp laid out in neat rows of tents and beside it an Indian village of tepees. On August 3, the show was performed for the home folks. Captain Bogardus and his sons performed their fancy shooting, the cowboys did a fast-riding pick-up act, and a melee of bucking horses and riders was turned loose in the arena for a wild spectacle. Harry Hill, now wearing a flowing blonde wig, and his son shot glass balls out of a girl's hand and then from her mouth; howling Indians charged a trapper's cabin; a horse thief was hanged; warriors attacked a Pony Express rider; and masked highwaymen held up an overland mail stage. Finally, an Indian group conducted a religious ceremony so the crowd could see how they worshiped at home.[17]

This, however, was the final performance of the Oklahoma Harry Hill Wild West Show. Despite the brave front it presented, the show had suffered heavy financial loses and could not continue. Most citizens of Wichita were much more interested in the prizefight between Paddy Shea and John W. Abbott, a black man, just across the border in the Indian Territory eight miles south of Arkansas City, than they were in imitation scenes of the old West. Speaking for many of the public, perhaps, was the man who yelled out "Rats!" when Captain Horne was making a speech promoting the show.

A benefit was held at the Crawford Opera House to raise money with which to pay the members of the show who "are a long ways from home, and in destitute circumstances."[18] A few days later, Hill took the

Indian members of the show to the railway station and saw them off for their homes in northeast Kansas. When he secured chair cars for the Indians rather than seats on the common coach of the train, some of the whites aboard the train were miffed.[19]

It was now suggested that members of the defunct Wild West show band could be incorporated into a brass band for Wichita.[20] The end of Hill's show was, perhaps, emblematic of the demise of the old West in Wichita. Even to the south now the Indian Territory was in the throes of becoming a civilized society with towns and government. Perhaps even more symbolic was the departure of Dutch Bill from Wichita.

At Burnett, Oklahoma Territory, Dutch Bill continued to raise racehorses and special strains of cattle, develop real estate, operate a merchandise store, and even dabble in some early oil exploration. His health turned bad and he finally went blind, but he stubbornly held onto life until September 26, 1899, when he succumbed to a stroke.[21]

Greiffenstein's body was returned to Wichita, appropriately, for burial. Those who knew him poured forth accolades of remembrance of the little German immigrant, frontiersman, Indian trader, friend to the red man, leader in civic and economic progress, a man who had experienced the old West in its infancy and had labored diligently to develop a "fair city" at the mouth of the Little Arkansas.

It was felt by many that no one represented the good part of the old West better than did Bill Greiffenstein. He had died almost as the clock of the century struck, leaving behind a Wichita that was on its way to becoming the largest city in Kansas, a modern metropolis on the Plains that would remember with pride its sometimes rowdy but always colorful western days.

Notes

Key to Abbreviations

NA — National Archives

OIA — Office of Indian Affairs

CoIA — Commissioner of Indian Affairs

LR — Letters received

OHS — Oklahoma Historical Society

OU Div./MS — Oklahoma University Division of Manuscripts

AGO — Adjutant General's Office

KHS — Kansas Historical Society

HofR — House of Representatives

Chapter One

1. *Arkansas Intelligencer*, May 19, October 27, 1849.
2. Ibid., June 2, 1849.
3. Bolton, *Coronado*, 288–89.
4. Translation of Castañeda, Winship, *The Coronado Expedition, 1540–1542*, 217.
5. *Arkansas Intelligencer*, May 19, 1849.
6. Bolton, *Coronado*, 29–93.
7. It is unclear as to whether the message was carved on a stone or wood. If stone was used, then it may well be that the historic marker still rests somewhere under the Kansas soil today.
8. Bolton, *Coronado*, 335–41; *Survey of Historic Sites*, 32.
9. Bolton, *Spanish Exploration*, 200–201.
10. Hammond and Rey, *Don Juan de Oñate*, 5: 416–19.
11. Ibid., 6: 746–60; Bolton, *Spanish Exploration*, 250–65. See also Newcomb and Campbell, "Southern Plains Ethnohistory," 30.
12. Hammond and Rey, *Don Juan de Oñate*, 754–55.
13. Ibid., 757.

14. Thomas, *After Coronado*, 8–9; Hyde, *Indians of the High Plains*, 13.
15. Thomas, *After Coronado*, 53.
16. Hyde, *The Pawnee Indians*, 39–72.
17. Nuttall, *Journal of Travels into the Arkansas Territory*, 109; Bentley, ed., *History of Wichita* 1: 115.
18. Barry, *The Beginning of the West*, 317.
19. Bolton and Stephens, eds., *French Intrusions into New Mexico*, 400–404.
20. Ibid., 396–98.
21. Bolton, *Athanase de Mézières and the Louisiana-Texas Frontier*, 48.
22. *Wichita Eagle*, August 30, 1872; July 20, 1882.
23. Lieutenant J. B. Wilkinson's Report, appendix 2 to part 2, Pike, *An Account of Expeditions to the Sources of the Mississippi*, 20–32.
24. Barry, *Beginning of the West*, 70.
25. "Journal of Jules De Mun," 55–56; Barry, *Beginning of the West*, 76–77.
26. Thwaites, ed., *James' Account of S. H. Long's Expedition*, 239.
27. Ibid.
28. Ibid.
29. Coues, ed., *The Journal of Jacob Fowler*, 18–19.
30. Thomas James, *Three Years among the Indians and Mexicans*, 161–81.
31. *Arkansas Intelligencer*, May 19, 1849.
32. *Arkansas Gazette*, June 8, 1831; January 18, 1832.
33. *Arkansas Intelligencer*, May 19, 1849.
34. Barry, *Beginning of the West*, 317.
35. *Arkansas Intelligencer*, June 2, 1849.
36. Ibid., May 19, October 24, 1849.
37. *Herald of Freedom* (Lawrence), December 5, 1857.

Chapter Two

1.   Bentley, ed., *History of Wichita* 1: 9; Mead, "The Little Arkansas," 7–14.
2.   Bentley, ed., *History of Wichita*, 1: 123; Mead, "Little Arkansas," 9.
3.   Mead, "Little Arkansas," 9.
4.   *Wichita Eagle*, July 10, 1873.
5.   Ibid., August 14, 1873.
6.   Bentley, ed., *History of Wichita*, 1: 116.
7.   *Wichita Eagle*, March 1, 1883; Early History of Wichita and Sedgwick County Scrapbook, compiled by Wichita Public Library, 1932, vol. 1 of 2 vols, 23–25; *Wichita Vidette*, August 13, 1870.
8.   Bentley, ed., *History of Wichita*, 1: 116, 125; Andreas, *History of the State of Kansas*, 2: 1384; Mead, "Little Arkansas," 9–10.
9.   Bentley, ed., *History of Wichita*, 1: 116; Mead, "Little Arkansas," 10.
10. Bentley, ed., *History of Wichita*, 1: 116; Andreas, *History of the State of Kansas*, 2: 1384, 1388.
11. *Report of the Commissioner of Indian Affairs, 1868*, 748–51;

Thoburn, "Battle with Comanches," 22–28.

12. *Report of the Commissioner of Indian Affairs, 1859*, 587.

13. U.S. War Department, *The War of Rebellion*, series 1, vol. 1, 648.

14. Mead, *Hunting and Trading*, 126, ns. 1, 2.

15. Thoburn, "Horace P. Jones," 383–85.

16. *Emporia News*, December 6, 1862.

17. Mead, *Hunting and Trading*, 151.

18. *Report of the Commissioner of Indian Affairs, 1864*, 30, 304. The Wichita chiefs also brought with them a large number of scalps and, wrapped in a rebel flag, papers belonging to the Wichita agency. *Report of the Commissioner of Indian Affairs, 1865*, 259.

19. Bentley, ed., *History of Wichita*, 1: 125.

20. Ibid.

21. Ibid., 529.

22. A short time before his death in 1910, Mead evidently told O. H. Bentley (*History of Wichita*, 1: 115) that in 1864 he built a trading post between the Great and Little Arkansas rivers. This was probably a memory failure, however, for in no other of his many accounts does Mead make this claim. He does say in several of his writings that he was a visitor to the Indian camps during 1864. See *Wichita Eagle*, March 7, 1890; Mead "The Little Arkansas," *Collections*, 11.

23. *Wichita Eagle*, March 7, 1890.

Chapter Three

1. Unrau, "Indian Agent vs. the Army," 129–52, provides a thorough discussion of the complex events leading up to the 1865 treaty.

2. Abel, *The Slaveholding Indians*, 274.

3. Sanborn to Leavenworth, August 14, 1865, Selected Letters by Office of Indian Affairs, 1864–68, Indian Archives, OHS; Hyde, *Life of George Bent*, 247.

4. Mead, *Hunting and Trading*, 176.

5. *Kansas Daily Tribune*, September 13, 14, October 5, 1865.

6. "Diary of Samuel A. Kingman," 442–50.

7. Ibid.

8. Mead, *Hunting and Trading*, 176.

9. Bentley, ed., *History of Wichita*, 1: 128.

10. *Report of the Commissioner of Indian Affairs, 1866*, 701–2.

11. "Diary of Samuel A. Kingman," 446.

12. *Report of the Commissioner of Indian Affairs, 1866*, 704.

13. Hyde, *Life of George Bent*, 248.

14. *Report of the Commissioner of Indian Affairs, 1866*, 709. The occasion referred to by Black Kettle was the 1825 peace-making expedition under Gen. Henry Atkinson.

15. Ibid., 717.

16. Ibid.

17. "Diary of Samuel A. Kingman," 447. Though his name was not

given, the black man from Texas may well have been Bret Johnson, whose family had been taken captive during a Kiowa raid in 1864. Hoig, *The Kiowas*, 93.

18. *Report of the Commissioner of Indian Affairs, 1866*, 718–19.
19. Ibid.
20. "Diary of Samuel A. Kingman," 448.
21. Ibid.
22. Ibid.
23. *Leavenworth Times*, November 26, 1865.

Chapter Four

1. Bentley, ed., *History of Wichita*, 1: 529.
2. Mead, *Hunting and Trading*, 152.
3. Ibid., 127, 535; Dorsey, *The Mythology of the Wichitas*, 1–7; *Report of the Commissioner of Indian Affairs, 1869*, 528.
4. Buntin, "The Removal of the Wichitas," 65, citing Byers to Gookins, February 28, 1866.
5. *Report of the Commissioner of Indian Affairs, 1866*, 220.
6. Gookins report, Wichita Agency, April 14, 1866, Indian Houses File, Kiowa Agency, Indian Archives, OHS.
7. Shanklin to Commissioner of Indian Affairs, Wichita Agency, July 6, 1866, Agents and Agency File, Kiowa Agency, Indian Archives, OHS.
8. Ibid.
9. Shanklin to Colonel E. Sells, July 13, 1866, Depredations File, Kiowa Agency, Indian Archives, OHS.
10. Shanklin to Commissioner of Indian Affairs, July 6, 1866, ibid.
11. Buntin, "Removal of the Wichitas," 66–67.
12. Ibid., 67–68.
13. Byers to Shanklin, November 20, 1866, Removal File, Kiowa Agency, Indian Archives, OHS.
14. *Report of the Commissioner of Indian Affairs, 1867*, 322.
15. Shanklin to Secretary of Interior, April 3, 1867, Removal File, Kiowa Agency, Indian Archives, OHS.
16. Shanklin letter, May 6, 1867, ibid.
17. Shanklin letter, May 21, 1867, ibid.
18. Shanklin to Taylor, Wichita Agency, June 1, 1867, ibid.
19. Buntin, "Removal of the Wichitas," 62.
20. Shanklin to Taylor, June 1, 1867, Removal File, Kiowa Agency, Indian Archives, OHS.
21. Wortham to Shanklin, July 16, 1867, ibid.
22. *Report of the Commissioner of Indian Affairs, 1866*, 330.
23. *Kansas Daily Tribune*, August 2, 1867.
24. Shanklin Report, Wichita Agency, September 1, 1867, partial copy in Kiowa Files, Indian Archives. OHS.
25. Shanklin to Wortham, August 12, 1867, ibid.

26. Wichita Scrapbooks, 1: 13–14, citing *Bulletin No. 83*, Bureau of American Ethnology article by Dr. Fordyce Grinnell, 1879.

27. *Wichita Eagle*, April 26, 1872.

28. U.S. War Department, *The War of Rebellion*, series 4, 1: 548; *Wichita Eagle*, March 1, 1883.

29. Shanklin to N. G. Taylor, Wichita Agency, June 1, 1867, Removal File, Kiowa Agency, Indian Archives, OHS.

30. Hyde, *Life of George Bent*, 280–81.

31. Ibid., 281.

32. Leavenworth to Mathewson, August 5, 1867, Selected Letters, Office of Indian Affairs, OHS.

33. Shanklin to Wortham, October 21, 1867, Removal File, Kiowa Agency, Indian Archives, OHS.

34. *Kansas Daily Tribune*, August 2, 1867.

35. Carolyn Thomas Foreman, "Black Beaver," 281–82.

36. *Leavenworth Daily Conservative*, November 21, 1867; *Report of the Commissioner of Indian Affairs, 1867*, 330–31.

37. McCusker to Murphy, November 15, 1867, Ltrs. OIA, Wichita Agency, 1867–75, M234, Roll 929, NA.

38. Butler, "Pioneer School Teaching," 489.

39. *Kansas Daily Tribune*, December 20, 1867.

Chapter Five

1. C. B. Johnson to Brig. Gen. William Steele, September 18, 1863, U.S. War Department, *The War of Rebellion*, I, 22, 2: 1020–21.

2. A letter from Chisholm to Agent Gookins dated February 6, 1865, issued claim against the Wichitas for their residing on his land, Chisholm Ranch. This implies that Chisholm arrived there before the Wichitas moved down from the Walnut. C. Ross Hume Collection, Box 29, Item 12, OU Div./MS.

3. For a full account of Chisholm's life, see Hoig, *Jesse Chisholm, Ambassador of the Plains*.

4. C.S.A. officer to Charles Johnson, December 16, 1862, Special Collections Department, University of Arkansas Library.

5. Letter from M. Gookins, November 1, 1864, *Emporia News*, November 12, 1864.

6. *Leavenworth Times*, January 28, February 8, 10, 11, 12, 16, 17, 28, 1864.

7. *Wichita Eagle*, March 7, 1890; Mead, *Hunting and Trading*, 194–95.

8. *Leavenworth Times*, September 8, 1865.

9. J. R. Mead, *Wichita Eagle*, March 7, 1890; *Daily Oklahoman*, November 17, 1907; Mead, "Trails in Southern Kansas," 93.

10. Mead, *Hunting and Trading*, 194.

11. *Daily Oklahoman*, November 17, 1907. On another occasion, Mead said that Chisholm returned to his former trading post, with trader Henry Donnell going along as far as the Red Fork

(Cimarron River). "On this Mr. Chisholm naturally selected the most direct and practicable route. This was the first wagon train to pass over the great trail that by common consent was given the name of 'Chisholm,' from the man who located it." *Wichita Eagle*, March 7, 1890.

12. Just when Chisholm made the trip that is said to have opened the trail between the Little Arkansas and Council Grove is unclear. Chisholm's adopted son George (also known as Vincente) said that Jesse's initial trip was made in the spring of 1865, following the faint trace left by the retreating Union forces in 1861. Taylor, *Jesse Chisholm*, 74–75.

13. Service of Jesse Chisholm, Selected Ltrs., Kiowa Agency, 1864–68, NA.

14. U.S. War Department, *The War of Rebellion*, series I, vol. 48, pt. 2, 1021.

15. Chisholm to Leavenworth, July 14, 1865, ibid.

16. Chisholm to Leavenworth, August 1, 1865, ibid. Jackson was a rescued Mexican captive whom Chisholm had taken into his family unit. After Jesse's death Jackson would marry Jesse's widow Sah-kah-kee.

17. *Emporia News*, December 24, 1866.

18. *Leavenworth Daily Conservative*, May 8, 1868.

19. Mead gives the date of Chisholm's death as March 4, 1868, and this has long been accepted by historians. However, the Chisholm family Bible indicates his death was April 4, and this is supported by newspaper records. Chisholm Family Bible, Jesse Chisholm File, Barker Texas History Collection, University of Texas; *Leavenworth Daily Conservative*, May 8, 1868.

20. *Wichita Eagle*, September 29, 1899.

21. *Portrait and Biographical Album of Sedgwick County*, 166–67. As Carson explained it: "Mr. Maxwell and I now rigged up a party of eighteen men to go trapping, I taking charge of them." Quaife, ed., *Kit Carson's Autobiography*, 146.

22. Andreas, *History of the State of Kansas*, 2: 1398.

23. Mead, *Hunting and Trading*, 178.

24. William Chisholm to Leavenworth, December 30, 1868, Ltrs. Recd., Kiowa Agency, 1869–70, NA.

25. Mead, *Hunting and Trading*, 196; McCoy, *Historic Sketches of the Cattle Trade*, 50–62.

26. Leavenworth to Commissioner of Indian Affairs, September 2, 1867, Ltrs. Recd., Kiowa Agency, 1864–68, NA.

27. *Wichita Eagle*, March 7, 1890.

28. *Kansas Daily Tribune*, May 12, 1868.

29. *Wichita Eagle*, March 7, 1890. As noted previously, Mead misremembered the date of Chisholm's death, which was April 4 rather than March 4, 1868.

30. *Leavenworth Daily Conservative*, May 8, 1868.

31. *Kansas Daily Tribune*, February 11, 21, 1868; *Emporia News*, December 20, 1867.

32. *Leavenworth Times*, February 26, 1867.

33. Ibid., January 31, 1867.

34. Ibid., June 25, 1867.

35. McCoy, *Historic Sketches of the Cattle Trade*, 50, 261.

36. Map of the Indian Territory by Alvin J. Johnson and Son, 1880, OHS; map accompanying William E. Strong, *Canadian River Hunt, 1876*.

37. McCusker ltr., November 15, 1867, Ltrs. Recd., OTA, Wichita Agency, 1867–75, Roll 78, NA.

Chapter Six

1. *Portrait and Biographical Album of Sedgwick County*, 162–66; Murdock, *Folks*, 5–8; *Wichita Eagle*, April 16, 1876; September 29, 1899.

2. *Wichita Eagle*, September, 28, 1899.

3. Ibid., September 29, 1899.

4. Ibid.

5. Ibid. Mead also tells of a time when a party of outlaws stopped a stage on which Greiffenstein was riding and robbed him. It may be that this story comes from the same incident. Mead, *Hunting and Trading*, 117.

6. *Wichita Eagle*, September, 29, 1899.

7. Mead, *Hunting and Trading*, 224.

8. *Wichita Eagle*, September 29, 1899.

9. Ibid.

10. Greiffenstein to Taylor, September 14, 1868, Ltrs. Recd., Kiowa Agency, 1865–68, NA.

11. *Portrait and Biographical Album of Sedgwick County*, 165.

12. Hyde, *Life of George Bent*, 282.

13. Walkley to Hazen, October 10, 1868, Rister Collection, OU Div./MS.

14. Connelley, "John McBee's Account," 361.

15. For a more detailed account of the march of the Nineteenth Kansas and the Washita battle see Hoig, *The Battle of the Washita*, 98–111.

16. The bodies of Major Elliott, Mrs. Blinn, and her child were taken to Fort Arbuckle and buried, later being moved to other burial sites.

17. Hazen to Nichols, November 25, 1868, Ltrs. Recd. Office of the AG, NA.

18. *Portrait and Biographical Album of Sedgwick County*, 165.

19. Ellington, "The Story Behind William Street," 6.

20. *Leavenworth Daily Conservative*, February 25, 1869.

21. Late in life James Mead said that he knew Sheridan's charges to

be valid (Mead, *Hunting*, 117, fn. 3); but in a letter to the *Wichita Eagle*, March 3, 1893, Mead said that Sheridan had ordered Dutch Bill out of the Territory because Greiffenstein had told the officer that Custer had made a mistake in striking a camp of friendly Indians.

22. Murdock, "Vision of Wichita," *Wichita Eagle*, June 30, 1929.
23. *Wichita Eagle*, November 29, 1899.
24. *Emporia News*, August 20, 1869.
25. Ibid.; *Kansas Daily Tribune*, September 4, 1869.
26. *Emporia News*, September 10, 1869.
27. *Portrait and Biographical Album of Sedgwick County*, 165; McIsaac, "William Greiffenstein," 20–21, citing *Collections of the KSHS, 1913–1914* 13: 371–77.

Chapter Seven

1. *Kansas Daily Tribune*, August 1, 1869.
2. Though Kansans today emphasize the "kansas" portion of the name of the Arkansas River, evidence that the "Ar'-kan-saw" pronunciation was used by early settlers can be found in the verse by early residents which appeared in the *Wichita Eagle* on September 9, 1875 and February 2 and March 9, 1882, where Arkansas is rhymed with "saw," "draw," "law," and "Wichita." In some cases the word was written as "Arkansaw."
3. September 14, 1866; Andreas, *History of the State of Kansas*, 2: 1385.
4. Bentley, ed., *History of Wichita*, 1: 7; *Wichita Eagle*, March 1, 1883; *Emporia News*, July 12, 1867.
5. Andreas, *History of the State of Kansas*, 2: 1385; *Wichita Eagle*, March 1, 1883; *Emporia News*, July 12, 1867.
6. *Emporia News*, December 20, 1867.
7. *Leavenworth Times and Conservative*, December 18, 1868.
8. Long, *Wichita Century*, 120; *Wichita Eagle*, May 4, 1888.
9. Andreas, *History of the State of Kansas*, 2: 1389; Bentley, ed., *History of Wichita*, 1: 6.
10. Mead, *Hunting and Trading*, 13.
11. *Kansas Daily Tribune*, May 31, 1868.
12. Campbell, "Camp Beecher," 173.
13. Runyon, "A. L. Runyon's Letters," 64.
14. Jenness, manuscript, 15–17.
15. Spotts, *Campaigning with Custer*, 51–52.
16. Miner, *Wichita*, 35.
17. Ibid., 174–78.
18. Ibid., 36–37.
19. *Wichita Eagle*, April 6, 1876.
20. Miner, *Wichita*, 27.
21. Ibid.
22. Andreas, *History of the State of Kansas*, 2: 135.

23. Campbell, "Camp Beecher," 175.
24. *Wichita Vidette*, August 13, 1870; *Wichita Tribune*, March 15, 1871; Root, "Ferries in Kansas," 186–87.
25. Root, "Ferries in Kansas," 186–87.
26. Wichita Scrapbook, 1: 269; Long, *Wichita Century*, 22; *Wichita Eagle*, October 3, 1920.
27. Murdock, "The Buckhorn Hotel."
28. Ibid.
29. Andreas, *History of the State of Kansas*, 2: 1389.
30. Ibid., 1385; Long, "Wichita Knew Cordiero as Picturesque Pioneer," 322–24.
31. *Wichita Tribune*, July 6, 1871; *Emporia News*, January 21, 1870.
32. Andreas, *History of the State of Kansas*, 2: 1389.
33. Ibid.
34. Ibid.
35. Coyne, "David L. Payne," 19; *Indian Chieftain*, December 1, 1884.
36. Spotts, *Campaigning with Custer*, 127.
37. *Wichita Vidette*, September 1, 1870.
38. Ibid., October 13, 1870.
39. *Emporia News*, December 16, 1870.
40. Ibid., November 18, 1870.
41. Ibid., December 16, 1870. The *Wichita Vidette* told the story much differently, claiming that Corbin had been captured by a settler and his two sons by tracking their stolen animals to the gang's camp. Attacking the hideout, the three killed several of the horse thieves and captured Corbin, who was promptly hanged. November 10 and December 8, 1870.
42. *Emporia News*, December 16, 1870.
43. *Wichita Eagle*, April 6, 1876; Andreas, *History of the State of Kansas*, 2: 1386.

Chapter Eight

1. Murdock, *Folks*, 5; *Wichita Eagle*, April 1, 1875; September 29, 1899.
2. *Wichita Eagle*, January 16, 1878.
3. Ibid., October 24, December 12, 1872; April 1, 1875; June 18, 1891; *Wichita City Directory and Immigrant's Guide*, 15.
4. Wichita Scrapbook 1: 235–36; Murdock, "Genius of Wichita's Father, Wm. Greiffenstein," *Wichita Eagle*, August 9, 1923.
5. *Wichita Tribune*, March 15, 1871.
6. *Wichita Eagle*, May 13, 1887; February 7, 1888.
7. American Guide project, Wichita State University, from *Edward's Historical Atlas*, 1882.
8. Andreas, *History of the State of Kansas* 2; 1389; Long, *Wichita Century*, 26; *Wichita Eagle*, May 24, 1872.
9. *Wichita Eagle*, December 12, 1872.
10. Ibid.

11. Andreas, *History of the State of Kansas* 2: 1391. By July 1870 the hotel was placed under the operation of P. C. Hubbard and renamed.
12. *Emporia News*, July 8, 1870.
13. Ibid.
14. Ibid.
15. Ibid., July 1, 1870.
16. Ibid.
17. Ibid., July 15, 1870.
18. Ibid.
19. Ibid.
20. Long, *Wichita Century*, 28–30; *Wichita Tribune*, March 15, 1871. An excellent account of the brief stay in Wichita of Billy the Kid and his family can be found in Koop, "Billy the Kid, the Trail of a Kansas Legend."
21. Koop, "Billy the Kid, the Trail of a Kansas Legend."
22. *Wichita Vidette*, August 13, 1870.
23. *White Cloud Chief*, March 28, 1872.
24. Ibid., March 28, 1870; Andreas, *History of the State of Kansas* 2: 1390.
25. *Wichita Vidette*, October 27, 1870.
26. Ibid., December 22, 1870.
27. Ibid., June 27, 1871.
28. Ibid., August 25, 1870.
29. *Wichita Tribune*, August 31, 1871.
30. Ibid., September 7, 1871.
31. Andreas, *History of the State of Kansas* 2: 1390.
32. Ibid.; *Wichita Eagle*, January 2, 1873; Murdock, "Pioneer Ferry," ibid., November 17, 1932; Root, "Ferries in Kansas," 186–89.
33. *Wichita Eagle*, September 29, 1899.
34. Ibid., April 6, 1876; *Wichita Tribune*, July 6, 1871.
35. Long, *Wichita Century*, 31, 82; *Wichita Eagle*, October 24, 1872.
36. *Wichita Eagle*, September 29, 1899.
37. Andreas, *History of the State of Kansas* 2: 1385.
38. *Wichita Eagle*, November 7, 1872.
39. Ibid., April 12, 1872.

Chapter Nine

1. *Wichita Eagle*, April 10, 1891.
2. McCoy, *Historic Sketches of the Cattle Trade* 148–49, 190, 201.
3. *Emporia News*, September 10, 1869.
4. *Kansas Daily Tribune*, September 17, 1869.
5. Ibid., August 1, 1871.
6. Ibid.
7. *Wichita Eagle*, August 14, 1873.
8. McCoy, *Historic Sketches of the Cattle Trade*, 412.
9. *Wichita Eagle*, February 28, 1884; Mead, *Hunting and Trading*, 232–34.

10. Mead, *Hunting and Trading*, 236–37.

11. *Wichita Eagle*, October 24, December 12, 1872.

12. Gard, *The Chisholm Cattle Trail*, 184; *Wichita Eagle*, April 19, 26; May 10, 24; June 7, 1872.

13. *Wichita Eagle*, July 10, 1873.

14. Ibid., May 29, 1873.

15. *Wichita Eagle*, April 12, 1872.

16. Ibid. January 9, April 24, 1873.

17. Ibid., March 20, 1873.

18. Ibid.

19. Ibid., January 2, February 13, 1873.

20. Ibid., July 10, 1873.

21. Ibid., February 13, 1873.

22. Ibid., March 27, 1873.

23. Ibid., May 1, 1873.

24. Ibid., May 22, 29; June 5, 1873.

25. Ibid., April 10, 1873.

26. Ibid., April 16, 1874.

27. Ibid., June 11, 25, 1874.

28. B. K. Wetherell letter, July 4, 1884, to Enoch Hoag, Kiowa Depredations File, Indian Archives, OHS; *Report of the Commissioner of Indian Affairs, 1874*, 234.

29. John D. Miles to Commissioner of Indian Affairs, July 7, 1874, in *Kansas Daily Tribune*, July 8, 1874.

30. *Wichita Eagle*, July 21, 1875.

Chapter Ten

1. Andreas, *History of the State of Kansas* 2: 1390.

2. Ibid., 2: 1393.

3. Ibid., 2: 1388; Miller and Snell, *Great Gunfighters*, 33–35.

4. *Wichita Vidette*, March 11, 1871; *Emporia News*, March 10, 1871.

5. Andreas, *History of the State of Kansas* 2: 1391.

6. *Wichita Eagle*, December 2, 1875.

7. Andreas, *History of the State of Kansas* 2: 1390; *Wichita Eagle*, December 5, 1885, quoting the *St. Louis Globe*, July 13, 1873.

8. *Wichita Eagle*, December 2, 1875.

9. Bentley, ed., *History of Wichita*, 1: 458–59.

10. Andreas, *History of the State of Kansas* 2: 1390.

11. Ibid.; *Wichita Eagle*, April 12, 1872.

12. June 22, 1871.

13. *Wichita Eagle*, October 3, 1872.

14. Wichita Scrapbook, 1: 317, clipping of Long, "Six-shooters Once Used as Fly-Swatters in Wichita"; *Wichita Eagle*, November 7, 1872.

15. Bentley, ed., *History of Wichita*, 1: 120, 133.

16. *St. Louis Globe*, July 13, 1873, as reprinted by the *Wichita Eagle*, December 5, 1885.

17. Ibid.
18. Ibid.
19. Ibid.
20. Ibid.
21. Ibid.
22. *Wichita Eagle*, October 24, 1872, citing the *Topeka Commonwealth*.
23. Ibid.
24. Ibid., January 16, 1873.
25. Miller and Snell, *Great Gunfighters*, 156–57.
26. *Wichita Eagle*, June 5, 1873.
27. Ibid., June 21, 1871, October 30, 1873; Andreas, *History of the State of Kansas* 2: 1389; Miller and Snell, *Great Gunfighters*, 158.
28. Miller and Snell, *Great Gunfighters*, 167–68.
29. *Wichita Eagle*, December 19, 1872.
30. Ibid., July 12, 1872.
31. Ibid., November 13, 1873.
32. Ibid., November 4, 1875.
33. Long, *Wichita Century*, 51.

Chapter Eleven

1. *Wichita Eagle*, April 6, 1876.
2. Miller and Snell, *Great Gunfighters*, 343–44.
3. Ibid., 575; *Wichita Eagle*, January 16, 1878, April 6, 1876; Andreas, *History of the State of Kansas* 2: 1388.
4. First Records of the City of Wichita, I, entry April 10, 1871.
5. Miller and Snell, *Great Gunfighters*, 346.
6. *Wichita Eagle*, October 10, 1872.
7. Ibid., October 29, 1874.
8. January 4, 1874.
9. *Wichita Beacon*, December 15, 1875.
10. Ibid., April 5, 1876.
11. Miller and Snell, *Great Gunfighters*, 90–91.
12. *Wichita Eagle*, January 4, 1877; Wichita Scrapbook, 1: 329–30.
13. *Wichita Eagle*, August 7, 1885.
14. *Caldwell Post*, April 8, 15, 1880; Miller and Snell, *Great Gunfighters*, 360.
15. November 5, 1881.
16. *Caldwell Post*, December 22, 1881.
17. Miller and Snell, *Great Gunfighters*, 361–67.
18. Ibid., 368.
19. *Caldwell Post*, December 22, 1881.

Chapter Twelve

1. *Wichita Eagle*, November 14, 1872.
2. Ibid., June 19, 1872.
3. Ibid., November 9, 1872.

4. Ibid., August 2, 1872.
5. Bentley, ed., *History of Wichita*, 1: 239.
6. *Wichita Eagle*, July 17, 1879.
7. Ibid., January 2, 1879.
8. April 25, 1878.
9. *Wichita Eagle*, ibid.
10. Ibid., January 31, February 28, 1878.
11. Ibid.
12. Ibid., July 17, 1885.
13. Ibid., August 7, 1885.
14. Ibid., October 3, 1878.
15. Wichita Scrapbook, 2: 539–44; Morehouse, "Memories of a Wichita Pageant Staged by Indians," *Wichita Eagle*, November 21, 1928.
16. *Wichita Eagle*, November 10, 1878.
17. Hoig, *Tribal Wars*, 294–95.
18. Ibid., December 26, 1878; *Congressional Record*, December 5, 1878.
19. *Wichita Eagle*, June 7, 1941.
20. Ibid., June 26, July 3, 1879.
21. Ibid., January 20, 1879.
22. Ibid., May 15, 1879.
23. Ibid., September 11, 1879.
24. Ibid., October 2, 1879.
25. Ibid., November 27, 1879.
26. Ibid., April 3, 1879, citing *North American Review*, April 1879.

Chapter Thirteen
1. *Wichita Eagle*, quoting W. D. Brewer, Newspaper Clipping, Athey Collection, OHS. For a complete account of Payne and the Oklahoma Boomer movement, see Hoig, *David L. Payne.*
2. Andreas, *History of the State of Kansas* 2: 1387; *Leavenworth Conservative*, March 5, 1868.
3. Andreas, *History of the State of Kansas* 2: 1387.
4. Coyne, "David L. Payne," 18.
5. Ibid., 26–27.
6. The Newton *Kansan*, November 8, 1877.
7. *HofR Report No. 29*, 46th Cong., 2d. sess., 1879, 104.
8. Woodward to Neil, May 8, 1879, LR/AGO, NA.
9. *Wichita Eagle*, August 5, 1880.
10. *Wichita Beacon*, January 14, 1880.
11. Hoig, *David L. Payne*, 64.
12. *Wichita Eagle*, February 19, 1880.
13. Bloss MS on David L. Payne, Athey Collection, OHS, 40–41.
14. Interview of Harry Hill, *New York Sun*, February 7, 1889; account of E. H. Kirk, Athley Collection; statement of Harry Stafford, *Oklahoma War Chief*, July 23, 1885.

15. *Federal Reporter* 7: 884.
16. Pardee to Pope, May 2, 1880, LR/AGO, NA.
17. Acct. of Second Expedition, Athey Collection; *Wichita Beacon*, July 21, 1880; *Caldwell Commercial*, August 3, 1880.
18. Bloss MS on David L. Payne, 55; Whipple to AAG, Fort Leavenworth, July 16, 1880, LR/AGO, NA.
19. Payne and others to Pope, August 2, 1880, LR/AGO, NA.
20. *Wichita Beacon*, September 8, 1880.
21. *Wichita Eagle*, September 9, 1880.
22. Acct. of Third Expedition, Athey Collection; Coyne, "David L. Payne," 64.
23. Telegram to Payne, Athey Collection.
24. May 5, 1881.
25. *Wichita Eagle*, August 25, 1881.
26. Osburn, "Tribute to Payne," *Wichita Beacon*, February 1, 1882.
27. Payne's Diary, Athey Collection.
28. Ibid.
29. Osburn, "Tribute to Payne," 13.
30. Taylor to Post Adj., Fort Reno, September 30, 1882, LR/AGO, NA.
31. Osburn, "Tribute to Payne," 23.
32. *Oklahoma War Chief*, March 23, 1883; Osburn, "Tribute to Payne," 27–28.
33. Couch to Payne, August 22, 1883, Athey Collection.
34. "Letters to Payne" File, Athey Collection; *Wichita Beacon*, February 13, April 30, 1884.
35. *Oklahoma War Chief*, April 26, 1884; July 9, 23, 1885.
36. Day to AAG Fort Reno, May 8, 1884, LR/AGO, NA.
37. *Oklahoma War Chief*, June 14, July 17, 1884; Hatch to AAG, June 22, 26, 1884, LR/AGO, NA.
38. Rogers to Hatch, July 25, 1885, LR/AGO, NA.
39. Payne's Diary, Athey Collection; Mosely Account, Athey Collection; Payne letters, *Historia* 8 (July 1, 1920).
40. Koller, "Boomer Days" pamphlet, Athey Collection; *Oklahoma War Chief*, April 1909.
41. *Wichita Eagle*, December 3, 1884.

Chapter Fourteen

1. *Wichita Eagle*, July 28, August 11, 18, 1881.
2. *Wichita Weekly Beacon*, June 1, 1887.
3. *Wichita Eagle*, April 13, 1882.
4. Ibid., April 27, 1882.
5. Ibid., April 20, 1882.
6. Ibid., March 23, 1882.
7. Ibid., September 27, 1883.
8. Ibid., November 8, 1883.
9. Ibid., December 13, 20, 27, 1883; January 24, 1884.

10. Ibid., February 28, 1884.
11. *Harper's Illustrated Weekly*, April 5, 1884.
12. Ibid.
13. Ibid., April 8, 1884; *Wichita Beacon*, April 16, 1884.
14. *Daily Oklahoman*, December 26, 1927.
15. *Wichita Eagle*, December 9, 1887.
16. Ibid., November 23, 1888.
17. *Wichita Beacon*, February 6, 1889; *Arkansas City Traveler*, February 14, 1889; *Wichita Eagle*, February 8, 1889.

Chapter Fifteen

1. *Wichita Beacon*, May 9, 16, 23, 1888.
2. Murdock, *Folks*, 147–48.
3. *Wichita Beacon*, December 12, 1883.
4. Ibid., December 12, 1883.
5. Ibid., July 22, 1885.
6. Murdock, *Folks*, 148.
7. *Wichita Eagle*, April 12, 1889.
8. Ibid.
9. Ibid.
10. *Caldwell Journal*, May 9, 1889.
11. *Wichita Eagle*, May 10, 1889, citing *Emporia Republican*.
12. *Wichita Beacon Evening News*, May 17, 1889.
13. Ibid., June 21, 1889.
14. Ibid., August 3, 1889.
15. Ibid.
16. *Wichita Eagle*, August 3, 1889.
17. Ibid., August 4, 1889.
18. *Wichita Beacon*, August 8, 1889.
19. *Wichita Eagle*, August 10, 1889.
20. *Wichita Beacon*, August 15, 1889.
21. *Wichita Eagle*, September 29, 1899; *Daily Oklahoman*, December 26, 1927.

Bibliography

Articles

Barry, Louise. "Kansas before 1854: A Revised Annal." *Kansas State Historical Quarterly* 27 (spring 1961) to 33 (autumn 1967).

———, ed. "With the First U.S. Cavalry in Indian Country, 1859–61." *Kansas State Historical Quarterly* 24 (autumn 1958).

Buntin, Martha. "The Removal of the Wichitas from Butler, County, Kansas, to the Present Agency." *Panhandle-Plains Historical Review* 4 (1931).

Butler, Josiah. "Pioneer School Teaching at the Comanche-Kiowa Agency School, 1870–73." *Chronicles of Oklahoma* 6 (December 1928).

Campbell, Hortense Balderston. "Camp Beecher." *Kansas State Historical Quarterly* 3 (May 1934).

Chapman, Berlin B. "Establishment of the Wichita Reservation." *Chronicles of Oklahoma* 11 (December 1933).

"The Chisholm Trail." *Kansas State Historical Quarterly* 33 (summer 1967).

Connelley, William E. "John McBee's Account of the Expedition of the Nineteenth Kansas." *Kansas Historical Collections* 17 (1926–28).

"Diary of Samuel A. Kingman at Indian Treaty in 1865." *Kansas State Historical Quarterly* 1 (November 1932).

Dorsey, George Amos. "The Mythology of the Wichitas." Carnegie Institution of Washington Publications. Washington, D.C., 1904.

Doty, Francis. "Early History of Sedgwick." Sedgwick *Pantagraph*, May 14, 1931, Wichita Public Library.

Ellis, Richard N., ed. "Bent, Carson, and the Indians, 1865." *Colorado Magazine* 46 (winter 1969).

Foreman, Carolyn Thomas. "Black Beaver." *Chronicles of Oklahoma* 24 (autumn 1946).

———. "Col. Jesse Henry Leavenworth." *Chronicles of Oklahoma* 13 (March 1935).

Foreman, Grant, ed. "Survey of a Wagon Road from Fort Smith to the Colorado River." *Chronicles of Oklahoma* 12 (March 1934).

Hadley, James A. "The Nineteenth Kansas Cavalry and the Conquest of the Plains Indians." *Transactions of the Kansas State Historical Society* 10 (1890).

Isely, Bliss. "Black Beaver Founded the Chisholm Trail." *Wichita Beacon*, November 8, 1925.

———. "The Grass Wigwam at Wichita." *Kansas State Historical Quarterly* 2 (February 1933).

"Journal of Jules De Mun." Translated by Nettie Harney Beauregard, edited by Thomas M. Marshall. *Missouri Historical Society Collections* 5 (1978).

Koop, W. E. "Billy the Kid, the Trail of a Kansas Legend." *The Trail Guide* 9 (September 1964).

Leahy, David D. "Pioneer Kansas Editor Told of Early Day Wichita Newspapermen." *Wichita Eagle*, December 21, 1931.

———. "Some Experiences of an Amateur Officer of the Law." *Wichita Sunday Eagle*, January 3, 1932.

Long, Dick. "Six-Shooters Once Used as Fly-Swatters in Wichita." Wichita Scrapbooks. Vol. 1. See also *Wichita Eagle*, July 5, 1926.

———. "Wichita Knew Cordiero as Picturesque Pioneer." Wichita Scrapbooks. Vol. 1. See also *Wichita Eagle*, December 26, 1926.

Masters, J. G. "Incident in Life of William Mathewson." *Omaha World-Herald*. Reprinted in *Lyons Daily News*, April 19, 1932.

Mead, James R. "The Little Arkansas." *Collections of the Kansas State Historical Society* 10 (1908).

———. "Trails in Southern Kansas." *Transactions of the Kansas State Historical Society, 1893–96* 5 (1896).

———. "The Wichita Indians in Kansas." *Collections of the Kansas State Historical Society* 8 (1904).

Miller, Nyle H., ed. "Surveying the Southern Boundary Line of Kansas." *Kansas State Historical Quarterly* 1 (February 1932).

Miller, Nyle H., and Joseph W. Snell. "Cowtown Police Officers and Gunfighters." *Kansas State Historical Quarterly* 26 (spring 1960) to 28 (autumn 1962).

Morehouse, George P. "Memories of a Wichita Pageant Staged by Indians." Wichita Scrapbooks. Vol. 2. See also *Wichita Eagle*, October 21, 1928.

Murdock, Victor. "The Buckhorn Hotel, Wichita, Kansas, Meals $25 Each." Wichita Scrapbooks. Vol. 1. See also *Wichita Eagle*, December 16, 1928.

———. "Genius of Wichita's Father, Wm. Greiffenstein." *Wichita Eagle*, August 9, 1923.

———. "How Douglas Avenue in Wichita Got Its Width." Wichita Scrapbooks. Vol. 1. See also *Wichita Eagle*, June 23, 1927.

———. "Pioneer Ferry." *Wichita Eagle*, November 1, 1932.

———. "Vision of Wichita that Sprang from a Sheridan Order." Wichita Scrapbooks. Vol. 1. See also *Wichita Eagle*, June 30, 1929.

———. "Wichita's First Schools." *Wichita Evening Eagle*, May 3, 1932.

———. "Wichita's First Social Event." *Wichita Evening Eagle*, November 14, 1932.

Newcomb, W. W., and T. N. Campbell. "Southern Plains Ethnohistory: A Re-Examination of the Escanjaques, Ahijados, and Cuitoas." Edited by Don G. Wyckoff and Jack L. Hofman. Oklahoma Anthropological Society, Memoir 3. Cross Timbers Heritage Association, Contributions 1, 1982.

Osburn, William. "A Tribute to Captain D. L. Payne by His Private Secretary, W. H. Osburn, Also Colony Secretary During the Fourth Raid." *Chronicles of Oklahoma* 8 (March 1930).

"Pioneer Scraps; History of Founding of Wichita." *Wichita Evening Eagle*, March 1 to May 6, 1933.

Richards, Ralph. "Wichita, Kansas, As I Knew It." *Wichita Eagle*, October 16 and November 3, 1936.

Root, George A. "Ferries in Kansas." *Kansas State Historical Quarterly* 5 (May 1936).

Rossel, John. "The Chisholm Trail." *Kansas State Historical Quarterly* 5 (February 1936).

Runyon, A. L. "A. L. Runyon's Letters from the Nineteenth Kansas Regiment." *Kansas State Historical Quarterly* 10 (1940).

Sowers, Frederick. "The Building of a City." *Carter's Monthly* 12 (July 1897).

Thoburn, Joseph B. "Battle with Comanches." *Sturm's Oklahoma Magazine* (August 1910).

———. "Horace P. Jones, Scout and Interpreter." *Chronicles of Oklahoma* 2 (December 1924).

"Two and Thirty Years Ago." Wichita Scrapbooks. Vol. 1. See also *Wichita Eagle*, January 1, 1909.

Unrau, William E. "Indian Agent vs. the Army: Some Background Notes on the Kiowa-Comanche Treaty of 1865." *Kansas Historical Quarterly* 30 (summer 1964).

Warden, Ernest. "Wichita's First Murder Trial." Wichita Scrapbooks. Vol. 1. See also *Wichita Eagle*, February 3, 10, 1929.

Wellman, Manly Wade. "The Killing of Jack Ledford, Early Wichita Hotel Proprietor." *Wichita Sunday Eagle*, March 27, 1932.

Wright, Muriel W. "A History of Fort Cobb." *Chronicles of Oklahoma* 34 (spring 1956).

Young, Joseph. "An Indian's View of Indian Affairs." *North American Review* 269 (April 1879).

Books

Abel, Annie Heloise. *The Slaveholding Indians*. Vol 2. *The American Indian as a Participant in the Civil War*. Cleveland: Arthur H. Clark, 1919.

Andreas, Alfred Theodore. *History of the State of Kansas.* 2 vols. Chicago: A. T. Andreas, 1883. Reprinted by Atchison County Historical Society, Topeka, 1976.

Barry, Louise. *The Beginning of the West: Annals of the Kansas Gateway to the American West, 1540–1854.* Topeka: Kansas State Historical Society, 1972.

Bentley, O. H., ed. *History of Wichita and Sedgwick County, Past and Present.* 2 vols. Chicago: C. F. Cooper, 1910.

Berthrong, Donald J. *The Southern Cheyennes.* Norman: University of Oklahoma Press, 1963.

Bolton, Herbert Eugene. *Athanase de Mézières and the Louisiana-Texas Frontier, 1768–1780.* 2 vols. Cleveland: Arthur H. Clark, 1914.

———. *Coronado, Knight of Pueblos and Plains.* Albuquerque: University of New Mexico Press, 1949.

———. *Spanish Exploration in the Southwest, 1542–1706.* New York: Charles Scribner's Sons, 1925.

Bolton, Herbert Eugene, and Henry Morse Stephens, eds. *French Intrusions into New Mexico, 1745–1752.* New York: Macmillan, 1917.

Coues, Elliott, ed. *The Journal of Jacob Fowler.* New York: Francis P. Harper, 1898.

Dorsey, George A. *The Mythology of the Wichitas.* Washington: Carnegie Institution of Washington, 1904.

Dykstra, Robert. *The Cattle Towns.* New York: Knopf, 1968.

Edwards, John P. *Historical Atlas of Sedgwick County, Kansas.* Philadelphia, 1882.

Gard, Wayne. *The Chisholm Trail.* Norman: University of Oklahoma Press, 1954.

Hammond, George P., and Agapito Rey. *Don Juan de Oñate, Colonizer of New Mexico, 1595–1628.* Coronado Historical Series, Vols. 5–6. Albuquerque: University of New Mexico Press, 1940.

———. *Narrative of the Coronado Expedition.* Albuquerque: University of New Mexico Press, 1940.

Hoig, Stan. *The Battle of the Washita.* New York: Doubleday, 1976.

———. *David L. Payne, the Oklahoma Boomer.* Oklahoma City: Heritage Books, 1980.

———. *Jesse Chisholm, Ambassador of the Plains.* Niwot, CO: University Press of Colorado, 1991; reprint: Norman: University of Oklahoma Press, 2005.

———. *The Kiowas and the Legend of Kicking Bird.* Boulder, CO: University Press of Colorado, 2000.

———. *Oklahoma Land Rush of 1889.* Oklahoma City: Oklahoma Historical Society, 1989.

———. *Tribal Wars of the Southern Plains.* Norman: University of Oklahoma Press, 1993.

Hyde, George E. *Indians of the High Plains.* Norman: University of Oklahoma Press, 1959.

———. *Life of George Bent Written from His Letters*. Edited by Savoie Lottinville. Norman: University of Oklahoma Press, 1968.

———. *The Pawnee Indians*. Norman: University of Oklahoma Press, 1974.

Illustrated History of Early Wichita. Compiled and written for the Daughters of the American Revolution. Wichita: DAR, Eunice Sterling Chapter, 1914.

Jackson, Mary E. *The Life of Nellie C. Bailey: or A Romance of the West*. Chicago: Donohue and Hennebery, 1885.

James, Edwin. *Account of an Expedition from Pittsburgh to the Rocky Mountains*. Ann Arbor, Michigan: University Microfilms, 1966.

James, Thomas. *Three Years among the Indians and the Mexicans*. Edited by W. B. Douglas. Chicago: Rio Grande Press, 1962.

Long, Richard M. *Wichita, Cradle Days of a Midwestern City*. Wichita: McCormick-Armstrong, 1945.

———. *Wichita Century*. Wichita: Wichita Historical Museum in cooperation with the Junior League of Wichita, 1969.

Long, Stephen Harriman. *Account of S. H. Long's Expedition, 1819–1820*. Compiled by Edwin James. Cleveland: Arthur H. Clark, 1905.

McCoy, Joseph G. *Historic Sketches of the Cattle Trade of the West and Southwest*. Kansas City, MO: J. T. Reton, 1874. Reprinted by the Rare Book Shop, Washington, D.C., 1932.

Mead, James R. *Hunting and Trading on the Great Plains, 1859–1875*. Edited by Schuyler Jones. Norman: University of Oklahoma Press, 1986.

Miller, Nyle H., and Joseph W. Snell. *Great Gunfighters of the Kansas Cowtowns, 1867–1886*. Lincoln: University of Nebraska Press, 1967.

Miner, H. Craig. *Wichita: The Early Years, 1865–80*. Lincoln: University of Nebraska Press, 1982.

Moses, L. G. *Wild West Shows and the Images of the American Indians, 1833–1883*. Albuquerque: University of New Mexico Press, 1996.

Murdock, Victor. *Folks*. New York: Macmillan, 1921.

Nuttall, Thomas. *Journal of Travels into the Arkansas Territory, During the Year 1819*. Philadelphia: Thos. H. Palmer, 1821.

Peerless Princess of the Plains. Compiled by Hal Ross, Hal Ottaway, and Jack Stewart. Wichita: Two Rivers, 1976.

Pike, Zebulon Montgomery. *An Account of the Expeditions to the Sources of the Mississippi and the Western Louisiana Territory*. Ann Arbor: University Microfilms, 1966.

Portrait and Biographical Album of Sedgwick County. Chicago: Chapman Bros., 1888.

Pratt, George B. *"Magic City," Wichita, Picturesque and Descriptive*. Neenah, WI: Art Publishing, 1889.

Quaife, Milo Milton, ed. *Kit Carson's Autobiography*. Chicago: R. R. Donnelley, 1935.

Ridings, Sam P. *The Chisholm Trail.* Guthrie: Co-operative Publishing, 1936.

Rister, Carl Coke. *Land Hunger.* Norman: University of Oklahoma Press, 1942.

Schmitt, Karl, and Iva Osanai Schmitt. *Wichita Kinship, Past and Present.* Norman: University of Oklahoma Press, 1953.

Simmons, Marc, *The Last Conquistador.* Norman: University of Oklahoma Press, 1991.

Souvenir 1895 of Wichita, the Commercial City of Kansas, Oklahoma and Indian Territory. Wichita: P. B. Dilday, 1895.

Spotts, David L. *Campaigning with Custer and the Nineteenth Kansas Volunteer Cavalry on the Washita Campaign, 1868–69.* Edited and arranged by E. A. Brininstool. Los Angeles: Wetzer, 1928.

Strong, General Wm. E. *Canadian River Hunt.* Norman: University of Oklahoma Press, 1960.

Survey of Historic Sites and Structures in Kansas. Topeka: Kansas State Historical Society, 1957.

Taylor, T. U. *The Chisholm Trail and Other Routes.* San Antonio, TX: Naylor, 1936.

———. *Jesse Chisholm.* Bandera, TX: Frontier Times, 1939.

Thoburn, Joseph H. *A Standard History of Oklahoma.* Chicago: American Historical Society, 1916.

Thoburn, Joseph H., and Muriel Wright. *Oklahoma, a History of the State and Its People.* 4 vols. New York: Lewis Historical, 1929.

Thomas, Alfred B. *After Coronado, Spanish Exploration Northeast of New Mexico, 1696–1727.* Norman: University of Oklahoma Press, 1966.

Thwaites, Reuben Gold, ed. *James' Account of S. H. Long's Expedition, 1819–1820.* Vol. 16, Pt. 3, *Early Western Travels.* 28 vols. Cleveland: Arthur H. Clark, 1905.

Wedel, Waldo R. *An Introduction to Kansas Archeology. Ethnology Bulletin No. 174.* Washington: GPO, 1959.

Wichita: An Illustrated Review of Its Progress and Importance. Wichita: Enterprise, 1886.

Wichita City Directory and Immigrant's Guide. Kansas City: Tierman and Wainwright, 1878.

Wichita Journal of Commerce. Wichita: Wichita Board of Trade, 1888.

Winship, George Parker. *The Coronado Expedition.* Chicago: Rio Grande Press, 1964.

Woodman, Rea. *Wichitana, 1877–1897.* Wichita, 1948.

Worchester, Don. *The Chisholm Trail, High Road of the Cattle Kingdom.* Lincoln: University of Nebraska Press, 1980.

Zornow, William Frank. *Kansas: A History of the Jayhawk State.* Norman: University of Oklahoma Press, 1957.

Government Documents—Published

HofR Report No. 29, 46th Cong., 2d. sess., 1879.

Reports of the Commissioner of Indian Affairs, 1858–80.

U.S. Bureau of Ethnology. *Bulletin No. 83* by Dr. Fordyce Grinnell. GPO: Washington, D.C., 1879.

U.S. War Department. *The War of Rebellion. A Compilation of the Official Records of the Union and Confederate Armies.* Four series, 128 vols. Washington, D.C.: GPO, 1880–91.

Government Documents—Unpublished

Office of Indian Affairs. Indian Archives, Division of Archives and Manuscripts, Oklahoma Historical Society.

Office of Indian Affairs. Selected Letters, Kiowa Agency, 1864-68, NA.

Office of Indian Affairs. Letters Received, Wichita Agency, 1857–75, NA.

Miscellaneous Sources

Account of Second Expedition. Athey Collection, Oklahoma Historical Society.

Account of Third Expedition. Athey Collection, Oklahoma Historical Society.

American Guide project. Wichita State University, from *Edward's Historical Atlas*, 1882.

Bloss Manuscript. Athey Collection, Oklahoma Historical Society.

Chisholm File. Barker Texas History Collection, University of Texas, Austin.

Coyne, Marjorie Aikman. "David L. Payne, the Father of Oklahoma." Ph.D Diss., University of Wichita, 1930.

Early History of Wichita and Sedgwick County, a Scrapbook. 2 vols. Wichita City Library, 1932.

Ellington, Bill. "The Story Behind William Street," Wichita Public Library.

First Records of the City of Wichita, Wichita Public Library.

Hume, C. Ross, Collection, Division of Manuscripts, University of Oklahoma.

Jenness, George B. Manuscript. Kansas State Historical Society.

Koller, John S. "Boomer Days" pamphlet. Athey Collection, Oklahoma Historical Society.

Map of the Indian Territory. Alvin J. Johnson and Son, 1880, Oklahoma Historical Society.

McIsaac, Robert Hugh. "William Greiffenstein and the Founding of Wichita." Master's thesis, University of Wichita, 1957.

Mead, James R. "Reminiscences of Frontier Life." Manuscript, Kansas State Historical Society.

Proceedings of the Town Trustees of the City Council of Wichita, 1870–75. Office of the City Clerk, Wichita, Kansas.

Rister Collection, Division of Manuscripts. University of Oklahoma, Norman.

Rodgers, Joseph Phelps. "A Few Years Experience on the Western Frontier." Manuscript, Kansas State Historical Society.

Special Collections Department, University of Arkansas Library.
Stories of Wichita as Related by Wichita Pioneers. Independent
   Business Men's Association, Wichita, 1938.
Wellman, Manly Wade. "The Builders of Wichita, 1934." Wichita
   City Library.
Wichita Court Records. Kansas State Historical Society.

Newspapers and Periodicals

Arkansas Gazette (Little Rock)
Arkansas Intelligencer (Van Buren)
Caldwell Commercial
Caldwell Journal
Caldwell Post
Cherokee Advocate (Tahlequah, Oklahoma)
Congressional Record
Daily Oklahoman
Emporia News
Federal Reporter
Herald of Freedom (Lawrence)
Historia (Oklahoma City)
Kansas Daily Tribune (Lawrence)
Leavenworth Daily Conservative
Leavenworth Times
Leavenworth Times and Conservative
Lyons Daily News
New York Sun
Newton *Kansan*
Niles Weekly Register
Oklahoma War Chief
Omaha World-Herald
Republican-Traveler (Arkansas City)
St. Louis Globe
Times and Conservative (Leavenworth)
White Cloud (Kansas) *Chief*
Wichita Beacon
Wichita Eagle
Wichita Eagle Sunday Magazine
Wichita Tribune
Wichita Vidette
Wichita Weekly Beacon

Index

Page numbers in italics indicate illustrations.

A-wa-he (O-was-he, Wichita chief), 39
Abbott, John W., prizefight of, 167
Abilene, Kansas, xi, 55, 66, 70, 85, 88, 102, 111; railhead at, 97
Abilene Trail, 55
Absentee Shawnee Indians, 23, 35, 40
Adobe Walls, attack on, 105
Alamo Varieties, 118
America, 59, 67, 112, 165
American West, 93; Wichita as model town of, x
Anadarko Indians, 32
Anderson, Bill, shooting of, 117
Anderson, James, Osage killing of, 73
Antelope Hills, 62, 64
Antrim, William H., 93
Apache Indians, 5, 7–9, 100, 105
Apiz, Charles, 99
Arapaho Indians, 12, 19, 25, 29, 31–32, 60–61, 64, 67, 105, 131–32, 134, 136; delegation of, 130
Arbuckle Branch of Chisholm Trail, 55, 144
Archuleta, Juan de, 6
Arikara Indians, 1
Arikaree River, battle on, 73, 81

Arizona, 12, 122, 124
Arkansas, 10–12, 145, 147; gold seekers from, 1
Arkansas City, Kansas, 54, 152, 157, 167; boomer headquarters moved to, 149
Arkansas River, xiii, 3–5, 7–8, 10–13, 15–16, 18–22, 24–25, 28–29, 32, 36, 39, 41–42, 45, 51, 54–55, 61, 63, 65, 70–72, 75, 77, 86, 90–94, 98–99, 112–14, 118, 137, 151; bridge for promoted, 76; gold search on, 2; harbor for Western adventure on, xiii; legend of gold on, 7; Texas herd fording of, 88; visit of gold seekers to, 1. *See also* Ne Shutsa
Arkansas River Bridge and Ferry Company, organizing of, 76
Arnold, C. C., 19
Atchison, Kansas, 28
Atchison, Topeka, and Santa Fe Railroad, connection of with Wichita & Southwestern line, 95
Atkinson, Gen. Henry, 1825 expedition of, 30
Augusta, Kansas, 86, 99

Baker's Ranch (Indian Territory), 106; trail stop at, 55, 105

Bancroft, E. P., townsite membership of, 73

Barr, Capt. Samuel L., as first commander of Camp Beecher, 75

Barrett, E. H., Wichita presence of, 105

Barrett-Stanley survey, 105

Battle of the Washita, 64

Bean, Richard, 11

Bean, Robert, 11

Beard, E. R. "Red," dance house operated by, 116; killing of, 117

Beard and Vance, wagon train of, 103

Beardstown, Illinois, 16

Beaver Creek, 63

Beecher, Lt. Fred, 73, 81

"Beecher," suggested name for Wichita, 73

Behrens, John, 121

Bell, Capt. John R., 10

Belmont, Kansas, 23

Bemis, H., 22

Bemis, William, 22, 28

Bent, George, 39–40, 62

Bent, William, 25, 27–28, 51; Cheyenne reservation proposed by, 29

Bent's New Fort, 51

Bent's (Old) Fort, 27

Big Bend, 10–11

Big Mouth (Arapaho chief), 29

Bigtree, Bob, 124–26

Billy the Kid, xiii, 153; presence of in Wichita, 93

Black, William, gold search led by, 12; gold-seeking story of, 11

Black Beaver (Delaware), 40–41, 45

Black Eagle (Kiowa chief), 31

Black Hills, 131, 166; gold rush to, 79

Black Kettle (Cheyenne chief), 19, 25, 39–40; attack on village of, 64; speech of, 30; village of, 82

Blackfoot Indians, 28

Blinn, Mrs. Clara, capture and death of, 64–65

Blinn, Willie, capture and death of, 64–65

Blue Front Store, trail herd registry kept at, 102

Bluff Creek, 50

Bogardus, Capt. A. G., 165; performance of, 167

Bogardus, Pete, shooting skills of, 165

Boggs, Rev. Dr. W. R., 90–91; early Wichita residence of, 76; Wichita Presbyterian Church organized by, 89

Bonney, William, alias Billy the Kid, 93. See also Henry McCarty

Boone, Albert G. (Indian Commissioner), 131

Boone, Daniel, 131

Boudinot, Elias C., 147; paper on Unassigned Lands by, 142

Bournett, Joe, 60

Brandley, Capt. Henry, 50

Bridger, Jim, death of, 153

Bridges, Jack, gunfight of, 110–11

Brimstone, Wichita compared to, 115

Brooks, Billy, 104

Browning, R. H., 36

Bryden, James, 102

Buckhorn Hotel, 77–78, 109; establishment of, 73

Buffalo Bessie, performance of, 167

"Buffalo Bill," nickname of William Mathewson, 51

buffalo, 8–10, 16–19, 104; barbeque of, 89, 92; hides and bones of, 98; slaughter of, 105; trail herd stampeded by, 102

Buffalo Bill's (Cody) Wild West show, 51, 163

Buffalo Charley, buffalo ride of, 166

Buffalo Goad (Wichita chief), 39

Buffalo Hump (Comanche chief), 29

buffalo hunt, 23, 51, 134; description of, 16–19, 90–91; Fourth of July event recounted, 89; staging of, 164

Buffalo hunters, Wichita presence of, 103

Buffalo Springs (Indian Territory), 40, 55, 106

Burnett, Abraham (Potawatomi chief), 67, 155

Burnett, Catherine, 67

Burnett (town of, Oklahoma Territory), 168

Burrow, James, 31

Burton Car Works of Wichita, 163

Butler, Josiah, 43

Butterfield, D. A., 74

Butterfield Overland Mail Line, 74

Byers, William, 35, 37

Cache Creek, 20

Caddo Indians, 23, 28, 32, 35, 40, 47

Caldwell, Kansas, xi, 55, 104, 124, 146, 151, 154, 157; gun battle at, 120, 124–25

Caldwell Board of Trade, 159

Caldwell Opera House, 125

Caldwell-Fort Sill stage line, 154

California, 10, 12, 47, 167

California Fran, performance of, 167

Callan, James, 11

Calloway, Thomas, 106

Calvert, A. B., 142

Camp Alice, Payne expedition to, 149

Camp Beecher, 74–75; establishment of, 63

Camp Butterfield, 74

Camp Davidson, early designation of Camp Beecher, 75

Camp Supply (Indian Territory), 64, 67, 106; creation of, 63

Canadian River, 10–11, 30, 41, 46, 50, 52, 105–6, 156

captives, 31, 46–47, 51, 63–65, 136; Kansas women held as, 141

Carey, Jacob, 19

Carlos, I. J. L., 24, 34

Carpenter, Col. C. C., 144; first Indian Territory invasion led by, 142

Carroll, Capt. Henry, Payne arrest of, 149

Carson, Kit, 27–29, 51

Catlin, George, 9

cattle buyers, Wichita presence of, 102

cattle drive, 48

cattle drovers, 111, 116

cattle herds, Wichita presence of, 124, 154

Cattle Towns, by Robert Dystra, x

cattle trade, demise of, 118

cattle trail, 79

cattlemen, opposition of to Oklahoma boomers, 159

cavalry troops, 98

Central Plains, 8, 12–13, 25, 29, 47, 60

Chelsea, Kansas, 50

Cherokee alphabet, 47

Cherokee country, 12, 47

Cherokee heritage, 47

Cherokee Indians, 11, 35, 47, 142: gold-seeking party of, 12

Cherokee Live Stock Association, 151

Cherokee Nation, 11, 46, 146

Cherokee Outlet, 150

chewing gum, 132

Cheyenne Dog Soldiers, 25, 27, 35, 40, 54–55, 61

Cheyenne Indians, 12, 19, 25, 28–32, 35–36, 39–41, 60–61, 64–65, 67, 73, 91, 105, 107, 131–34, 136, 141; delegation of, 135; exile of, 107; Hennessey train massacred by, 106; impersonation of, 164; robes of, 62

Cheyenne Jack, 64–65

Cheyenne Jennie, 60–61; role of in captive rescue, 62–63

Cheyenne/Arapaho agency, 55;
establishment of, 67;
Wichita trade with, 103
Cheyenne-Arapaho caravan, 136
Cheyenne-Arapaho scouts, 145
Chicago, 99, 166
Chickasaw Indians, 21, 35
Chikaskia River, 148, 150
Chisholm, Jesse, ix, xiv, 7, 11, 25, 28,
31, 39–40, 46, 47, 50–51,
arrival at Wichita of, 24, 45;
cattle drive of to Wichita
site, 48; Council Grove post
of, 53; death of, 53; frontier
service of, 49; Little
Arkansas ranch of, 35;
member of gold seeking
party, 1; trading camp of, 53
Chisholm Cattle Trail, xiii, 46,
52–55, 71, 103, 105, 124, 126,
144, 154; beginning of, 48
Chisholm Creek, 45, 102, 120
Chivington, Col. John M., 25,
29–30
Choctaw Indians, 21
cholera, 38–40, 43
Chollar, J. J., 36, 40
Chouteau, A. P., trapping party
of, 10
Chouteau's Island, battle of, 10
Cimarron Crossing, 55
Cimarron River, 41, 43, 53, 55, 63,
105–6, 144, 149–50, 154, 156
Cincinnati Chamber of
Commerce, 157
Civil War, 12, 20–21, 24–25, 45, 47,
75, 92, 137, 141, 144; post war
immigration, xiii
Clanton gang, 124
Clark, George, saloon of, 77
Clearwater River, 55
Cody, Mrs. Sam, Jr., 164
Cody, Sam, Jr., 164
Cody, William F. (Buffalo Bill),
51, 148
Coffee Creek (Indian Territory), 144
Coffeyville, Kansas, 143; Texas
cattle shipped from, 98, 101

Colley, Dennis N. (Commissioner
of Indian Affairs), 35
Colorado, 8, 10, 12, 25, 28, 64, 66, 131
Comanche Bill, 125–26
Comanche Indians, 7–8, 11, 13,
20–21, 25, 30–32, 40–41,
46–47, 49, 51, 103; attacked
by Van Dorn, 21; captive of,
136; drovers attacked by, 99;
robes of, 62
Concord Stage, 135
Confederacy, 23, 31, 39, 45, 47, 99
Cook, Ed, 106
Corbin, Jack, hanging of, 82; service of as Custer scout, 82
Cordiero, M. R. "Charlie," 92; eat-
ing place of, 77; man killed
by, 78–79; prejudice against,
79; Texas House operated
by, 113
Coronado, Francisco Vásquez de,
expedition of, 1–4, 6, 8,
33–34
Couch, William, 157; boomer expe-
dition led by, 150; Lillie seen
as threat by, 159; successor
of to Payne, 149, 152
Council Grove (Indian Territory),
47–48, 53, 55, 61, 145, 150
Covington, J. A., 134
Cow Creek, 4, 27
Cowskin Creek, 20, 42, 50, 103;
Greiffenstein post on, 71
Cowskin Grove, 20
Cowskin ranch, 61, 63; Piley-
Vandervort operation of, 81
Cox, Fannie, 53
Craddock, Tom, 147
Crawford, Gov. Samuel J., 63, 74,
141; townsite membership
of, 73
Crawford, Thompson, 19
Crawford County, Arkansas, 12
Crawford Opera House, 157, 167
Creek Indians, 11, 35, 47, 81, 160;
treaty with, 142–43, 150
Crook, Gen. George, Wichita visit
of, 133

Curry, Jim (Kid Curry), 93
Custer, Lt. Col. George A., 81–82,
    131; Indian Territory inva-
    sion of, 63–64; Texas
    Panhandle expedition of, 141

Dagner's cigar store, 110
Daily Kansas Commercial, 116
Daisey, O. C., 113
Daniels, J. W. (Indian
    Commissioner), 131
Darling, Capt. E. N., 54
Darlington, Brinton, 55, 67
Darington Agency, 99, 105–7,
    131–32, 136–37
Daugherty, James M., 52
Day, Lt. M. W., 150
De Mun, Jules, trapping party
    of, 10
DeBarnard Hotel, Wellington,
    Kansas, 151
Declaration of Independence, 92;
    reading of at Wichita, 89
Deep Fork (Indian Territory), 145,
    147–48
Deer Creek (Indian Territory), 126
Delano (West Wichita), saloon at,
    117; rough reputation of, 115
Delaware Indians, 22–23, 35, 40
Democratic Party, 142
DeMoore, George, saloon of, 110
Denison, Texas, 62, 147
Dennison, E. B., 123
Denton County, Texas, 52
Denver, Colorado, 25, 71, 117
Department of the Missouri, 145
Derusha, Edward, 154–55
Deutcher Brothers ranch, 126
Dixon, Billy, 105
Dodge, Col. Henry, 20
Dodge City, Kansas, xi, 82, 103,
    118, 122
Doniphan County, Kansas, 142;
    Payne's homestead in, 141
Donnell, Sgt. Tom, 145, 155
Douglas Avenue, Wichita, x, 87–88,
    96, 124, 134–35, 143; Payne's
    office on, 145; smell of beer
on, 154; Steven A. Douglas
    namesake for, 86
Douglas Hotel, 162, construction
    of, 96
Douglass, Kansas, 82
Dray, Mike, 82
Drovers' Wichita Headquarters, 102
Dry Creek, 24, 81, 89, 141
du Pratz, Antoine W. Le Page, map
    by, 7
Dull Knife (Northern Cheyenne
    chief), 137
Dunlap, Robert 19
Dunn, Sam, Osage killing of, 73
Durackin, Robert, 19
Durfee, E. H., Company, 50, 72;
    post of operated by
    Greiffenstein, 86; trading
    post of, 77
Dystra, Robert, x

Eagle Drinking (Comanche chief),
    29–31
Eagle Hall, 131, 146
Eagle Head (Cheyenne chief), 135
Earp, Wyatt, xiii, 59, 113, 119; battle
    of at O.K. corral, 124; broth-
    ers of, 122; dismissal of, 121;
    honesty of, 122; lawman
    activities of, 121
Eddleman, Dick, 124–25
Edmond Station (Indian
    Territory), stage stop at, 160
Edwards, Eliza, 47
Eighteenth Kansas Volunteer regi-
    ment, 38, 141
El Curatelejo, Indian settlement of, 6
El Dorado, Kansas, 50, 69; found-
    ing of, 22
El Paso, Texas, 47
Elliott, Maj. Joel, death of, 64
Ellsworth, Kansas, xi, 102, 115;
    competition of, 101; drum-
    mers working for, 103; Texas
    cattle shipped from, 98
Emory, Col. William H., 21
Empire House hotel, 109;
    Greiffenstein building of, 88

Emporia, Kansas, 38, 50, 61, 69, 72, 76, 79, 87, 93, 166; citizens of visit Wichita's Fourth of July celebration, 89; Wild West show parade at, 166

Emporia News, 24; Wichita's Fourth of July notice in, 89

English, N. A., 94; actions of to protect Wichita's trail herd business, 101–2; early Wichita residency of, 76; role of in railroad development, 95

English Street, 132

Escanjaque Indians, battle with Oñate, 6; Rayado village looted by, 6

Eureka (Indian Territory), 43

Ewing, Gen./Senator Tom, 144

Ewing (Indian Territory), first Payne settlement of, 144

Fand, George, 106

farmers, resistance of to Texas cattle, 99

fast women, Wichita presence of, 154

Fenlon, Thomas, 148

Ferdinandina, 20

ferry, operation of, 76

Fifth U.S. Cavalry, 110

Fifth U.S. Infantry, 74–75

financial panic of 1873, 98

Finn, William, Wichita survey by, 86

First Colorado Cavalry, 28

Fisher, Frank, 143

Fitzpatrick, Thomas, 29

Flint Hills, 69

Florida, 107, 132–33, 135

Ford, Robert, kills Jesse James, 153

Forsyth, Maj. George, 81

Fort Arbuckle, 21–22, 40, 49, 51, 99

Fort Bascom, New Mexico, 28

Fort Belknap, Texas, 54

Fort Cobb, Oklahoma, 21–22, 40–41, 53–54, 62, 65–66, 141

Fort Dodge, Kansas, 137

Fort Gibson, Oklahoma, 2, 12; founding of as cantonment, 1

Fort Harker, Kansas 38, 88; military road from, 75

Fort Hays, Kansas, 116

Fort Laramie, Wyoming, 25

Fort Larned, Kansas, 41, 61, 75

Fort Leavenworth, Kansas, 25, 48, 137, 145; Payne as postmaster at, 141

Fort Lyon, Colorado, 25, 65

Fort Marion, Florida, 107, 132

Fort Reno, Oklahoma, 107, 145, 148, 154; Payne arrested by troops of, 147, 149

Fort Riley, Kansas, 28, 54

Fort Robinson, Nebraska, 137

Fort Sill, Oklahoma, 67, 81, 99–100, 106, 122, 136, 141; establishment of, 66; Mead trading post at, 103; military road to, 75; ox trains to and from, 88

Fort Smith, Arkansas, 10–11, 50, 145–46, 148; Payne taken to, 151

Fort Sumner, New Mexico, 153

Fort Towson (Indian Territory), 11

Fort Worth, Texas, 154

Fossett. W. D., 125

Fouquet, L. C., 77

Fourth of July celebration, 92, 100; first Wichita event held for, 89

Fowler, Jacob, journal of, 10

Franciscan friars, 5

Franklin County, Kansas, 65

Fredericksburgh, Texas, 31

Freedmen, delegation of, 149; Unassigned Lands designated for, 143

French, Arkansas River post of, 7; explorations of, 7; soldiers of, 7; trade with, 8

French-Spanish struggle, 8

Friend, Lee Temple, capture of, 136

Friend, Rev. Leonard S., 136

frontier, existence of in Indian Territory, 154

frontier travel, perils of, 156
frontiersmen, Wichita presence of, 154
fur trade, ix, 23

Gainesville, Texas, 147, 152, 157
Gale, Lt. G. H. G., 145
gamblers, 111, 115; Wichita presence of, 154
Garrett, Maj. C. F., 40–41
Garrett, Sheriff Pat, Billy the Kid killed by, 152
Georgetown, Texas, 31
Germain (or German) sisters, capture of, 135
German, 57, 59–62, 67, 95, 137, 168
Gessley, Professor S., 111
Gifford, Jim, 72
Glenn, Hugh, trapping party of, 10
Glenn-Fowler party, 10
Goddess of Liberty, 92
gold, 11, 13, 45, legend of, 2, 4, 7, 12; search for, 2, 6, 12
Gookins, Maj. Milo, 35, 47, treatment of Wichitas by, 34
governor of Kansas, 65
Grand Saline (Indian Territory), 11
Grant, President Ulysses S., 75
grasshoppers, images of, 156
Great Bend of Arkansas River, 8, 51, 71
Great Father, 31
Greenlee, Dr. D. R. B., 143
Greenway, Alonzo F., 50, 53, 76–77; buffalo hunt of, 16–19
Greiffenstein, Beate, 59
Greiffenstein, Catherine, 86; place of on Potawatomi roles, 157
Greiffenstein, Charles, 59, 156
Greiffenstein, William (Dutch Bill), ix, xiv, 28, 39–40, 55, *58*, 63, 92, 137, 156; affinity of for the Indian Territory, 155; Arkansas Bridge Company organized by, 94; arrival of at Wichita, 86; called the "Father of Wichita," 85; called the "George Washington of Wichita," 85; charged with selling arms, 66; civic projects of, 94–95; connection of with Wild West show, 164; Cow Creek trading post of, 27; Cowskin trading house of, 50; description of, 57–59; dog feast of, 135; effort of to rescue Mrs. Blinn and son, 64–65; election as mayor of Wichita, 131; Emporia trade of, 62; first Fourth of July celebration urged by, 89; first lumber house erected by, 87; friendship with Indians, 129; home development of, 88; home of, 86, 132; host to Indians, 130–32; known to friends as "Uncle Billy," 94; land for stockyards donation by, 95; last days and death of, 168; leadership of in civic and commercial projects, 93; marriage of to Catherine Burnett, 67; marriage of to Cheyenne Jennie, 60–61; meeting of with Sheridan, 133; opposition of to Payne, 146; post of on the Washita, 53; Quakers led to Indian Territory by, 66–67; role of in Wichita settlement, 83; tenure of as Wichita's mayor, 134; toast of to Chisholm, 53; trading activities of, 60–62; trading post of at Wichita, 77; trip of to Indian Territory, 155; trip of with Corn Train, 157
Grey Beard (Cheyenne chief), death of, 135
GTT (Gone to Texas), 117
Guthrie Station, Oklahoma, 144, 160

Haines, Anna, 142, 151

Haines, George, 142
Hallowell, J. R., opposition of to Payne, 143–44
"Hamilton," name of suggested for Wichita, 73
Harney, Maj. Gen. William, 27–28, 30
Harper's Illustrated Weekly, 156
Harrington, W. T., 65
Harris House, 109–10
Harrison, President Benjamin, proclamation opening Oklahoma issued by, 160
Harrison, President William Henry, 53
Harvey County, Kansas, 141
Hatch, Col. Edward, Payne's Rock Falls settlement destroyed by, 150–51
Hayes, President Rutherford B., proclamation outlawing Oklahoma settlement issued by, 143
Hays Brothers Company, 107
Hays City, Kansas, 110
Hazen, Maj. Gen. William B., 62, 66–67
Hennessey, Patrick, massacre of, 106
Hennessey Massacre, staging of, 164
Henrietta, Texas, 148
Hermann, Missouri, 59
Herrington, G. H., 129
Herrington, Kansas, 5
Hibben, Harry, 150
Hill, Doug, 124–26
Hill, Harry L. (Oklahoma Harry), 144, 158–62, 164, 168; show promotion of, 167; show troubles of, 166; sketch of, 159; stables of, 163; state line operated by, 160; Wild West show of, x
Hill's Drug Store, 123
Hoag, Enoch, 66
Holliday, Doc, 124
Hope's saloon, 123

Horne, Capt. Harry, 165, 167
Horner, A. F., townsite membership of, 73
Horse Back (Comanche chief), 29
horse racing, Wichita sport of, 118
Horse Thief Corner, 89
horse thieves, 105; lynching of, 82
houses of ill repute, 111, 115, 154
Hubbard, Phares C., 71–72; land claims of purchased by Greiffenstein, 86; Wichita residency of, 76
Hubbard and Mason mercantile store, 77
Hull's Ranch, 103
Humaña, Antonio Gutierrez de, unauthorized expedition of, 5
Hunnewell, Kansas, 138, 151, 159
Hunter, Charlie, 72
Hutchison, W. B. "Hutch," 93, 149; *Caldwell Post* edited by, 124

Illinois, 86, 116, 158–59, 166–67
Indian Appropriations Bill, 160
Indian battles, staging of, 164
Indian Bureau, official of, 142, 151
Indian conflict, 105
Indian dog feast, 135
Indian photographic display, 135
Indian Territory, ix-xi, 1, 21, 25, 30–32, 35–36, 38–41, 45, 47–55, 61–64, 66–67, 70, 75, 81–82, 97, 101, 103, 111, 121, 126, 129–31, 133–36, 138, 140–48, 150, 152, 154–55, 157, 159, 162, 164, 167; cattlemen of challenged, 159; conflict in, 105; crossing of by Santa Fe Railroad, 157; freighting operations to, 106; hostile tribes in, 74; Indian agencies of, 88; settlement of, 89, 139; stage line to, 104–5; survey of, 105; trail herds driven across, 98–99; Wichita trade with, 103
Indian War of 1864, 25

Indian warfare, 106–7
Ioni Indians, 32
Iowa Indians, 15, 131
Iron Mountain (Comanche chief), 31

Jackson, President Andrew, 39
James, Jesse, killing of, 153
Jenness, Capt. George, pre-city view of Wichita site given by, 75
Jester, Alexander, 82
Johnson, Charles B., 35–36
Jones, Oklahoma, Payne intrusion to, 148
Joseph (Nez Perce chief), Wichita visit of, 137–38
Junction City, Kansas, 28

Kansa (Kaw) Indians, 13, 15, 43; migration of through Wichita, 130. *See also* Kaw Indians
Kansas, x, 2–8, 11–12, 16, 22–23, 25, 28–30, 32, 35–37, 39, 41, 47–48, 50–51, 53–54, 60–66, 69, 75, 82–83, 93–94, 98, 101, 103–4, 106, 131, 136, 141–44, 148–50, 155–56, 158, 168, 173; border of, 47, 55, 144–45, 147; farmers of, 101; governor of, 76; hostile tribes in, 74; Indian Territory freighting operations of, 106; legislature of, 54, 89, 140–41; locust swarms of, 156; men of feted, 157; Oklahoma boomer lobby of, 160; outlaw elements of, 119; railheads of, 45, 55, 97; Senate of, 141–42; statutes of, 77
Kansas City, Kansas/Missouri, 114, 118, 157, 166
Kansas City Times, 148; Oklahoma boomer movement supported by, 142–43
Kansas Historical Society, xi
Kansas Pacific Railroad, 29, 37, 101, 103, 110

Kaw (Kansa) Indians, 67
Kellogg, Dr., 38
Kellogg, Milo, arrival of, 72
Kelly, Fanny, 135; redress sought by, 136
keno, 113, 115
Kichai (Keechi) Indians, 23, 28, 32, 35, 41
Kickapoo Indians, 131
Kicking Bird (Kicking Eagle, Kiowa chief), 31, 135
Kingfisher Creek (Indian Territory), 53, 55, 106
Kingfisher Station (Indian Territory), 106, 160
Kingman, Kansas, 155
Kingman, Samuel W., 30, 32–33; treaty council diary of, 28
Kiowa Indians, 13, 19–20, 25, 29–32, 40–41, 46, 49, 61–62, 103; attack of on drovers, 99
Kirk, E. H., 144
Kohn, Sol, 94

La Harpe, Bernard de, exploration of, 7
Lafflin wagon train, 103, 106
Lakin, Kansas, 10
Lamar, Colorado, 51
Lanford, Professor, hot air balloon feat of, 165
Larned, Kansas, 3
Lawrence, Kansas, 36, 54, 60, 99, 135
Lawrence, W. H. H., townsite membership of, 73
Lawrence *Daily Tribune*, 69
Lawton, John, murder of, 72
Lean Bear (Cheyenne chief), murder of, 25
Leased District (Indian Territory), 21–22, 35–36, 40–41, 43, 47, 62, 103
Leavenworth, Gen. Henry, 25
Leavenworth, Jesse, 25, 27, 27–28, 39–41, 49–52, 71, 74
Leavenworth, Kansas, 24, 50, 74, 114

Leavenworth, Lawrence and
   Galveston Railroad, 101
Leavenworth Times, 71
Ledford, Jack, 79; Buckhorn inci-
   dent of, 78; civic activity of,
   109; fatal gunfight of, 110;
   sheriff's office sought by,
   119–20
Ledford, Mrs. Jack, 110
Ledrick, Philip, 72
Leeper, Mathew, 22
Levy, M. W., 94
Lewellen, Doc, log house of, 80;
   Wichita mercantile store of,
   72, 77, 79–80
Lewellen's Hall, 80
Lewis and Clark expedition, 1, 8
Lexington, battle remembrance
   of, 89
Leyva y Bonilla, Francisco de,
   unauthorized expedition
   of, 5
Lillie, Maj. Gordon W. (Pawnee
   Bill), 158–61, *162*; Oklahoma
   boomer movement placed
   under, 161; show people of,
   163. *See also* Pawnee Bill
Lillie, Miss May, trick shooting
   of, 161
Lincoln, President Abraham, 25
Lincoln, Secretary of War Robert
   T., 149; sued by Payne, 147
Little Arkansas Agency, 41
Little Arkansas peace commission, 28–32
Little Arkansas River, 2, 4, 8–13,
   15–16, 18–20, 22–25, 27–28,
   31–33, 36–37, 40–41, 43,
   45–46, 48, 50–52, 54–55, 63,
   66, 71–72, 74, 76–77, 86, 112,
   129, 131, 137, 168; known to
   early residents as "Little
   River," 70; treaty council at,
   27–32. *See also* Ne Shutsa
   Shinka
Little Missouri River, 137
Little Mountain (Kiowa chief), 25,
   29, 31. *See also* To-haw-son

Little Mountain (moundlike
   hill), 53
Little Raven (Arapaho chief), 29
Little River (Little Arkansas), 4
Little Robe (Cheyenne chief),
   29, 132
Little Rock, Arkansas, 8
Little Wolf (Northern Cheyenne
   chief), 137
Lone Tree Massacre, 136
Lone Wolf (Kiowa chief), 31, 135
Long, Stephen H., expedition
   of, 10
longhorn cattle, 40, 45, 52. *See also*
   Texas longhorns
lost gold mine, story of, 11
Louisiana, 7
Louisiana Territory, 8
Louisville, Kentucky, 166
Love, Tom, 124–25
Lowe, Rowdy Joe, 113, 115–16; Red
   Beard Shot by, 117; sketch of,
   113–14
Lowe, Rowdy Kate, 115, girls of, 116
Lutheran Church, 59
Lyons, Kansas, 4

Maidt, H. M., 146
Main Street, Wichita, 86–87, 112–13,
   124, 134–35
Malto (Spanish Queen), riding
   performance of, 167
Man Afraid of His Horses (Sioux
   chief), 131
Mansur, Charles H. (Missouri
   Representative), 158
Marion Center, Kansas, 50, 76
Martin, Hurricane Bill, arrest of,
   88–89
Martin, Jim, 124–26
Masterson, Bat, xiii, ix, 154; aging
   of, 153
Mathewson, Lizzie, 53
Mathewson, William "Buffalo Bill,"
   25, 28, *37*, 40–41, 43, 66, 106;
   background of, 50–51; early
   Wichita residency of, 76;
   Indian Territory trading

operations of, 103; wagon
trains of, 105
May, Ida, as Wichita "madam," 93;
bawdy house operated
by, 112
McCarty, Mrs. Catherine, 93
McCarty, Henry, alias William
Bonney or Billy the Kid, 93
McClain's Ranch, 55
McClure, W. P., 94
McCoy, Joseph G., 52, 151; hiring
of, 102
McCusker, Philip, 55, 130; Wichita
death march report of, 41–42
McDonald, Mrs. Caroline, 31
McDonald, Rebecca, 31
McElroy children, 63
McKnight-James group, 10–11
McNab, James, 11
McNair, Nicholas, 11
Mead, James, ix, xiv, 11, 16, 22,
28–29, 39, *49*, 52–53, 60–61;
Arkansas Bridge Company
role of, 76, 94; early Wichita
residency of, 76; friend of
Mathewson, 51; gold search
story told by, 7; Indian
Territory trading operations
of, 103; Jesse Chisholm
friendship of, 48; quotation
from, 45; railway promotion
by, 95; Spanish hieroglyphics related by, 8; Towanda
trading post of, 61, 69; townsite survey run by, 73; trading operations of, 23–24,
105; trail herd business promoted by, 101–2; Wichita
Indians described by, 33–34
Mead, Maj. Gen. Ebenezer, 23
Mead addition, development
of, 88
Meagher, John, 107, *120*, 121, 144;
move of to Darlington, 155
Meagher, Mike, ix, 107, 117, *120*,
120–22, 146, 155; death of,
126; Fort Sill prisoners taken
by, 106; gun battle of, 123–25;

move to Caldwell of, 124;
police force headed by, 113;
praised by *Wichita Eagle*,
119; saloon padlocked by,
121; serves as U.S. Marshal,
121; trail herd business pro-
tected by, 101–2; Wichita
burial of, 127
Meagher, Molly, 120
Meagher, Timothy, 120
Medicine Bluff Creek, 65
Medicine Lodge peace council, 41
Medicine Water (Cheyenne chief),
135–36
Mexican Rafael, performance of, 167
Mexico, 30, 47, 65, 70, 99; cowboys
of, 79, 100, 113; silver of, 12;
traders from, 19
Miles, John D. (Indian Agent),
131–32, 137; flight of, 106–7
Miles, Gen. Nelson, 134
Miller, W. H., 147
Miner, H. Craig, x; tells of military
influence on early
Wichita, 75
Minimic (Cheyenne chief), 132, 137
Mississippi River, 23
Missouri, ix, 8–9, 15, 59, 149,
153, 158
Missouri Indians, 13
Missouri River, 1, 8, 51, 59, 119
Missouri-Kansas-Texas Railroad,
131, 156
Montana, 81, 133, 137
Moore, A. A. "Lank," claim pur-
chased by Greiffenstein, 86
Moores Brothers' saloon, 125
Morehouse, George P., 134
Morgan, Jim, 154–55
Morris, Dr., 82
Mosely, Ed, 19
Moseley and Maxley, trading post
of, 19
Mosier, Burr, ranch of, 106
Mulberry Creek, 106
Munford, Dr. Morrison, 148
Munger, D. S., 73; townsite mem-
bership of, 73

Munger House, 76, *87*
Munger townsite, 86, 120
Munsen, Bob, 124–26
Murdock, Marsh, *104*, 131, 135–36, 142, 146, 149, 153, 158–59; admiration of Nez Perce voiced by, 138; changing views of, 140; end of Oklahoma boom predicted by, 147; Oklahoma movement scorned by, 139; Oklahoma settlement supported by, 157; Payne opposition led by, 145; protection of buffalo voiced by, 103; Washington contact of, 143
Murdock, R. P., 61; Emporia store of, 62
Murdock, Victor, 161; Wichita history written by, 136
Murphy, Thomas (Indian Superintendent), 27–28
Murray, George P., 81–82
Muskogee (Indian Territory), 131, 146

Ne Shutsa Shinka (Little Arkansas), 15, 67
Ne Shutsa (Arkansas River), 15
Nebraska, 10, 15, 25
Negro, 99; rights of under Indian treaties, 143
Neosho River, 11
New Mexico, ix–x, 1, 3–7, 10, 12, 28, 32, 48, 50, 60, 93, 105, 153
New Orleans, 1, 12, 47
New York, 14, 50
Newton, Kansas, xi, 111, 118, 134, 142; railhead at, 97
Nez Perce Indians, 131, 137, 144; Wichita visit of, 138
Nineteenth Kansas Volunteer Cavalry, 63–64, 75, 81, 89, 141
Ninnescah River, 9, 55, 71, 91, 101–2
Ninth U.S. Cavalry, 81, 151
Non-Intercourse Act, 147
North Canadian River, 47–48, 53, 55, 105, 144, 148–49, 156

North Fork of Red River, 20
North Mosely Street, 142
Northern Cheyennes, escape homeward of, 136–37
Northwest Fur Company, 50
Nugent, E. H., 149

Occidental Hotel, 101, 112, 132
Odell, Daniel, 150
Ohio, 23, 158, 166
Ohio River, 166
Ohio Valley, flood victims of, 156
Oklahoma, x, 7, 20, 47, 55, 142–44, 146–48, 150, 152, 157, 160, 163–65; settlement of, 144, 161, 157–59. *See also* Indian Territory
Oklahoma Bill, 159
Oklahoma Boomer Movement, 131, 139, 145, 149, 152, 157; Payne leader of, 89, 139, 145–46, 157–58; limbo status of, 152; railroad activity of, 157
Oklahoma Harry Hill's Wild West Show, 163, departure of from Wichita, 165; last performance of, 167
Oklahoma Historical Society, xi
Oklahoma Land Rush of 1889, 160
Oklahoma Panhandle, 3
Oklahoma proclamation, 160
Oklahoma question, Wichita conference on, 158
Oklahoma Station, 47, 55, 144, 152, 160,
Oklahoma War Chief, 149–50; building of destroyed, 151
"Old Chisholm Trail," cowboy song of, 97
Old Oxheart, David L. Payne nickname of, 89
Old West, xi, 71, 167; last flicker of, 161; trappings of, 155
"On to Oklahoma," Payne motto of, 143
Oñate, Don Juan de, expedition of, 5–6

Oregon, 131, 142
Osage City, 140
Osage Crossing, 16, 19, 23
Osage Indians, 8–11, 13, 15–16,
    18–19, 24, 31–32, 36, 39, 41,
    54–55, 67, 77, 105–6, 131;
    Kansas lands of, 32; land
    cession of, 53; reservation
    of, 16; settlers attacked by,
    73; scouts of, 81; warrior
    sketch of, 9
Osage Trail, 16
Osage Trust Lands, 54, 73, 76
Osburn, William, 148; arrest resis-
    ted by, 149
Otoe Indians, 131
Ottawa, Kansas, 65
outlaws, presence of in Indian
    Territory, 154

Padilla, Father Juan de, 3; murder
    of, 5
Palo Duro Canyon, 3
Pardee, Lt. J. H., 144–45
Park City, county seat denied for,
    76; founding of, 19
Parker, Judge Isaac C., court of,
    145–46
Parsons, Charles F., 154–55
Paul's Ranch, 35
Pawnee Bill, 161, *162. See also* Maj.
    Gordon W. Lillie
Pawnee Bill Circus, disbandment
    of at Wichita, 162
Pawnee Bill Wild West Show, 158,
    161; Wichita playing of, 161;
    Wichita reception of, 159
Pawnee Indians, 6, 10, 13, 15, 19, 131
Payne, David L., ix, 82, 140, 143–44,
    149, 154, 157, 159; arrest of,
    144–45; boomer activities of,
    142–43, 147–48; buffalo hunt
    led by, 90–91; capture of
    staged, 164; death of, 140,
    151–52, 162; Fourth of July
    celebration plans of, 92; his-
    tory of, 141; Non-Intercourse
    law broken by, 147;

Oklahoma boomer move-
    ment led by, 139; Oklahoma
    Colony of, 148; ranch of, 94,
    141–42; repute of as "Father
    of Oklahoma," 89; role as
    director of Arkansas Bridge
    Company, 94; role as
    Wichita's Grand Marshal of
    July 4 celebration, 89;
    Washington visit of, 150;
    Wichita homestead of, 81;
    Wichita office of, 143;
    Wichita reception of, 146
Peerless Princess of the Plains, xiii
Peyton, Uncle Jack, oration on
    theology by, 80–81
Philibert, Joseph, trapping party
    of, 10
Pierce, A. H. "Shanghai," called
    upon to promote
    Wichita, 102
Pierce, President Franklin, 39
Pierce, H. L., money for Oklahoma
    conference raised by, 158
Pike, Albert, 47
Pike, Lt. Zebulon M., expedition
    of, 1, 8
Pinkerton men, 166
Plains Apache Indians, 30–32
Plains Indian warfare, staging
    of, 164
Plains Indians, x, 25, 41, 61
Platte River, 25, 29, 37, 61
Pliley, A. J., 81–82
Plumb, Preston B., 150
Polecat Creek (Indian Territory),
    104, 145
Polk, Col. J. W., 142
Polk, President James, 47
Ponca City, Oklahoma, 20
Ponca Reservation, 134–35, 144
Pond Creek, 126
Pony Express rider, show perform-
    ance of, 167
Pope, General John A., 145, 147, 149
Potawatomi Indians, 60, 131, 157;
    reservation of, 155, 157; show
    biz role of, 164

Powell, Sylvester, 122–23; Meagher's killing of, 124

Price, Hiram (Commissioner of Indian Affairs), 150

Pryor, Nathaniel, 11–12; gold search led by, 1–2

Pueblo Indians, 3, 5

Quakers, Indian agency role of, 66–67

Quimby, Douglas merchant, 82

Quivira, 2–8; legend of, 2; village of, 5

Railway service, 118; arrival of first train in Wichita, 95

Randall, Capt. G. W., 110

Ransom, George, 51–52

Rathbun, Ed, 126

Rayado Indians, village of, 6

Rector, Frank A., 37, 100

Red Beard's saloon and dance house, 113, 117

Red Dog (Sioux chief), 131

Red Fork Ranch, 55, 105–6, 155

Red River, 11, 20–21, 46

Republic of Texas, 46

Republican Party, 142–43

Republican River, 29

Rich, Joe, Wild West show financed by, 163

Rock Falls (Indian Territory), 151; expedition to, 148; Payne settlement at, 150

Rocky Mountains, 7, 10–11, 51

Ross, John, 20

Ross, Mrs. John, 20

Round Pond Creek, 55, 67, 103–4, 106–7

Rowdy Joe's saloon, 113–17

Runyon, A. L., pre-settlement Wichita site described by, 75

Rush Creek, 20–21

Sac and Fox Agency, 48

Sac and Fox Indians, 131

Sacred Heart Mission, 156

Sadawah (Wichita chief), 105

Sage, Madam, 112

Sah-kah-kee, 47

St. Louis, 36, 59, 146–7, 150; journalist from, 115

St. Louis Globe, lurid account of Wichita printed by, 114

St. Joseph, Missouri, 153

Salina, Kansas, 8, 60–61

Saline County, Kansas, 54

Saline River, 23, 60

saloonkeepers, 111

Salt Creek, 53

Salt Fork of Arkansas, 23, 99

Salt Plains, 30, 41, 61

Sanborn, Gen. John B., 27–29

Sand Creek (Colorado), 25

Sand Creek Massacre, 25, 28–30

Sand Hills, Indian fight at, 107

Sand Hills battlefield, pictures of, 135

Sandoval, Felipe de, visit of to Arkansas River, 7–8

Santa Fe, 2, 6–7, 91

Santa Fe Railroad; extension of across Indian Territory, 152, 157; officials of enlisted to promote Wichita, 102

Santa Fe Trail, 12, 19, 25, 29–30, 51, 59, 61, 64

Santa Cruz, steer-riding performance of, 167

Satank (Kiowa chief), 29

Saxby, Brother, first Wichita sermon by, 76

Schurz, Secretary of Interior Carl, Wichita visit of, 137

Scott, Dr., 54

Scott City, Kansas, 6

Second U.S. Mounted Infantry, 28

Sedgwick, Maj. Gen. John, 75

Sedgwick County, 15, 76, 109, 120, 141, 157; creation of, 75; economic advancement of, 156; lawless days of, 82; namesake of, 75

Sedgwick County Corn Train, 156

Sedgwick County Fair, events at, 134

Sedrick, Henry, post of at Great Bend, 71
Seger, J. G., 134
Seger Colony Industrial School, 134
Seminole Indians, 160; treaty with, 142–43
Seventh U. S. Cavalry Regiment, Indian Territory invasion of, 63–64
Sewell Ranch (Indian Territory), 105
Shanklin, Maj. Henry M., 35–37, 39, 41, 102; cattle-shipping competition of, 101–2
Shattner's Saloon, 77
Shawnee Indians, 22, 36, 60; Kansas lands of, 36
Shawnee reservation, 60
Shea, Paddy, prizefight of, 167
Sheridan, Gen. Phil, 63, 137; 1885 visit to Wichita, 133–34; field order of, 66, 74; Greiffenstein charged by, 66; Indian Territory campaign of, 8, 64, 141
Sherman, Texas, 35
Shirley, John, 31
Shirley, William, 31
Short, Mrs. Celia C., 135–36
Short, O. F., massacre of, 135–36
Silver Broach (Comanche chief), 31
Singleton, Al, 123
Sioux Indians, 25, 61; Wichita visit of, 131
Sioux-Cheyenne Indians, 137
Sixth U.S. Cavalry, 116
Skeleton Creek, 43, 45, 104, 107
Sluss, Henry C., early Wichita residency of, 76
Smith, John Simpson, 27–29
Smith, William, 120–22
Smoky Hill River, 8, 23, 25, 29, 37, 60
Smoot, Col. Samuel S., 54
South Canadian River, 55
South Dakota, 131
South Haven, Kansas, 144, 148
South Platte River, 12

South Water Street, 94; location of for first lumber house, 87
Southwest Colony Town and Mining Company, 143
Southwestern Stage Company, 61, 81, 95, 122; relay station established by, 103–4
Sowers, F. A., 93
Spaniards, 1–8, 12; fight with Escanjaques, 6; Pike captured by, 1; story of gold search by, 12
Spanish conquistadors, ix, 2
Spanish Forts, Texas, 20
Spanish hieroglyphics, 8
Speers, George, 124, 126
Spotted Tail (Sioux chief), delegation led by, 131
Spotts, David L., pre-settlement view of Wichita site given by, 75
Springer, William M. (Illinois Representative), 158; Oklahoma Bill sponsored by, 159
Springfield, Illinois, 167
Stafford, Harry, 144
stage line, 103; Harry Hill establishment of, 163; Wichita service of, 96
Stanley, Henry M., Mathewson's post visited by, 51
Star of the West dance hall, 153
Steele, Judge James, 27–28
Steele, John, 92, 94, 120, 127, 135, 143; cattle business protected by, 101–2; departure of, 153, 155; early Wichita residency of, 76
Steen, Capt. Enoch, 12
Stein and Dunlap trading firm, 22
Stevens, Henry T., 154–55
Stevens, John, 48
Stewart, Lee, 110
Stillwater, Oklahoma, Couch expedition to, 152
Stinking Saddle Cloth (Kiowa chief), 31

stockyards, creation of, 95
Stone, George, 100
Storm (Arapaho chief), 29
"Strawberry Hill" (Greiffenstein's
home), 87
street peddlers, Wichita presence
of, 154
Sunset Ranch, 71
surveyors, 98, 105; massacre of,
135–36

Tacoma, Washington, 153
Talbot, Jim, 124–26
Talbot, Mrs. Jim, 125
Taos Indians, 6
Tawakoni Indians, 28, 32, 35, 38, 41
Taylor, Lt. C. W., 148
Taylor, Dorcas, 31
Taylor, James, 31
Taylor, N. G. (Commissioner of
Indian Affairs), 62
Taylor, Robert H., 40, 51
Ten Bears (Comanche chief), 40,
50, 53
Texas, 7, 22, 25, 30–31, 35, 39–40,
46–47, 51–52, 54–55, 62, 66,
70, 88, 97, 100, 136, 147–48,
152, 157, 163, 167; panhandle
of, 3, 103, 105, 129
Texas cattle (trail herds), xiii, 42,
47, 52, 54, 66, 70, 76, 79,
98–99, 101–2, 114, 164;
Arkansas River forded by,
88; first shipment of from
Wichita, 95; growing trade
of, 76; Indian attack on, 99
Texas Charley, 165–66
Texas Confederates, 22
Texas cowboys (drovers), 70, 101,
111–12, 114; celebrations in
Wichita saloons by, 88;
Wichita presence of, 102
Texas fever, 54, 101
Texas House, 113
Texas Tom, performance of, 167
Third U.S. Infantry, 81
Thrarsber, Capt., 54
To-haw-son (Kiowa chief), 25. See

also Little Mountain
Tombstone, Arizona, 122, 124
Tonkawa Indians, 22–23
Topeka, Kansas, 60, 63, 66–67,
76–77, 110, 114, 140–41; town-
site group of, 73; visitors
from, 78
Towanda, Kansas, 42, 69, 81;
founding of, 23
trail herds, x, 55; periods of in
Wichita, 113
Treaty of Comanche Peak, 47
Treaty of Little Arkansas, 27, 39,
49, 51, 72; Greiffenstein's role
at, 62
Treaty of Medicine Lodge, 40,
51–52, 54
Turk, the, 1–4
Turkey Red winter wheat, 118

U.G.R.R. (underground railroad), 90
U.S. Army, 19, 138; removal of
Indian Territory intruders
by, 143; troops of, 21, 25, 66,
105, 142, 152, 159; Wichita
camp of, 73
U.S. Cavalry, 163
U.S. commissioners; treaty efforts
of, 73
U.S. Congress, 35, 39, 136, 157,
159–60; Osage Trust Lands
opened by, 76; protection of
buffalo requested of, 103
U.S. District Court, 155
U.S. government, 24, 27, 41, 45,
131, 148
Unassigned District/Lands, 139,
143, 147, 150, 152, 155, 157, 159
Union, 21, 23, 31, 92; army of, 137
United States, 8, 46, 59, 63, 75, 150

Van Dorn, Maj. Earl, 21, 30
Vandervort, Jesse, 81
variety shows, 111
Verdigris River, 11
Vigus, Henry W., 77–78, 80; arrival
of at Wichita, 72; Buckhorn
hotel and saloon of, 77;

death of, 153; hotel opened
by, 73
Vigus, Mrs. Henry, 77
Vigus, Will, 153

Waco Indians, 23, 28, 32, 35, 41–42
Wade, John, 79
Wakarusa River, 60
Wakarusa trading post, 60
Walker, W. N., 109, 120
Walker, Wash, 124
Walkley, S. T., 63
Walnut Creek, 2, 11, 20, 22–23, 54,
61, 69, 73
Walnut Creek ranch, 60
Wantland Crutch-O Ranch, 144
Washington, D.C., 31, 36, 47, 66, 97,
130, 137, 148, 150, 158–59;
Payne on police force of, 142;
visited by Greiffenstein, 157
Washington, state of, 153, 155
Washita River, 21–22, 40, 53, 66, 82;
battle on, 64; Greiffenstein
trading post on, 65
Water Street, 130, 132; northwest
corner of known as "Horse
Thief Corner," 89
Waterman, Eli P., arrival of, 72
Waterman Addition, 88
Waterman's Grove, 92
Watkins, William, 106
Weaver, James B. (Iowa
Representative), 158
Wellington, Kansas, xi; Payne bur-
ial at, 151
Wells, Tom, 72
West Wichita (Delano), 113, 115,
117–18
Westport, Missouri, 153
Wheeler, Col. G. W., 52
White, Capt. Will, 133
Whitewater River, 36, 69
Whitman, O. J., killing of, 78–79
Whittaker, Charles, 50; claim of on
Little Arkansas, 71, 94; trading post of, 55
Wichita, ix–x, xiii–xiv, 19–20, 27, 33,
35, 37, 39, 45, 52, 61, 66, 69,
80, 82–83, 89–92, 97–100, 103,
105, 107, 118–19, 121–24, 130,
132–34, 137, 140, 142–44,
147–48, 152–53, 155, 158, 160,
162, 166–67; ancestral pride
of, xiv; border toughs at, 127;
cattle trail period of, 85;
demise of Old West in, 168;
development as a cattle
shipping point, 95; early
businesses of, 77; early days
of recalled, 135; economic
advancement of, 156; 1870s
transformation of, 101; emer-
gence of as commercial center, 154; first construction at,
87; first log house at site of,
10; freighters of killed, 106;
frontier life in, 88; host to
Indians, 129; incorporation
of as town of "third class,"
93; Indian scare of, 136;
influence of military camp
on, 75; modern era of, 3;
musical performances in,
112; name of first appears in
print, 73; Nineteenth
Volunteer Cavalry passes
through, 141; Oklahoma
Boomer headquarters at,
139; Oklahoma story covered
by newspapers at, 139; pioneer family of, 120; railway
service for, 95, 97; reign of as
cattle town, 111; rise of law
and order in, 154; Sioux delegation arrives at, 131; site of,
50; soldier views of, 75;
stagecoach line to, 96; Texas
cattle shipped from, 98;
town plat of drawn on old
flour sack, 86; town status
requested for, 93; townsite
claims filed for, 76; trail herd
promotion of, 102; traveling
show from, 161; visitor's view
of, 88; Wild West mystique
of, ix–xx, 78, 109

Wichita, the Early Years, x

Wichita Agency (Indian Territory), 37, 103; trade with, 103; uprising at, 47

Wichita & Southwestern Railroad Company, promotion of, 95

Wichita Beacon, 133, 143; Democratic allegiance of, 140; Wyatt Earp praised by, 121–22

Wichita Board of Trade, 161–62, 165; moves to regain boomer lead, 158; protest against Lillie sent to, 159

Wichita City Library, xi

Wichita Corn Train, sketch of, 158

Wichita Coronet Band, 92

Wichita Cowtown Museum, xi; original log-house replicated by, 73

Wichita Eagle, 102–4, 116, 118, 121, 131–32, 153, 156, 163; Chief Joseph quote of, 138; Greiffenstein-Sheridan meeting reported by, 133–34; Indian Territory events covered by, ix; O.K. Corral story of, 124; opposition to Payne led by, 145; Payne given credit by, 147; Republican allegiance of, 139; support for "new empire" voiced by, 157

Wichita fairgrounds, 167

Wichita House, 92; Empire Hotel renamed as, 88

Wichita Indians, 3, 7, 9–10, 15, 20, 28, 32–33, 35, 38–39, 41, 43, 46, 55, 101, 103; burial methods of, 38; business leaders of, 157; chief of murdered, 105; departure and return of, 23; description of, 34; homes of, 3–4; lodges of, 77; Oklahoma colony members from, 149; original settlement of, 67; outpost days of, 69–83; raucous social event at, 80–81; removal of, 37–39; reporter visit to, 69–70; retreat of, 22; teamsters of, 106; war party of, 39

Wichita Mountains, 20

Wichita racetrack, 134

Wichita stockyards, 101

Wichita Vidette, beginning of, 93; report of, 86

Wichita Wheat Market, 118

Wichita-Sedgwick County Historical Museum, xi

Wild West, aspects of, 161; Wichita period of, x, 164

Wild West shows, 153, 159, 163; band of, 168; exhibits of, 165; wild animals of, 154

Wilkinson, Lt. James B., exploration of, 8–10

Wilmarth, Mrs. Margaret, 29

Wilson, John, 124–25

Wolf Creek (Indian Territory), 63–64

Wood, Sam, prophecy of, 32

Woodman, E. C., as pioneer banker of Wichita, 156

Woods, Professor, 165

Wortham, James, 37

Wynkoop, Maj. E. W., 25

Yellowstone River, 51, 138

Yellowstone Vic, 165